FLANNERY O'CONNOR'S
RELIGIOUS IMAGINATION

◑

A World with Everything Off Balance

FLANNERY O'CONNOR'S RELIGIOUS IMAGINATION

A World with Everything Off Balance

George A. Kilcourse, Jr.

PAULIST PRESS ❉ NEW YORK/ Mahwah, n.j.

LIBRARY OF CONGRESS CATALOGING-IN-PUBLICATION DATA

Kilcourse, George, 1947-
    Flannery O'Connor's religious imagination : a world with everything off balance / George A. Kilcourse, Jr.
        p. cm.
    Includes bibliographical references.
    ISBN 0-8091-4005-5
    1. O'Connor, Flannery—Criticism and interpretation. 2. Christianity and literature— United States—History—20th century. 3. Christian fiction, American—History and criticism. 4. O'Connor, Flannery—Religion. I. Title.

PS3565.C57 Z728 2001
813'.54—dc21

2001036004

Published by Paulist Press
997 Macarthur Boulevard
Mahwah, New Jersey 07430

www.paulistpress.com

Printed and bound in the United States of America

Contents

For my sister, Kathy,

who blesses us with love and laughter

Preface

The genesis of this book lies somewhere in laughter—the rollicking, face-creasing kind of laughter that I enjoy whenever I read Flannery O'Connor. From a puzzled first brush with her work as a college student, through my ongoing rereading of her fiction, prose, and those inimitably comic and porous letters she wrote, I delight in the spirit and faith of this woman whose life among us was interrupted at the age of thirty-nine.

As I came to appreciate O'Connor's imagination, I began to examine more carefully the theological dimensions of her art. Now I see her as a contemporary American Doctor of the Church. This book is an effort to communicate how and why her deep experience of the Catholic ethos bears an urgent insight for our ongoing renewal as Church.

I owe special thanks to Thomas Stransky, C.S.P., who graciously welcomed me as a visiting scholar at the Tantur Ecumenical Institute in Jerusalem for the fall 1998 semester. There, on the troubled border between the West Bank and the ancient city, where peacemakers summon all to recognize a common human dignity, I invested myself in research on the prophets and dialogue at the interreligious frontier. My sojourn in this desert land proved to be important environs in which to reread and ponder Flannery O'Connor's works. Father Mark O'Keefe, O.S.B., extended warm hospitality for my spring 1999 semester as a scholar in residence at St. Meinrad School of Theology in Indiana. The wonderful library and rhythms of monastic prayer at the archabbey afforded me a quiet habitat where I drafted initial sections of this book.

Every author relies on the assistance of especially patient and capable friends. John D. Boyd, S.J., my mentor at Fordham

University, first awakened my theologian's mind to the interdisciplinary study of theology and literature and ably equipped me to undertake the writing of this book. To Kimberly Baker I owe a great debt of gratitude for her careful reading of these chapters and suggestions for making them more reader-friendly. Sara Crutchfield's expertise with word processing and its mysteries, as well as her expert secretarial skills transformed the tangled script of my editorial changes into readable prose.

To Joe Scott, my editor at Paulist Press, I want to express thanks for a new friendship with a fellow Flannery fan and for the good humor and expertise with which he helped to make this book a better tool for readers.

3 August 2000
26th anniversary of Flannery O'Connor's death

Introduction

On my second visit to Flannery O'Connor's hometown of Milledgeville, Georgia, in May 1993, what impressed me deeply were the quiet morning Masses at her parish, Sacred Heart Church. The interior of this diminutive brick edifice, erected in 1874, has undergone minimal renovations since O'Connor's death. Materials from the elegant Lafayette Hotel, which previously occupied this site, were utilized in the main body of the church. The Gothic-arched clear glass windows are said to have been salvaged from the hotel, and were used to harmonize with the Gothic architecture of the nearby old capitol. The church structure mingles secular and sacred much like O'Connor's fiction. Both the worship space and ritual at Sacred Heart reflect the liturgical reforms of the Second Vatican Council (1962–65), which was still in session when she died on 3 August 1964, at the age of thirty-nine. The gospel reading on one of those sunny spring mornings was from John 17—the story of the risen Jesus interrogating Simon Peter at the Sea of Tiberias—"Do you love me?" In the story Christ goes on to commission the rehabilitated disciple, "Feed my sheep," and again invites him, "Follow me!" Here was the refined kind of storytelling that Flannery O'Connor relished. And something more on that May day, when the last pastels were fading from the emerald Georgia landscape, riveted my attention. It was the voice of the lector, clipping past words minus the clanging g's at the end: "…seein',…comin',… readin'…."

Elizabeth Horne, the lector, was introduced to me after Mass by the Australian pastor (with Irish roots and the surname to match). I waited on the small, open porch at the church entrance to express my gratitude and to meet the handful of people who were participating in the liturgy. I overheard one woman ask prayers for her daughter who had lost twins in the third month of her pregnancy. An elderly man preceded her, seeking consolation for the chronic infirmities of age. The pastor exclaimed to me, "You must be a Flannery person!" Whenever new faces appeared at a weekday Mass, he indicated, the regulars at the parish drew that conclusion.

When I inquired about the O'Connor family's life at Sacred Heart Parish, the friendly pastor (who was divesting of his chasuble and alb on the porch) pointed to Elizabeth and identified her as a "long-timer" who had known both Flannery and her mother, Regina Cline O'Connor. He pointed out a pew in church, next to a pole, as her habitual seat. Elizabeth corrected him with a whiplash turn and interruption, "Flannery sat in the *fifth* pew on the *right* side." I asked if she had been a daily communicant. "During Lent," said Elizabeth. "And oftentimes she came on First Fridays. The First Fridays were a big observance at the parish," she explained.

The parish hall had recently been named and dedicated to Flannery, so I asked if I might visit there. We moved through a door just to the right of the sanctuary and were suddenly in a space that had the incomparable look and asbestos floor-wax scent of a Catholic auditorium-cafeteria. A setting of tables was arranged in a large square, lunch that day to be served for the Knights of Columbus. A plaque and photograph on the far wall identified this place as "The Flannery O'Connor Hall." In the familiar portrait a young Flannery holds her delicate piano fingers meshed before her and her eyes sparkle above her smile, lit with a radiant joy.

When I coaxed Elizabeth to talk more about Flannery, she had only good reminiscences. The O'Connors, she remarked, came to everything at the parish, "They were great supporters." She recalled vivid stories related to the community's brief five-year effort to support a parochial school. Regina and Flannery invited the children out to their farm, Andalusia, each spring—"When the young animals were born," Elizabeth emphasized, "for a picnic." She waved her hands high to demonstrate how Flannery wore her big straw hat and maneuvered on her crutches for one such occasion. "There was one little girl, slightly retarded," Elizabeth remembered, "whom Flannery observed. She was approaching a duck's nest that was laden with eggs. 'How much you wanta bet she steps on it?'" she described Flannery asking her. "Sure enough, she did," laughed Elizabeth. "Just like Flannery would have done as a mischievous child!"

The Cline family's monetary support for the small Milledgeville Catholic community grew legendary. Elizabeth told how the pastor used to boast about the $2.50 often received in collections. Flannery's maternal great-grandfather, Hugh Donnelly Treanor, would take a generous check to the pastor each week, she explained. "When the school was struggling to begin, Flannery took piano lessons from one of the sisters. It was a way for Flannery to give them money," Elizabeth emphasized. She had already taken piano lessons when she was six years old. "Regina tells the story," Elizabeth laughed, "how she had to spank Flannery to get her to put on hose and a dress for her first recital." An auspicious debut for any artist.

Elizabeth was reminded of her many conversations with Flannery on this same church porch before and after Masses. "Flannery always said something to amuse you," she noted. One trait of her famous writer-friend remains indelible in Elizabeth's memory: "How observant Flannery was!" Asked about her own reading of O'Connor, Elizabeth reported that she liked the stories but took them at their *literal* level. She claimed that she, like others in Milledgeville, was surprised at all the interest in Flannery's stories, the "implications" scholars and readers found. This was all the more striking, Elizabeth insisted, because "we experienced her as plain folks." She described the Milledgeville tea and book-signing event for Flannery's first novel, *Wise Blood*. Her cousin Kate ordered five copies of the book to give to friends. "She read the first chapter and sent four of the copies back," whispered Elizabeth. "At the signing, Regina and Louise, Flannery's cousin, sat on the margins and tried to maintain an affirming but detached posture of support," Elizabeth laughingly recollected.

The brief life of Flannery O'Connor (1925–64) encompasses a brilliant literary career. By the time of her death at the age of thirty-nine, she had three times won first prize in the O. Henry Awards for short story writing. *The Complete Short Stories,* published three years after her death, received the National Book Award. In addition to two collections of short stories, O'Connor authored two novels that attest to her gifts as an accomplished fiction writer, who effectively matured as a writer beyond the genre of her forte, the short story. *The Habit of Being,* a collection of her posthumously published letters, perdures in American religious and literary circles as a benchmark of candor, humor, and intellectual rigor.

Studies at the State University of Iowa and its renowned Writers' Workshop under the direction of Paul Engle brought forth O'Connor's literary talents. Her subsequent invitation from the Yaddo Foundation to participate in its artists' colony near Saratoga Springs, New York, in 1948 led to her lifelong friendship with literary figures such as Robert Lowell and Robert Penn Warren; these eventually led to contacts with Allen Tate, Caroline Gordon, and a host of major American writers. In 1949, after a brief period when she lived in New York City, O'Connor met poet and translator Robert Fitzgerald and his wife, Sally. She accepted their invitation to move to their Connecticut home to assist with child care; she discovered in their friendship the encouragement to develop as a writer—a lifelong blessing.

Throughout her adult life, O'Connor suffered a debilitating physical condition that was first diagnosed as acute rheumatoid arthritis. However, by early 1951 doctors confirmed that she had inherited disseminated lupus erythematosus, the disease that had taken her father's life a decade earlier. By this time, her widowed mother, Regina Cline O'Connor, was operating a dairy farm near Milledgeville, the original antebellum capital of Georgia. The young O'Connor insisted on using the farm's original name, Andalusia, and took enormous pleasure enjoying its rural setting. Flannery's Catholic ancestors had settled there by the mid-nineteenth century and prospered, with large land holdings. Her grandfather, Peter James Cline, was elected Milledgeville's first Catholic mayor in 1888. She spent the remainder of her life at Andalusia, except for occasional visits as a speaker on college and university campuses—or to hospitals.

O'Connor disciplined herself to write for several hours each morning, as her energies allowed. The only references she makes to her infirmity appear in letters, where she is self-deprecating and never complains about the suffering or the difficulties of confinement. She treats with wry humor her life restricted to the farm under the watchful eye of a protective, strong-willed mother—and transforms local figures (including Regina and residents from the nearby state mental health facility) into characters for her fiction. Eventually the lupus required her to use crutches and further restricted her mobility. Medications caused bone damage as a side effect and compounded her physical deterioration.

A fuller appreciation of Flannery O'Connor inevitably leads to her Catholic faith. Born in Savannah, Georgia, on the feast of the Annunciation (25 March 1925), she lived her first thirteen years in a middle-class row house in the shadow of the spire of the Cathedral of St. John in Lafayette Square. As part of a minority Catholic enclave living in the Protestant "Bible Belt," Flannery O'Connor was venturing forth as an ecumenical pioneer before the Second Vatican Council approved or popularized the term. Her essays and letters repeatedly return to the identity of the Catholic fiction writer vis-à-vis the secularization process in the wider culture. She finds in the Protestant South a striking religious literacy and demonstrates how these unique environs promote her task as a creative Catholic writer. O'Connor's Catholic imagination peoples her fiction with backwoods fundamentalists and grotesque eccentrics who ironically enable her to create an imaginative sacramental universe. Her essays refine a modern understanding of American culture that both retrieves essentials of Catholic identity and honestly faces the realities of a post-Christian world.

Flannery O'Connor speaks unashamedly of her life of prayer, spirituality, and the curiosity of a Catholic intellectual at a time of great ferment in the Church. These very characteristics help to identify her as a modern Catholic contemplative. She remained single and celibate for fear of passing on her hereditary lupus to any children she might bear. The remote locale of Andalusia and its peaceful environment, along with her diligent, disciplined work habits, combined for a quasi-monastic life. Most importantly, this life as a creative artist afforded her the distance and perspective in which to recognize the spiritual crisis in our culture's unhealthy illusions. O'Connor's fiction challenges readers to recognize these illusions and to discover an alternative vision of a spiritually wholesome reality.

Three striking coincidences in my life have converged to prompt this study of Flannery O'Connor's fiction. The first occurred during my undergraduate education as an English major. A gifted teacher, herself a native of Georgia, Joan Tucker Brittain, guided me through two semesters' study of American literature. The mother of four, Joan had followed her own love of literature and launched a second career with doctoral studies and one of the first dissertations on her fellow Georgian, Flannery O'Connor. She and her mentor, Leon Driskell, went on to publish one of the earliest critical studies of O'Connor, *The Eternal Crossroads*.[1] Their book perdures as a watershed volume warranting serious attention. Joan Tucker Brittain taught me how to read fiction. Her intellect and enthusiasm were contagious. Joan's voice with its Georgia vowels and cadences held me spellbound as she ushered my imagination into the precincts of Flannery's world. I was hooked. Years later Joan "converted" and entered the Roman Catholic Church. She is a witness to the power and depths of O'Connor's art and faith.

The second coincidence nurturing my study of O'Connor came when I discovered Thomas Merton heralding her fiction in a prose elegy in which he compared her to Sophocles: "I write her name with honor, for all the truth and all the craft with which she shows man's fall and his dishonor."[2] In those half dozen pages, the Kentucky Trappist monk coaxed readers of Flannery's fiction to appreciate the religious vision that is still so easily eclipsed or blithely dismissed in critical appraisals of her work. I can think of no better orientation for readers of O'Connor than to be alert to Merton's identification of her "dry-eyed irony." My own study of Merton as a wisdom critic of modern literature[3] contributes to a contemplative interpretation of O'Connor's fiction in this study. It is unfortunate that the two writers never met or corresponded, but their publisher and mutual friend Robert Giroux provided a conduit to keep them apprised of each other's work and to provide them with one another's texts. As I indicate throughout these pages, Merton and O'Connor were not only contemporaries but also genuinely kindred contemplative spirits.[4]

The third unexpected turn in my recurring interest in Flannery O'Connor came during a 1979 trip to Atlanta to participate in the National Workshop on Christian Unity. Catholics are still comparatively scarce in the southeastern states of America, so O'Connor's title for her essay, "A Catholic Novelist in the Protestant South," offers even today an apt description of that particular geography and its religious demographics. Nonetheless, at breakfast one morning I found myself in conversation with one of the few Atlanta priests present at the national workshop. Father John Mulroy was pastor at a suburban parish. I inquired about his experiences with Archbishop Paul J. Hallinan, who had been one of the most intelligent members of the United States Catholic hierarchy when it came to implementing the Vatican Council II renewal and reforms; one of Hallinan's auxiliary bishops and apprentices had been then-Bishop Joseph Bernardin. In the midst of our lively conversation, I spontaneously asked Father Mulroy how far it would be to drive from

Atlanta to Milledgeville, where Flannery O'Connor had lived. I had heard that Georgia College was entrusted with the collection of her literary archives and with establishing the definitive scholarly collection of works published about her life and writings. He indicated it would be a day's endeavor to make the round trip and spend any time there. I decided to postpone the pilgrimage on this occasion.

As I checked out of the hotel the next morning, the desk clerk handed me an envelope with my name handwritten across it and the return address indicating "Holy Spirit Church." Puzzled, I opened it as the taxi drove me to the airport. Father John Mulroy[5] had penned a brief note and attached a copy of a baptismal certificate. His explanation referred to my question the day before about Flannery's correspondent whose identity had been protected by designating her "A" in the collection of her letters, *The Habit of Being*.[6] Flannery had been the sponsor for "A" when she was received into the Catholic Church. The certificates for baptism (31 March 1956) and confirmation (10 June 1957) inscribed "A's" name, respectively, as "Magdalen Hazel Elizabeth Hester" and "Mary M. Hester" (Gertrude being her chosen confirmation name). John's note added, "Now you and I are the only priests to know her identity." It was several years before I pursued this revelation. On my first visit to Georgia College's O'Connor Collection I asked the librarian if that name was familiar to her. She referred me to Sarah Gordon, the resident O'Connor scholar and editor of *The Flannery O'Connor Bulletin*.

In the end, I wrote to Sally Fitzgerald, editor of O'Connor's work and her trusted friend and biographer. In a lengthy and beautiful letter of response and also a telephone conversation, she advised me that it would be more prudent not to contact "A" because her mental stability was precarious. As Sally indicated, "A" did well when she was with her books and cats, but would not be reliable for an interview because she had a propensity to read herself into the characters in Flannery's stories. Sally did emphasize what became more and more apparent: in her letters to

"A" Flannery worked diligently to articulate how she integrated her faith and her literary artist's identity. Sally puts it well in her introduction to *The Habit of Being* where she describes Flannery's Catholic faith as "her intellectual and spiritual taproot" that continued to deepen and expand throughout her life.[7] This unparalleled collection of her correspondence affords a unique matrix for understanding O'Connor's fiction. In these pages I return often to her letters to "A."

I decided not to disturb "A" by requesting an interview. By this time I had learned from a fellow-priest's reply to a letter I had written to Father Mulroy that he had died of cancer in September 1982. I would not use my own identity as a priest or as an acquaintance of Father Mulroy to gain access to "A," this fragile, vulnerable, but talented woman who had been Flannery's friend and most important correspondent. In the middle of my 1998–99 sabbatical year as I was researching for this book, I went to the Flannery O'Connor web site on the Internet. One article indicated that a longtime O'Connor friend had died. I held my breath as I clicked the computer's mouse on this item, concerned about the aging Sally Fitzgerald, who was completing the long awaited O'Connor biography, to be entitled *The Mansions of the South*. It was almost like opening another page of Flannery's short stories. (Though Sally Fitzgerald did subsequently die in early summer, 2000.)

Instead, I learned that on the day after Christmas, 26 December 1998, "A" had taken her own life with a hand revolver. Violence and the trademark O'Connor struggle to enter the kingdom of God echoed in this sorrow. The day of "A's" death had been St. Stephen's Day, the feast of the Church's first martyr. Uncanny coincidence? Rereading the letters to "A," it now strikes me how Flannery's epistles manifest a compassionate outreach to a searching pilgrim. Hers is a very personal response and a profoundly Catholic form of evangelization, which O'Connor once clarified: "There is a better sense in which [compassion] can be used but seldom is—the sense of being in travail with and for creation in its subjection to vanity. This is a sense which implies a recognition of sin; there is a suffering-with, but one which blunts no edges and makes no excuses. When infused into novels, it is forbidding. Our age doesn't go for it."[8] This same countercultural truth radiates through the urgent insight of her stories and novels, and in the integrity of her life as a Catholic fiction writer.

As a theologian I gravitate to Flannery O'Connor's fiction because she personifies the way in which the imagination theologizes. William F. Lynch, S.J.,[9] best articulated this axiom, and O'Connor read and carefully annotated his work. This book explores how her fiction as literary art compels us to discover within ourselves "the kind of mind that is willing to have its sense of mystery deepened by contact with reality, and its sense of reality deepened by contact with mystery."[10] I am the kind of theologian she once characterized as having learned that he cannot ignore the fiction writer's "image of ultimate reality as it is glimpsed in some aspect of the human situation"[11] or in the mystery of existence. For Flannery that invariably meant crafting stories where readers can experience "the action of grace in territory held largely by the devil"[12]—and possibly discover in their own lives this same redemptive action.

Whenever I have mentioned writing this book, numerous acquaintances have responded, "Do people still read Flannery O'Connor?" It's a bit like meeting someone at a college reunion and having them pause uncomfortably when you mention that you are again reading Dante or Euripides or W. H. Auden or Mark's gospel—while they remark with sophistication that they have moved onto postmodern novelists like Stephen King or Danielle Steele or John Grisham. In an early version of O'Connor's essay, "The Catholic Novelist in the Protestant South," she employed the term "post-Christian"[13] to identify our modern predicament as Christians. It describes one pole in her survey of the modern world. The opposite pole (which she located in the South within a half hour's ride from the post-Christian pole) was the "Bible Belt," a metaphor of disdain coined in 1919 by H. L. Mencken but the designation of a cultural asset in O'Connor's purview.[14] What she next proposes in that essay is a pioneering ecumenical initiative that professional ecumenists have ignored. I reserve particular energy in chapter 5 to assess that unique ecumenical dialogue she explains. O'Connor was convinced that the American Catholic artist could best recover from five centuries of the Church's overemphasis upon the abstract and the absolute by reclaiming from the biblically rooted Protestant South the twin antidotes of existentially grounded faith and religious passion. She concluded that the "Hebrew genius for making the absolute concrete has conditioned the Southerner's way of looking at things." And it was better to live with less than ideal results than with the abstraction because "a distorted image of Christ is better than no image at all."[15]

O'Connor's diagnosis of the malaise of the American Catholic imagination rings as true today as when she made this observation in 1963. Perhaps the current symptoms are even more alarming; we self-congratulate while Catholic identity and the Christian mystery continue to be diluted vis-à-vis secularism. O'Connor perceptively analyzed the deeper malady: "[W]e are beginning to realize that an impoverishment of the imagination means an impoverishment of the religious life as well."[16] The epigraph for her contemporary the American Catholic novelist Walker Percy's *The Moviegoer*, quoting the Danish theologian Søren Kierkegaard, comes to mind: "The true character of despair is that it is unaware of itself as despair."[17] Flannery O'Connor acknowledged the collaborative interest of theologians in appreciating the modern novel amid the temptation to despair, "because there [the theologian] sees reflected the man of our time, the unbeliever, who is nevertheless grappling in a desperate and honest way with intense problems of the spirit."[18]

Shortly after the publication of her second novel, *The Violent Bear It Away*, in 1960, O'Connor is quoted as saying, "I can wait fifty years, a hundred years, for it to be understood."[19] I contend that we are now closer to an authentic understanding of her fiction because we are closer to admitting the challenge of the "post-Christian" environs in which we find ourselves. Such an honest self-scrutiny makes possible an awakening to our predicament and a fresh awareness of the innate religious possibilities that O'Connor's fiction dramatizes.

Flannery O'Connor mentions the name of "Jesus" or "Christ" 147 times in *Wise Blood;* 84 times in *A Good Man Is Hard to Find;* 61 times in *The Violent Bear It Away;* and 36 times in *Everything That Rises Must Converge.* The frequent placement of the Christian Redeemer's name throughout her fiction echoes her description of the South as "Christ-haunted, not Christ-centered."[20] Even more telling is how her characters frequently use the name of the second person of the Trinity in a nonchalant utterance of profanity or, ironically, as the literal evidence of their lack of Christian faith and their capitulation to a post-Christian void. It is from this concrete, given world that O'Connor's imagination summons and awakens her characters and her audience so that they might live alternatively with faith as "the concrete expression of mystery—mystery that is lived" (988).[21]

Religious educators and catechumens especially are encouraged to read Flannery O'Connor's stories in concert with this book. I invite my fellow priests and other ministers in the churches to do the same: to comb her stories for insights and clarity about the lifelong ongoing conversion process and to sharpen your own homiletic skills by appreciating her uncommon gift for story-telling. When adults denigrate the religious interest of teenagers, I challenge them to reclaim her stories with their initially bewildering, grotesque distortions. Imagine how a youth group or youth retreat discussion of "Everything That Rises Must Converge"—the tragedy of Julian and his mother—or the other parent-and-son/-daughter stories that dominate this collection might relieve the alienation that manacles both adults and teens and keeps them from expressions of a spiritually healthy affective life. Imagine the conversation among a circle of fledgling catechumens in the wake of their reading "A Good Man Is Hard to

Find" or any of the other stories from her first collection of short stories under that same title. Or imagine a liturgy of reconciliation and penance in which the examination of conscience retraces Ruby Turpin's coming to grips with her own pride in "Revelation." The genius of O'Connor's Catholic imagination awaits only the discovery by gifted pastoral ministers and pastoral theologians. Every baptized person can wrestle with *The Violent Bear It Away* and rediscover some dimension of their own prophetic call through following Tarwater's sidestepping and then reclaiming "the terrible speed of mercy" (478).

Near the end of "A Good Man Is Hard to Find," O'Connor's character, the escaped criminal who calls himself The Misfit, announces, "Jesus thown [sic] everything off balance" (151). He comes to blame Jesus for upsetting things by raising the dead. "He shouldn't have done it" (152), he protests. The great christological mystery of the incarnate Jesus' life, death, and resurrection as the redemptive act of unconditional love pulses at the heart of Flannery O'Connor's art. I can think of no title more apt for a study that investigates how her Catholic imagination theologizes than to fathom the meaning of Jesus throwing everything (and everyone) off balance. Her stories of conversion summon us time and again to contemplate the mystery of the Christ who throws off balance every status quo that threatens to seduce and paralyze us with its tempting illusion.

Chapter One

Discovering the Audience

It is a matter of getting across the reality of grace...plus making FIRST their God believable. To, as I have said before, an audience not adequately equipped to believe anything.
—Letter to "A," 5 July 1958

Something of the pundit echoes throughout Flannery O'Connor's honest appraisals of her audience's strengths and limitations. When a student once wrote to inquire about "what enlightenment" she was expected to get from her stories, O'Connor-the-author suspected that this request betrayed the assignment to write a paper and an effort to "figure out" the stories. She wisely replied, "I wrote her back to forget about the enlightenment and just try to enjoy them."[1] O'Connor personifies this love of literature's capacity to re-create in readers an experience of joy. Yet she admits that most people misread her own stories as "hard, hopeless, and brutal." She intended to write them as stories "about the action of grace on a character who is not very willing to support it." No sooner had O'Connor staked out her parameters than she admitted the difficulty of writing "for an audience that doesn't know what grace is and doesn't recognize it when they see it" (1067).

A pair of major obstacles confront this Georgia Catholic fiction writer and her literary peers: (1) the functional illiteracy of generations of readers who do not know how to read or understand fiction; and (2) the absence of a religious culture to help these readers interpret the deeper meaning of fiction. O'Connor turned to Joseph Conrad's definition of the aim of a fiction writer: "to render the highest possible justice to the visible universe...because it suggested an invisible one." Her trenchant essay entitled "The Nature and Aim of Fiction" borrowed his insights to orient her own efforts:

> My task which I am trying to achieve is, by the power of the written word, to make you hear, to make you feel—it is, before all, to make you *see*. That—and no more, and it is everything. If I succeed, you shall find there, according to your deserts, encouragement, consolation, fear, charm, all you demand—and, perhaps, also that glimpse of truth for which you have forgotten to ask.[2]

The leaven of O'Connor's humor appears often when she ponders our neglect of ultimate questions and the consequences of missing the glimpse of truth offered in literature. She reports about one startling talk she gave to a ladies club: "The heart of my message to them was that they would all fry in hell if they didn't quit reading trash" (922).[3] She does not abandon this audience but challenges them. In another essay, she refers to a letter from a Californian who had informed her that tired readers come home at night and want to be "lifted up" by what they read. "And it seems," writes Flannery, "that her heart had not been lifted up by anything of mine she had read." "You may say that the serious writer doesn't have to bother about the tired reader," she reflects, "but he does, because they are all tired. One old lady who wants her heart lifted up wouldn't be bad, but you multiply her two hundred and fifty thousand times and what you get is a book club." She does not dismiss such tired readers (although she does reject the writers who pander to them) but reminds her California correspondent, "if [your] heart had been in the right place, it would have been lifted up (819–20)."[4]

Flannery O'Connor often tutors readers of her essays that the *form* of a story gives it meaning. No wonder she spent countless hours with numerous drafts in the effort to craft the form of her fiction. She claimed that the result of such attention to the form of the story would be "contemplation of the mystery embodied in it." To illustrate her point she recorded the incident of an English teacher asking students to name "the moral" of Nathaniel Hawthorne's novel, *The Scarlet Letter*. "[O]ne answer she got," O'Connor reports with chagrin, "was that the moral of *The Scarlet Letter* was, think twice before you commit adultery."[5] She insists that to reduce the reading of fiction to the decoding of moral propositions or simply to replace the short story or novel with a paraphrase shortchanges the reader. "When you can state the theme of a story, when you can separate it from the story itself," O'Connor warns, "then you can make sure the story is not a very good one."[6]

O'Connor cautions against subordinating literature to some other discipline. She laments the way that literature has been taught as psychology or sociology but not as literary art. She recounts one visit to a high school where all the subjects were renamed "activities" and integrated to the point that there were no distinct subjects to teach. O'Connor finds the proliferation of creative writing classes only worsens things. With her ironic flair she announces, "There's many a best-seller that could have been prevented by a good teacher."[7] O'Connor chastens such teaching and its results: people learn to write badly enough to make a great deal of money—"and in a way it seems a shame to deny them this opportunity." But she precipitates a collective examination of conscience—"unless the college is a trade school, it still has its responsibility to truth, and I believe myself that these people should be stifled with all deliberate speed."[8] She insists that the basis of art is imaginative truth.[9] "For the fiction writer," she argues, "the whole story is the meaning, because it is an experience, not an abstraction."[10] This book is a study of that dynamic in her fiction.

Few writers evidence as much sensitivity to both the limits and the potential of her audience as Flannery O'Connor does. If she is skeptical about a "false sophistication" that interferes with understanding fiction, she admits the real potential of the general audience of readers for whom she writes. "The type of mind that can understand good fiction is not necessarily the educated mind," she reminds us, "but it is at all times the kind of mind that is willing to have its sense of mystery deepened by contact with reality, and its sense of reality deepened by contact with mystery."[11] Flannery O'Connor insists upon the power of art to reveal "the image of ultimate reality as it can be glimpsed in some aspect of the human situation." That glimpse of Ultimacy enlarges into a worldview throughout her stories and novels. She trusts her ability as a fiction writer to awaken her readers to recognize the religious horizon. In the end, O'Connor brings both her characters and her audience to the brink of conversion; some of the characters even give ample evidence of the fact that they are initiated into a profoundly religious transformation. In such fiction, O'Connor claims, we see "reflected the man of our time, the unbeliever, who is nevertheless grappling in a desperate and honest way with intense problems of the spirit."[12]

But Flannery O'Connor was not naïve about her audience's limitations. One of the most direct O'Connor portraits of secular indifference disguised as Christian faith comes in her character Mrs. May in the short story "Greenleaf": "She thought the word *Jesus* should be kept inside the church building like other words inside the bedroom. She was a good Christian woman with a large respect for religion, though she did not, of course, believe any of it was true" (506). Mrs. May's stance mirrors a common predicament O'Connor encounters in the nonbelieving audience for her own fiction. On the one hand is the residue of Christianity, a superficial veneer or empty etiquette. On the other hand, Mrs. May personifies a typical protagonist in O'Connor's fiction because she eventually does come to an honest grappling with the most intense spiritual problems. The meaning of Mrs. May's violent death at the end of the story inevitably escapes those O'Connor called "casual readers." "Our age does not only not have a very sharp eye for the almost imperceptible intrusions of grace," she points out, " it no longer has much feeling for the nature of the violences which precede and follow them."[13]

O'Connor appeals to the writer and audience to be "more trustful of the blind imagination"[14] which yokes together art and belief in fiction such as hers. To appreciate O'Connor's genius, I first need to refine O'Connor's sense of the audience; then, to look at her own understanding of story as it unfolds in both her collections of short stories and her two novels; and thirdly, to attend to O'Connor's reflections on her identity as a Catholic fiction writer. We are blessed with an uncommon bounty in the triptych of her essays, her vast correspondence, and her fiction. These diverse types of writing prove mutually clarifying; they function like the three panels of religious icons, hinged together with an integral unity. This chapter concludes with brief orientation notes about five key elements operative in Flannery O'Connor's fiction. It alerts readers how to discover meaning as a function of the stories in terms of: (1) grace; (2) character; (3) distortion; (4) violence; and (5) vision. In the following chapters this matrix of her imagination will figure prominently in the interpretations of her short stories and novels.

AUDIENCE

In one of her memorable exaggerations, O'Connor once compared people who had the skill to read the entire telephone book to readers who claimed the ability to read a novel (811).[15] She protests that sheer endurance in scanning printer's type and turning pages cannot compare with the reader's skills needed for understanding fiction. In another context she cautions teachers to avoid the presumption that you can teach students techniques about how to write. Instead she recommends the potential of such classes "to teach you the limits and possibilities of words and the respect due them."[16]

O'Connor compares the writers of novels with the readers of novels in order to share an even more revealing insight about her audience. "People without hope not only don't write novels, but what is more to the point, they don't read them." She explains that their reason for neglecting novels is rooted in the fact that, "They don't take long looks at anything because they lack the courage." O'Connor alerts her audience to the genuine demands made by fiction, especially the novel. Readers are expected to do considerable work in reading a novel. "The way to despair is to refuse to have any kind of experience, and the novel," she asserts, "of course is a way to have experience." She admits that for both the artist and the audience fiction is a "plunge into reality" (not an escape from reality) and "very shocking to the system." She describes the writer as "sustained by the hope of salvation"—and invites the reader to make the same discovery by fathoming the depth of experience re-created in the novel.[17]

O'Connor offers a helpful analogy for her readers who struggle with fiction—hers and other writers'. It points to the interactive quality of her fiction. She makes demands upon an active reader; and she expects certain skills in her audience, skills equipping readers to be more than passive. She compares reading a story to the initial moment when a person stands in front of an impressionistic painting. Only when the viewer learns to move back gradually does the painting come into focus. "When you reach the right distance, you suddenly see that a world has been created—and a world in action—and that a complete story has been told, by a wonderful kind of understatement. It has been told more by showing what happens around the story than by touching directly on the story itself."[18]

Flannery O'Connor relies upon this same metaphor to describe the prophetic vision of the fiction writer. She is careful to avoid defining prophecy in terms of predicting the future; instead, she asserts that prophecy is "dependent on the imaginative and not the moral faculty....The prophet is a realist of distances, and it is this kind of realism that goes into great novels," she offers, "the realism which does not hesitate to distort appearances in order to show a hidden truth."[19] The analogy between impressionistic painting and fiction writing clarifies for the reader an integral dynamic of O'Connor's art. I return to it when discussing (below) the key element of distortion.

STORY

With her graphic imagination, O'Connor discredits discussions of story writing in terms of plot, character, and theme. She compares this to "trying to describe the expression on a face by saying where the eyes, nose, and mouth are."[20] A purely technical analysis of fiction fails by O'Connor's standards. In search of a definition of a story, she reminds us that "the obvious things are the hardest to define." But we also risk substituting almost anything for the definition—a story reminiscence, episode, opinion, anecdote, and so forth. She offers a straightforward, organic definition of "story" as found in fiction:

> A story is a complete dramatic action—and in good stories, the characters are shown through the action and the action is controlled through the characters, and the result of this is meaning that derives from the whole presented experience. I myself prefer to say that a story is a dramatic event that involves a person because he is a person, and a particular person—that is, because he shares in the general human condition and in some

specific human situation. A story always involves, in a dramatic way, the mystery of personality.[21]

We find here some of the key elements that operate in her fiction. O'Connor emphasizes the underlying drama that works as the mainspring of fiction. She subscribes to the playwright's axiom: If a gun is conspicuously present at the beginning of a dramatic literary work, it had better be fired before the conclusion! The literary artist achieves meaning out of this organic nexus of dramatic action and character. O'Connor describes a complete story as "one in which the action fully illuminates the meaning." There is no other access to meaning in fiction than through the characters-in-action. She describes it well in an early essay: "If you start with a real personality, a real character, then something is bound to happen and you don't have to know what before you begin."[22] Much later, in a December 1956 letter to "A" she points out that a fiction writer does not have to have a plot in mind. "You would probably do just as well to get that plot business out of your head and simply start with a character or anything that you can make come alive," she advises, adding, "when you have a character he will create his own situation and his situation will suggest some kind of resolution as you get into it" (1013). O'Connor reminds "A" that it is "better to discover a meaning in what you write than to impose one" (1013).

For this reason Flannery O'Connor never tires of reminding us that "fiction has to be largely presented rather than reported." This is what she means when she says that "fiction is narrative art, it relies heavily on the element of drama."[23] She returns to the analogy of the artist's painting and remarks how many fiction writers paint because it helps them become better writers. "It forces them to look at things," she emphasizes. "Fiction writing is seldom a matter of saying things; it is a matter of showing things." And the concrete details that the fiction writer chooses attest to the selective eye of the artist. "What is there is essential and creates movement," O'Connor adds, returning to the dramatic hallmark.

It becomes a matter of making "the concrete work double time" for the fiction writer.[24]

Such carefully crafted fiction demonstrates how a dramatic truth can be experienced only through the organic reality of the specific short story or novel. It yields a unique work of art and meaning. O'Connor speaks of the world a writer creates through the kinds of character and details found there. She terms it an "investment" on the author's part; in that imaginative world we discover a dramatic truth. When she comments on her own short stories, O'Connor offers a major clue to any successful fiction:

> I often ask myself what makes a story work, and what makes it hold up as a story, and I have decided that it is probably some action, some gesture of a character that is unlike any other in the story, one which indicates where the real heart of the story lies. This would have to be an action or a gesture, which was both totally right and totally unexpected; it would have to be one that was both in character and beyond character; it would have to suggest both the world and eternity.[25]

But it is only in and through the character and concrete details found in the story or novel that the reader can find what O'Connor calls the "intellectual meaning" of the work. Again, she compares it to painting—in this case, to the specific apples and particular tablecloth of a Cezanne painting:

> The novelist makes his statements by selection, and if he is any good, he selects every word *for a reason,* every detail *for a reason,* every incident *for a reason,* and arranges them in a certain time-sequence *for a reason.* He demonstrates something that cannot possibly be demonstrated any other way than with a whole novel.[26]

O'Connor distinguishes between two characteristics of fiction. The "literal surface" of fiction yields entertainment to one type of reader; but she insists that "the selfsame surface can be made to yield meaning to the person equipped to experience it there." Her conclusions are striking. "Meaning is what keeps a short story from being short." And the meaning of fiction is not abstract—it is "experienced meaning." You decide if you have written a complete story, she reminds us, if it bears up under the scrutiny of whether "the action fully illuminates the meaning."[27]

The fiction writer's task in creating a story is complex. Its complexity becomes more apparent when we appreciate the key elements of Catholic beliefs and character development in O'Connor's imagination.

THE WRITER'S CATHOLIC BELIEFS

With a stern voice O'Connor declares for her readers that she does not write fiction "primarily [as] a missionary activity."[28] She recognizes the hazards of being misunderstood on this point because her essays are unashamedly outspoken about her Catholic identity and faith. Her short stories and novels invariably offer the epiphany of a religious horizon. But this religious horizon is problematic for many readers to discern. Her many essays on this topic enlighten her audience to the subtleties of imagination vis-à-vis beliefs and faith. How ironic that these essays are often neglected and even occasionally discredited when it comes to a discussion of the integrity of her life as a writer and a believing Catholic Christian.

Flannery O'Connor's imagination theologizes on the central Christian mystery of the Christ and what he has done for us. This is not to muddy distinctions between the disciplines of theology and literature. The integrity of her literary gifts was self-evident to O'Connor, who declares, "Our final standard for [the novelist] will have to be the demands of art, which are a good deal more exacting than the demands of the Church. There are good novels a writer might write and remain a good Catholic, which his conscience as an artist would not allow him to perpetrate."[29] Instead,

O'Connor realizes a more fundamental truth: "[W]e are beginning to realize that an impoverishment of imagination means an impoverishment of the religious life as well."[30] Because she defines faith as "a 'walking in darkness' and not a theological solution to mystery,"[31] the following chapters tease out the meaning of O'Connor's appeal that the writer and audience be "more trustful of the blind imagination,"[32] which yokes together art and belief in fiction such as hers.

Flannery O'Connor insists that she writes from "the standpoint of Christian Orthodoxy." She unequivocally declares, "This means that for me the meaning of life is centered in our Redemption by Christ and what I see in the world I see in its relation to that."[33] She admits the difficulty in making that mystery transparent in fiction, but goes on to claim this yoking together of art and Catholic belief through her fiction: "Dogma is an instrument for penetrating reality. Christian dogma is about the only thing left in the world that surely guards and respects mystery."[34] O'Connor embraces her vocation as both a novelist and a Catholic believer through the invisible but effective bonds of the Judaeo-Christian tradition. "When one speaks as a novelist, he must speak as he writes—with the whole personality"[35]—meaning that her own faith commitment is integral to her personality and aesthetics as a fiction writer.

For this unashamedly Catholic fiction writer, born on March 25, the feast of the Annunciation, this means that the novelist and short story writer's "theology, even in its most remote reaches, will have a direct bearing" on artistic judgment.[36] It comes as no surprise that O'Connor concludes, "I shall have to speak, without apology, of the Church, even when the Church is absent; of Christ, even when Christ is not recognized."[37] To eclipse her identity as a believing Catholic Christian or her integrity as a fiction writer who claims that the Christian mystery "should enlarge not narrow" her "field of vision"[38] is to risk missing O'Connor's achievement as an imaginative literary artist.[39] She never improved upon her succinct observation that the larger part of her modern audience took exception to the underlying Christian assumptions of her worldview: "About this I can only say that there are perhaps other ways than my own in which this story could be read, but none other by which it could have been written. Belief, in my own case anyway, is the engine that makes perception operate."[40] O'Connor never forces her art to proselytize readers or to coerce them to believe; but neither does she make excuses for her Catholic faith as an integral part of her personality and imagination.

GRACE

Catholic theologians define grace as a twofold mystery: God's loving presence and the human person's transformation in that presence.[41] Karl Rahner describes grace in terms of a person who "confronts the abyss of his existence." Such an honest encounter with the depths of human existence does not lead to despair but to hope. Rahner reminds us that our always already graced human experience reveals our orientation toward self-transcendence and God's self-communication in love.

> ...[A] person who opens himself...experiences that this holy mystery is also a hidden closeness, a forgiving intimacy, his real home, that it is a love which shares itself, something familiar which he can approach and turn to from the estrangement of his own perilous and empty life. It is the person who in the forlornness of his guilt still turns in trust to the mystery of his existence which is quietly present, and surrenders himself as one who even in his guilt no longer wants to understand himself in a self-centered and self-sufficient way, it is this person who experiences himself as one...who is forgiven, and he experiences this forgiveness which he receives as the hidden, forgiving and liberating love of God himself, who forgives *in that* he gives himself, because only in this way can there really be forgiveness once and for all.[42]

Flannery O'Connor's fiction offers compelling imaginative presentations of this mystery of the absolute closeness that God communicates to her characters who discover the "forgiving and liberating love of God." Rahner names well the existential theological dynamics that O'Connor dramatizes: "When a person... confronts the abyss of his existence...and when this person has the courage to look into himself and to find in these depths his ultimate truth, there he can also have the experience that this abyss accepts him as his true and forgiving security." The irony of what Rahner calls "apparently so ordinary an experience" yields ultimate depth and ultimate truth when a person "comes into the presence of himself and of the holy mystery" of God's grace as God's self-communicating intimacy and unconditional love.[43]

One of the most able commentators on Rahner's revisionist Catholic theology of grace, Brian McDermott, offers a helpful insight that bears upon O'Connor's fiction. The doctrine of original sin, says McDermott, attempts to express the role that sin plays in human life before we exercise our human freedom. Rahner himself acknowledges the traditional understanding of original sin as depriving us of sanctifying grace. McDermott emphasizes, however, that Rahner "does maintain that two unequal forces influence everyone born into the world: the power of God's redeeming love in Christ and the power of sin opposed to Christ." In Rahner's theology, these two fundamental realities are "existentials" of our life from the beginning. These two conflicting orientations—sin and grace—become actual only through what McDermott describes as the "'free' complicity of the person." Our freedom ultimately permits either sin or grace to become the defining horizon of our life. But just as our family of origin or our genetic inheritance may be either a real curse or a real blessing, the "existentials" of sin or grace alone do not exclusively influence our salvation. "Christian faith maintains that God's *redeeming* love and the freedom of the person blessed by that redemption are the most powerful circumstances in human life."[44] Few writers present a more convincing imaginative drama of this central Christian mystery of grace and human freedom than does O'Connor.

O'Connor readily admits the challenge she faces in writing about grace for her contemporary audience. In a 1956 letter she remarks: "It's almost impossible to write about supernatural Grace in fiction" (988). She defines art in this same letter as "something that one experiences alone and for the purpose of realizing in a fresh way, through the senses, the mystery of existence." O'Connor includes a trademark comment, "Part of that mystery of existence is sin" (988). It is no wonder that in a 1963 letter (less than four months before her death) she would reiterate her life's task in a strikingly powerful statement: "The writer has to make corruption believable before he can make the grace meaningful" (1182). There is no better compass to orient us to her fiction. She adds a second insight in a letter written two weeks later to Cecil Dawkins. She chides her dissatisfaction with the Catholic Church and blames it on her "incomplete understanding of sin." She adds that she is wrong in expecting the successors of Peter—who denied Christ three times—to walk on water. Writing on grace in this context, O'Connor offers a simple and straightforward reflection on the mystery of human freedom:

> All human nature vigorously resists grace because grace changes us and the change is painful. To have the Church be what you want it to be would require the continuous miraculous meddling of God in human affairs, whereas it is our dignity that we are allowed more or less to get on with those graces that come through faith and the sacraments and which work through our human nature. God has chosen to operate in this manner. We can't understand this but we can't reject it without rejecting life.
>
> Human nature is so faulty that it can resist any amount of grace and most of the time it does. The Church does well to hold her own; you are asking that she show a profit. When she shows a profit you have a saint, not necessarily a canonized one.

...It is what is invisible that God sees and that the Christian must look for. Because he knows the consequences of sin, he knows how deep in you have to go to find love. (1084–85)

O'Connor affords her readers a third critical insight about the theology of grace in an early 1960 letter to Andrew Lytle. She alludes to her more frequent reflections about "the presentation of love and charity, or better call it grace" in her writing. She explains her word choice: "love suggests tenderness, whereas grace can be violent or would have to be to compete with the kind of evil I make concrete" (1121). Time and again her readers encounter the radical conversions of her characters portrayed in shocking and violent images. But O'Connor also points out that the frequent rejection of grace in her stories—most obvious in The Misfit who shoots the grandmother in "A Good Man Is Hard to Find"—relates to another dimension of her imagination. "This moment of grace excites the devil to frenzy" (1121). In order to make the reality of grace credible, O'Connor admits that her fiction first has to dramatize evil and to make it recognizable. It is for this reason that she volunteers, "my subject in fiction is the action of grace in territory held largely by the devil." The irony lies in her equally emphatic perception that she writes about this subject for "an audience which puts little stock either in grace or the devil."[45]

Flannery O'Connor insists that "grace is not lacking" despite the audience's disbelief. "There is a moment in every great story," O'Connor explains, "in which the presence of grace can be felt as it waits to be accepted or rejected, even though the reader may not recognize this moment." She admits the irony of the action where "the devil has been the unwilling instrument of grace." Alongside this surprise, O'Connor admits that it is not something she consciously imports into her stories, but "a discovery I get out of them." She repeats her conviction that the fulcrum for grace is a dramatic action "that is totally unexpected, yet totally believable."[46] Grace is offered, and the question remains open as to whether the protagonist in her story will perceive its presence and accept or reject its transforming effects. In the letter where she bluntly admits the challenge of writing about supernatural grace in fiction, she adds: "We almost have to approach it negatively. As to natural Grace, we have to take that the way it comes—through nature. In any case, it operates surrounded by evil."[47]

A key to understanding O'Connor's imagination is her realization of a flaw in the modern reader's consciousness. She points to both storytellers' and listeners' expectation of a "redemptive act"—what falls must be offered a chance to be restored. "The reader of today looks for this motion," O'Connor concedes, "but what he has forgotten is the cost of it. His sense of evil is diluted or lacking altogether and so he has forgotten the price of restoration"(820).[48] From this realization springs the dramatic action at the heart of O'Connor's fiction. Her sense of the "grotesque" in her fiction functions ironically to awaken both her protagonists and her readers to grace as God's loving presence and the human person's transformation in that presence.

One diagnosis offered by O'Connor helps the reader to recognize grace in her stories. In an important essay entitled "Novelist and Believer" she identifies the separation of nature and grace as the culprit. Catholic theology's axiom is uncompromising: grace builds on nature. She finds her reader, "if he believes in grace at all," preferring to have grace "served to him raw as Instant Uplift." This reader's favorite word, she notices, is "compassion." But O'Connor echoes the German Lutheran theologian Dietrich Bonhoeffer who ridiculed modern Christians for their superficial faith—what he named "cheap grace."[49] She likewise prefers to define compassion as "being in travail with and for creation in its subjection to vanity" because this clearly "implies a recognition of sin."[50] It is no wonder that O'Connor's masterpiece essay, "The Catholic Novelist in the Protestant South," insists upon this principle when she names the great misunderstanding of "what the operation of grace can look like in fiction."

The sentimental temptation looms large. "The reader wants his grace warm and binding," O'Connor protests, "not dark and disruptive."[51] The imaginative use of distortion and violence in her fiction is a metaphor for grace seen from this perspective.

An analysis of O'Connor's theology of grace would be incomplete without pointing out what she considers most damaging to fiction. In the same 1956 letter in which she admits the impossibility of writing about supernatural grace in fiction ("We almost have to approach it negatively"), she complains: "The two worst sins of bad taste in fiction are pornography and sentimentality." O'Connor defines the former as "too much sex" and the latter as "too much sentiment." "You have to have enough of either to prove your point but no more." This echoes a conviction she voices earlier in the letter, that the fiction writer has to use "as many aspects of life as are necessary to make his total picture convincing." In her often-quoted words, "The fiction writer doesn't state, he shows, renders" (988). The subject of sentimentalism in writing occupies O'Connor's attention seven months earlier in some of her first letters to "A." She responds to a book of Nelson Algren that "A" had sent to her. She is offended by the way Algren sentimentalizes the poor. "The particular appeal of the poor for the fiction writer is existential not economic" (947–48), she reminds her.

In September of 1956 O'Connor goes so far as to suspect "A" of being a "Romantic" because "A" argues that the truths of faith—or specifically, Christ's incarnation—have to be "emotionally satisfying to be right." O'Connor points out how "the very notion of God's existence is not emotionally satisfying for great numbers of people, which does not mean that God ceases to exist." She names Jean Paul Sartre as an example.

> The truth does not change according to our ability to stomach it emotionally. A higher paradox confounds emotion as well as reason and there are long periods in the lives of all of us, and of the saints, when the truth revealed by faith is

hideous, emotionally disturbing, downright repulsive. Witness the dark night of the soul in individual saints. Right now the whole world seems to be going through a dark night of the soul.

There is a question whether faith can or is supposed to be emotionally satisfying. I must say that the thought of everyone lolling about in an emotionally satisfying faith is repugnant to me. I believe that we are ultimately directed Godward but that this journey is often impeded by emotion. (982)

Two examples from O'Connor's Catholic life clarify her meaning. In her second letter to "A," the letter where O'Connor identifies her work with "Christian Realism," she remarks her distrust of "pious phrases," especially when she finds herself using them. "I try militantly never to be affected by the pious language of the faithful but it is always coming out when you least expect it. In contrast to the pious language of the faithful, the liturgy is beautifully flat" (943–44). The genius of the Roman Catholic liturgy is precisely that emotionally "flat" language, the un-Romantic aesthetics that O'Connor associates with it. Readers find a second example to illustrate her aversion to emotion and sentimentality in the often-quoted April 1958 letter to "A" where she says, "all good stories are about conversion." Even though she describes the action of grace changing a character, she adds, "Grace can't be experienced in itself." As an example she points to receiving Communion. "[W]hen you go to Communion, you receive grace but you experience nothing; or if you do experience something what you experience is not the grace but an emotion caused by it." For that very reason O'Connor admits "that in a story all you can do with grace is to show that it is changing the character" (1067).

CHARACTER

O'Connor's definition of story signals the pivotal role of character. She points to an action, a gesture of a character unlike any other in the story—yet an action or gesture that is "both totally right and totally unexpected,...both in character and beyond character"—as the "real heart" of the story. She describes a bad story, "where the writer has thought of some action and then scrounged up a character to perform it." In contrast, she states, "In most good stories it is the character's personality that creates the action of the story." A key to understanding her fiction lies in appreciating her own discovery in the process of writing about such real personalities, such real characters. Time and again, O'Connor admits the truth that with such characters "something is bound to happen; and you don't have to know what beforehand."[52]

The drama of sin and grace is central to the imagination of Flannery O'Connor when she creates characters. She explains this dynamic:

> The serious writer has always taken the flaw in human nature for his starting point, usually the flaw in an otherwise admirable character. Drama usually bases itself on the bedrock of original sin, whether the writer thinks in theological terms or not. Then, too, the character in a serious novel is supposed to carry a burden of meaning larger than himself. The novelist doesn't write about people in a vacuum: he writes about people in a world where something is obviously lacking, where there is the general mystery of incompleteness and the particular tragedy of our times to be demonstrated, and the novelist tries to give you, within the form of the book, a total experience of human nature at the time. For this reason the greatest dramas naturally involve the salvation or loss of the soul. Where there is no belief in the soul, there is very little drama. The Christian novelist is distinguished from his pagan colleagues by recognizing sin as sin.

> According to his heritage he sees it not as sickness or accident
> of environment, but as a responsible choice of offense against
> God which involves his eternal future. Either one is serious
> about salvation or one is not.[53]

One cannot find a better synthesis of the elements of the drama initiated by O'Connor's characters than this presentation of her task. It is no wonder that she describes the nine short stories comprising her first collection, *A Good Man Is Hard to Find,* as "nine stories about original sin" (927).[54]

At this juncture she introduces a subtle note about the fiction writer's development of characters. Her Catholic tradition and its emphasis upon the intellect, "faith seeking understanding," come into play. O'Connor explores how "great fiction involves the whole range of human judgment." The author, she explains, "finds a symbol and a way of lodging it which tells the intelligent reader whether this feeling is adequate or inadequate, whether it is moral or immoral, whether it is good or evil."[55] The reader recalls her emphasis upon details and the reasons the author has for their specific choice. "For the fiction writer, judgment begins in the details he sees and how he sees them."[56]

When she calls fiction an "incarnational art," there is a wealth of understanding of the mystery of Christ as a source for her imagination. She describes the materials of the fiction writer as "the humblest." "Fiction is about everything human and we are made out of dust, and if you scorn getting yourself dusty, then you shouldn't try to write fiction."[57] This "dusty" human nature of her characters (many of whom are touched by the spirit and given the life of grace) figures prominently in my interpretation of her short stories and novels vis-à-vis the mystery of Christ's humility. The God who becomes incarnate in Christ reveals the innate dignity of the human person; therefore, whenever O'Connor's protagonists come to discover this same human dignity in themselves and especially in those they have wrongly judged to be lacking in worth, the dramatic climax of her stories unfolds. Taking my cue from Thomas Merton's sterling elegy on O'Connor, I explore how the words *contempt* and *respect* offer a key to interpreting her stories.[58]

The O'Connor characters who respond to grace, we discover, are analogues of Christ, the God-Man of Christian tradition— recovering their identity as the image and likeness of God. Christ recovered this identity, lost in sin, in the redemptive drama of his life, death, and resurrection. Her characters are, first and foremost, characters whose freedom is essential to their identity. In this light, O'Connor perceives that "the general intelligent reader today is not a believer" because "he does not understand the character motivated by faith."[59] Contemporary Catholic moral theology's understanding of "fundamental option"[60] helps to interpret her characters in light of this insistence upon a transcendental freedom. Such freedom involves the choice of one's deepest identity. This involves two moments in the development of character. At one point, we find characters discovering how they have exercised their "fundamental option" as a negative stance toward self, toward others, toward God, and toward all reality. At a later point, some of her protagonists recognize and respond to the offer of grace, revealing their own capacity to change to an affirmative stance toward self, others, God, and even toward the cosmic reality.

Such an ironic sense of this fundamental option operates at the opening of O'Connor's short story, "The Displaced Person." When the xenophobic Mrs. Shortley descends from her hilltop vantage and meets the Polish immigrant family, O'Connor describes more than the literal scene: "{S]he moved down from her elevation and went forward to be introduced to them, as if she meant to find out at once what they were capable of." Storytelling, however, only gradually unfolds the *capacity* of free characters in terms of both sin and grace—in this case, those capacities dramatized through the immigrant Mr. Guizac *and* Mrs. Shortley herself.

Flannery O'Connor's genius will be evident whenever she appropriates from her Catholic ethos the truth that only free human characters create the credible action of a story. The extent to which she depends upon this tradition can be found expressed in the art of her fiction, but also explicated in her prose:

> [T]he novelist does not write about general beliefs but about men with free will, and...there is nothing in our faith that implies a foregone optimism for man so free that with his last breath he can say *No*. All Catholic literature will be positive in the sense that we hold this freedom to exist, but the Church has never encouraged us to believe that hell is not a going concern. The writer uses his eyes on what he happens to be facing....He does not decide what would be good for the Christian body and then deliver it. Like a very doubtful Jacob, he confronts what stands in his path and wonders if he will come out of the struggle at all.[61]

DISTORTION AND "THE GROTESQUE"

An O'Connor essay entitled "On Her Own Work" in the posthumously published collection *Mystery and Manners* acknowledges that her short story, "A Good Man Is Hard to Find," had been called "grotesque." She responds, "I prefer to call it literal." Then she proceeds to compare how a good story is literal "in the same sense that a child's drawing is literal." She remarks how a child's drawing does not intend to distort but to put down accurately "what he sees." As a result, the child "sees the lines that create motion." By analogy, O'Connor explains, the "lines of motion" that interest the writer are "lines of spiritual motion"—in the sense of the action of grace.[62] She writes to Carl Hartman in a March 1954 letter about *Wise Blood* and the grotesque "penances" ("acts of assertion") undertaken by Hazel Motes. She explains that the "mild horror" Hartman experiences when he realizes that she believes in the Christian mysteries (free choice, conscience, and Redemption) is "one reason my book is grotesque" to unbelievers (921–22). An August 1955 letter to

"A" already mentions that she is at work on her AAUW [American Association of University Women] lecture for Spring 1956 in Lansing, Michigan, where she attempts to justify "the distortion in fiction." She suggests that she is going to call it "The Freak in Modern Fiction." In a June 1957 letter to Cecil Dawkins she again takes up the question of Catholic belief in her stories. Returning once more to "A Good Man Is Hard to Find," O'Connor insists that the religion in her stories "concerns specifically Christ and the Incarnation." She refuses to reduce her fiction to the Golden Rule of "Do unto others" because more than an ethic, a religious mystery is at stake. She quotes The Misfit's protest that Jesus "th[r]own everything off balance" and the alternatives are clear: either "follow Him or find some meanness." Without a hesitation she explains: "That is the fulcrum that lifts my particular stories. I'm a Catholic but this is in orthodox Protestantism also, though out of context—which makes it grow into grotesque forms. The Catholic, using his own eyes and the eyes of the Church (when he is inclined to open them) is in a most favorable position to recognize the grotesque" (1035).

But it is O'Connor's 1960 essay, "Some Aspects of the Grotesque in Southern Fiction," that best defines her sense of the grotesque. She sloughs off misapplications of the term (such as northern readers pejoratively calling grotesque fiction "realistic"). "In these grotesque works," explains O'Connor, "we find that the writer has made alive some experience which we are not accustomed to observe everyday, or which the ordinary man may never experience in his ordinary life." The realism of each novelist, she argues, depends upon the writer's "view of the ultimate reaches of reality" (815). For these reasons she credits the grotesque in fiction for its interest in "what we don't understand rather than what we do." Imaginative possibility is preferred over probability. She describes both the creator and the characters as modern Don Quixotes. The concrete will be employed by such a writer, but "much more obviously by the way of distortion"—like the child's revelatory drawing. O'Connor uses the adjectives "wild," "violent," and "comic" to describe the "discrepancies" that grotesque fiction seeks to combine (816). She admits the American tendency to confuse the grotesque with "the sentimental" by mistaking it for "compassion." O'Connor remains consistent. She discredits the use of the grotesque as feeling or sentiment; instead she recognizes how the legitimate use of the grotesque implies intellectual and moral judgments.

For these reasons O'Connor identifies the grotesque in modern fiction with prophetic vision. "In the novelist's case," she insists, "prophecy is a matter of seeing near things with their extensions of meaning and thus of seeing far things close up. The prophet is a realist of distances, and it is this kind of realism that you find in the best modern instances of the grotesque" (817). She returns to the metaphor of the "freak," explaining how southern writers still recognize the freak because their general conception of the human is "in the main, theological." Her familiar verdict that the South is "hardly Christ-centered" but "Christ-haunted" (818) follows. In this sense, the modern fiction writer's irony serves well the prophetic task of the grotesque genre of literature: "[I]t is when the freak can be sensed as a figure for our essential displacement that he attains some depth in literature" (818). This irony is apparent in an early short story like "The Displaced Person," but will mature and become subtler in O'Connor's later fiction. Her attention to her audience of readers factors into the choice of the grotesque for her fiction. "We must remember that [the novelist's] vision has to be transmitted," cautions O'Connor, "and that the limitations and blind spots of his audience will very definitely affect the way he is able to show what he sees" (819). For O'Connor that meant a greater tendency to rely upon the grotesque. One has no doubt about the choice she makes when she compares the past with the present: "There are ages when it is possible to woo the reader; there are others when something more drastic is necessary" (820). For that very reason she chose to give her readers not the novels they wanted but the kind that interested her as a novelist (821).

One of O'Connor's most quotable lines captures her imaginative sense of the need for distortion to reach her "tired readers." She adjusts to the fact that her audience does not hold the same foundational beliefs and declares, "[T]hen you have to make your vision apparent by shock—to the hard of hearing you shout, and for the almost blind you draw large and startling figures" (804–5).[63]

An early example from an essay clarifies O'Connor's strategy. She points to Franz Kafka's classic short story, "The Metamorphosis." When the protagonist of that story awakens as a cockroach, O'Connor does not dismiss the story as surreal or alienating to the reader. She notes that the man who wakes up has not discarded his human nature. "[T]his situation is accepted by the reader because the concrete detail is absolutely convincing. The fact is that the story describes the dual nature of man in such a realistic fashion that it is almost unbearable." She is quick to point out that Kafka does not distort the truth, "but rather, a certain distortion is used to get at the truth." O'Connor follows the classical distinction between appearances and reality, allowing the artist the liberty "to make certain rearrangements of nature if these will lead to greater depth of vision."[64]

Flannery O'Connor's imagination is superbly ironic. She shares William F. Lynch's appreciation of the modern propensity for irony: one thing is said and something quite opposite is meant or implied.[65] I am reminded of the character Mrs. Freeman in her short story "Good Country People," which opens: "Besides the neutral expression that she wore when she was alone, Mrs. Freeman had two others, forward and reverse, that she used for all her human dealings" (263).[66] The ironic imagination makes shocking demands on an audience inclined to purely superficial or literal readings of a story—and the forward/reverse directions of the ironic imagination are equally stark opposites.

In this same vein, I interpret O'Connor's fiction and its distortions in light of recent scholarship on the parables of the New Testament as a unique access to an understanding of the historical Jesus and the Christ of faith. The parables' shock effect and reversal of audience expectations afford a valuable paradigm for appreciating O'Connor's urgent stories. Because she claims to be a "realist of distances" it is essential to appreciate her impulse "to distort appearances to show a hidden truth."

VIOLENCE

The very title of O'Connor's second novel, *The Violent Bear It Away,* suggests the centrality of this symbolic action in her fiction. In a letter only two years before her death she hints at the lengthy process of developing sanctity when she writes to a friend who is reporting on Monsignor Ivan Illich's school for missionaries in Cuernevaca, Mexico. "This is surely what it means to bear away the kingdom of heaven with violence: the violence is directed inward" (1171).[67] She returns to her own work to defend the use of so much violence.

> ...I have found that violence is strangely capable of returning my characters to reality and preparing them to accept their moment of grace. Their heads are so hard that almost nothing else will do the work. This idea, that reality is something to which we must be returned at considerable cost, is one which is seldom understood by the casual reader, but it is one which is implicit in the Christian view of the world.[68]

There are strong echoes of the Franciscan tradition and spirituality throughout O'Connor's work. The thirteenth-century Franciscan theologian John Duns Scotus speaks of *haeceitas,* the "this-ness" or distinctiveness that gives everything in creation its unique identity. The Jesuit Gerard Manley Hopkins is the great modern master of this Scotist spirituality in his poetry. O'Connor does the same by insisting on the union of imagination and reason: "For [the artist], to be reasonable is to find, in the object, in the situation, in the sequence, the spirit which makes it itself." She warns that it is neither easy nor simple to do. "It is to intrude upon the timeless, and that is only done by the violence of a single-minded respect for the truth."[69] Here her uses of distortion and violence coincide.

O'Connor nuances her meaning about the imaginative use of violence. She asserts that "violence is never an end in itself" but describes it as "the extreme situation that best reveals what we are essentially."[70] This ironic use of violence resonates with the work of contemporary theologians whose interpretations of the Christ orient us to what Edward Schillebeeckx calls "negative experiences of contrast."[71] By its absence, we imaginatively arrive at the presence of the human essence. Flannery O'Connor reminds us how we come to an appreciation of "the whole man" through the fiction writer's use of symbolic violence: "[T]he man in the violent situation reveals those qualities least dispensable to his personality, those qualities which are all he will have to take into eternity with him...."[72]

She understood well how "human nature vigorously resists grace because grace changes us and all change is painful." Rather than finding God "meddling" in our human lives, O'Connor reverences the mystery: "Human nature is so faulty that it can resist any amount of grace and most of the time it does." She dramatizes the "hidden love" that invites human freedom to invest itself in response to God's grace (1084).[73] It is no wonder that this highly symbolic violence is central to her fiction, a predictable instrument of distortion to awaken her audience to the higher truth. As O'Connor admits in one of her letters to "A," "The friends of God suffer." Therefore, as a fiction writer, she explains, "It has always seemed necessary to me to throw the weight of circumstances against the character" (973).[74]

The caliber of evil in the world O'Connor shows to her readers demands an equivalent drama of grace. I appraise her fiction in the same light because she understands Christ to be such a realist. In her incomparable words to "A," "As for Jesus' being a realist: if He was not God, He was no realist, only a liar, and the crucifixion an act of justice" (943).[75] A theological appreciation of the violence that Jesus suffers in redemptive love helps O'Connor's readers to interpret the presence of "violent" grace in her fiction.

VISION

Every genuine artist offers the audience a vision of who they might become. Literary art invites the reader to inhabit an alternative world, a world imaginatively made real. So that, at the conclusion, every good short story or novel offers an unfinished future in terms of the possibility of the reader's personal transformation. O'Connor's reservations about creative writing classes salt her insights with humor on this score:

> [Y]ou almost feel that any idiot with a nickel's worth of talent can emerge from a writing class able to write a competent story. In fact, so many people can now write competent stories that the short story as a medium is in danger of dying of competence. We want competence, but competence itself is deadly. What is needed is the vision to go with it, and you do not get this from a writing class.[76]

O'Connor emphasizes the artist's "angle of vision" when she considers what the artist shows to the reader. In this sense, she reminds us, "he begins to see before he gets to the surface and he continues to see after he has gone past it." She finds the artist beginning to see "the bedrock of all human experience" in "the depths of himself"—that is, "the experience of limitation or, if you will, poverty." For this reason she finds most fiction writers irresistibly attracted to the poor because of their involvement in both "manners" and "mystery."[77] Editors Sally and Robert Fitzgerald perceived the importance of that pair of terms in O'Connor's vocabulary and entitled the posthumous collection of her essays *Mystery and Manners*. O'Connor borrows again from Henry James to define her terms: "The mystery he [James] was talking about is the mystery of our position on earth, and the manners are those conventions which, in the hands of the artist, reveal that central mystery." She recognizes that mystery is "an embarrassment for the modern mind," something to be eliminated by an audience convinced "that what can't be done with figures [arithmetic] isn't worth doing." Flannery O'Connor found a genuine contact with lived mystery in Bible Belt religion and a powerful expression of manners in the texture of southern culture. She combines the two so that "fiction becomes very disturbing" to otherwise complacent readers.[78]

No doubt the abundance of "eye" imagery in O'Connor's short stories and the two novels provides telling metaphors for vision. Everywhere her characters symbolically stare, squint, pierce with their eyes, nervously glance, or look off toward a distant treeline. The author's own insistence upon showing the details of the story demands the alert eyes of her readers. Spectacles and blindness— both are often used ironically—become familiar symbols in this O'Connor universe. Her first novel, *Wise Blood*, reverberates with biblical echoes of Paul of Tarsus, struck blind on the road to Damascus and healed with the new vision of faith, merging with the blind Oedipus from classical literature.[79] Even in O'Connor's writing about her treasured peacocks, the eye and vision imagery dominates. She describes the peacock as "a careful and dignified investigator" with "a beady, pleasure-taking eye"—and already you are reminded of O'Connor's own demeanor as a writer: "When my mother and I arrived at the station, the crate was on the platform and from one end of it protruded a long, royal blue neck and crested head. A white line above and below each eye gave the investigating head an expression of alert composure."[80]

The alert composure of O'Connor has its source in a religious vision. She probes this in an important letter to a college student who wrote to her about an experience of losing his faith. In this context she points to the ambivalence of college life: one result is the stimulation of the intellect, the other result is "a shrinking of the imaginative life." O'Connor defines faith as the opposite of "absolute solutions." "Faith is what you have in the absence of knowledge," she reminds, and recommends that we thrive on different questions—just as she calls us to glimpse the ultimate questions we have forgotten to ask. Doubt, too, is an integral moment in the act of faith for Flannery O'Connor. She summons a larger religious vision when she reflects upon her own college skepticism born of Christian faith: "It always says: wait, don't bite on this, get a wider picture, continue to read." Vision begins where easy answers end: "[Faith] will keep you free—not free to do anything you please, but free to be formed by something larger than your own intellect or the intellects of those around you" (1163–65).[81] I interpret O'Connor's vision by paying particular attention to the characters in her stories who absolutely rely on scientific knowledge and exclude faith. Her stories unfold the dramatic peril that inevitably confronts such characters.

In this sense I find O'Connor's vision ultimately rooted in the contemplative stream of the Catholic tradition. Using a definition of contemplation as "anything that penetrates illusion and touches reality,"[82] my interpretation of her fiction offers new readings of familiar stories. It explains her insistence: "For me dogma is only a gateway to contemplation and is an instrument of freedom and not of restriction. It preserves mystery in the human mind" (943).[83] O'Connor's art becomes sublimely contemplative because she is such a realist of distances. She not only penetrated illusion and touched reality in her own life; she offers her audience a mimetic fiction that resonates with the contemplative eye and heart of the living Catholic tradition.

Chapter Two

Making God-in-Christ Believable: *Wise Blood*

Let me assure you that no one but a Catholic could have written Wise Blood *even though it is a book about a kind of Protestant saint.*
— Letter to Ben Griffith, 3 March 1954

Wise Blood is the work of a twenty-six-year-old novelist who greeted her 1952 audience with a challenge. Post–World War II America was priding itself upon military victories in Europe and the Pacific in 1945. The 1950–53 American campaign in South Korea proved to be a sequel in the battle against the threat of Communist world domination. The Eisenhower presidency, launched in 1952, ushered in the decade of peace, economic prosperity, and the birth of suburbia. A new generation was living the American dream, while on the distant horizon the grim specter of the Cold War[1] era went virtually unnoticed.

It was also a time of expansive church growth. Religion flourished as witnessed by the growth in churches and synagogues.

American Protestantism in the fifties had its conservative spokesman in Norman Vincent Peale and his 1952 best-seller, *The Power of Positive Thinking;*[2] American Catholicism had an equally dramatic celebrity in the television personality Bishop Fulton J. Sheen, author of the 1949 book *Peace of Soul;*[3] American Judaism began its recovery after the World War II Holocaust with an influx of European immigrants and found a prominent conservative spokesperson in Joshua L. Liebman, author of the 1946 title *Peace of Mind.*[4] Across this spectrum, religious certitudes were coupled with the Puritan ethic. The formula was simple: belong to visible religious institutions and be blessed with success. As Flannery O'Connor wrote in a letter to her friends Brainard and Francis Neel Cheney, "Woe to you who are filled, for you shall hunger."[5] The deeper human hungers for faith and meaning ultimately concern her in *Wise Blood.* The superficiality of both American religion and post–World War II American culture at the advent of the fifties figures prominently in this first novel.

Early reviewers tended to misread *Wise Blood* as an attack upon southern religious fundamentalism. O'Connor keenly appreciates the predicament of her American audience. She recognizes that they are "not adequately equipped to believe anything,"[6] but nonetheless she accepts her task as a fiction writer to awaken them to the possibility of authentic Christian faith. At the end of the first chapter, O'Connor has the train porter respond to Hazel Motes's repeated curse, "Jesus," with a telling appraisal: "The porter didn't move. 'Jesus been a long time gone,' he said in a sour triumphant voice" (14). The porter delivers more than a statement about the historical Jesus; it is an observation about a culture where religion has become confused with sentimentality and success. When Haze's landlady, Mrs. Flood, discovers his penitential acts of self-inflicted corporal punishment in the concluding chapter of *Wise Blood,* Haze contradicts her judgment that "It's not natural." She persists and unwittingly exiles the essence of Christian faith along with other grotesque behaviors: "'Well, its [sic] not normal. It's like one of them gory stories, it's something that people have quit doing—like boiling in oil or being a saint or walling up cats,' she said. 'There's no reason for it. People have quit doing it'" (127).

Four years before the publication of *Wise Blood,* a very kindred spirit, the Trappist monk Thomas Merton, had narrated how faith could be reclaimed as a dramatic countercultural act in his phenomenally best-selling autobiography of religious conversion, *The Seven Storey Mountain.* It was his Columbia University classmate Robert Lax who had asked him, "What do you want to be?" Lax's rejoinder to Merton's reply that he wanted to be "a good Catholic" disarmed Thomas Merton: "[W]hat you should say is that you want to be a saint."[7] It awakened Merton's mind and heart to the fact that the desire to be a saint was all that was necessary. No wonder that O'Connor herself would describe Hazel Motes as "a kind of Protestant saint" (923).

The voice of a Jewish contemporary of O'Connor, Abraham Joshua Heschel, spoke of the emptiness of American religion at this very same juncture. Few could rival his interreligious sensitivity or his hope for a Christian renewal that would enable people to be authentically Christian and in dialogue with their Jewish roots. Heschel summarizes the religious predicament with which O'Connor wrestles in *Wise Blood* when he enumerates the failures of a faithless people:

> Little does contemporary religion ask of man.
> It is ready to offer comfort; it has no courage to challenge. It is ready to offer edification; it has no courage to break the idols, to shatter callousness.
> The trouble is that religion has become "religion"— institution, dogma, ritual. It is no longer an event. Its acceptance involves neither risk nor strain. Religion has achieved respectability by the grace of society, and its representatives publish as a frontispiece the *nihil obstat* signed by social scientists.
> We define self-reliance and call it faith, shrewdness and call it wisdom, anthropology and call it ethics, literature and call

it Bible, inner security and call it religion, conscience and call it God. However, nothing counterfeit can endure forever.

It is customary to blame secular science and antireligious philosophy for the eclipse of religion in modern society. It would be more honest to blame religion for its own defeats. Religion declined not because it was refuted, but because it became irrelevant, dull, oppressive, insipid.

When faith is completely replaced by creed, worship by discipline, love by habit; when the crisis of today is ignored because of the splendor of the past; when faith becomes an heirloom rather than a living fountain; when religion speaks only in the name of authority rather than with the voice of compassion, its message becomes meaningless.[8]

It would be almost a decade after the publication of *Wise Blood* before American theologians debated the assets and liabilities of the "God Is Dead Theology"[9] which debuted in the mid-1960s in the United States. O'Connor's novel deserves to be described as brilliant because of the way her imagination anticipates their subtle (and much misunderstood) theological critique of the culture. But the origins of this modern dilemma lay much earlier.

With a characteristic bluntness O'Connor's first letter to "A" delivers a memorable metaphor to expose the spiritual void in American culture during the 1950s: "[I]t is easy to see that the moral sense has been bred out of certain sections of the population, like the wings have been bred off certain chickens to produce more white meat on them. This is a generation of wingless chickens," she lamented, "which I suppose is what Nietzsche meant when he said God was dead" (942). To trace the erosion of religious faith, O'Connor points first to the atheism of the modern philosopher Friedrich Nietzsche (1844–1900). It was his "Parable of the Madman" that ushered in the shocking realization that by our indifference to religious mystery we modern persons were behaving *as if* God were dead.

It helps to look carefully at the narrative of Nietzsche's parable. It begins with a man coming to the central marketplace at dawn.

He carries a superfluous lantern as the brilliant light of day comes with sunrise. He exclaims incessantly, "I am looking for God! I am looking for God!" The crowd in the marketplace mocks him with taunting responses, "Have you lost him then?" "Did he lose his way like a child?" "Has God gone on a voyage?" The madman speaks at length.

> "Where has God gone?" he cried. "I shall tell you. *We have killed him*—you and I. We are his murderers. But how have we done this? How were we able to drink up the sea? Who gave us the sponge to wipe away the entire horizon? What did we do when we unchained this earth from its sun? Whither are we moving now?...Are we not straying as through an infinite nothing? Do we not feel the breath of empty space?...Must not lanterns be lit in the morning? Do we not hear anything yet of the noise of the gravediggers who are burying God?"[10]

He concludes, "God is dead. God remains dead. And we have killed him. How shall we, murderers of all murderers, console ourselves?" But he warns the listeners that "the greatness of this deed [is] too great for us." He cautions that humanity does not yet realize the enormity of this murder and employs a powerful metaphor: "...the light of the stars requires time...[and] this deed is still more distant from [humanity] than the most distant stars...." In the end, he goes to the nearby church and there sings the *Requiem,* the Catholic Church's traditional funeral song, but this time with supreme irony—he prayerfully sings to God, "May God rest in peace!" And the haunting question that earns for Nietzsche's story its literary (and religious) caliber as a parable follows: "What are these churches now if they are not the tombs and sepulchres of God?"[11]

Nietzsche's parable is the late nineteenth century's stinging indictment of institutional Christianity. It is not a metaphysical statement about God, not meant as an argument to refute the existence of the Creator or the Divine Being. Rather, Nietzsche has confronted the modern world and honestly indicted a fraud-ulent Christianity because he sees Christians behaving *as if* God were dead. There is an unmistakable echo of Nietzsche in Heschel's verdict: "It would be more honest to blame religion for its own defeats. Religion declined, not because it was refuted, but because it became irrelevant, dull, oppressive, insipid." One can-not appreciate Flannery O'Connor's *Wise Blood* without a sense of the origins of the cultural collapse of Christianity, which Nietzsche witnessed.

Nietzsche's "Parable of the Madman" marked the first sign of the waning of Christianity as the dominant culture and the beginnings of the "post-Christian" world. Five weeks after her first letter to "A," O'Connor writes again to her, "[I]f you live today you breathe in nihilism. In or out of the Church, it's the gas you breathe" (949). But this Georgia Catholic fiction writer refused to be immobilized or deterred by the galloping progress of seculariza-tion and its companion, philosophical nihilism.

Wise Blood stands out in O'Connor's fiction for the sheer fre-quency of her use of the names of "Jesus" and "Christ." "Jesus" appears eighty-four times in the novel; "Christ" appears thirty-eight times.[12] In no other work of fiction does she make such explicit mention of the second person of the Christian Trinity. While the characters, particularly Hazel Motes, frequently use the name of the Redeemer in blasphemy, this ironic action serves O'Connor's dramatic purpose. Midway in the first chapter of the novel Haze twice confronts Mrs. Hitchcock with a revealing pre-occupation: "I reckon you think you been redeemed" (6). This dramatic dialogue ironically personifies Haze as O'Connor's "Christ-haunted" nonbelieving protagonist. It repeats on the fol-lowing page when he ventures to the train's dining car. Sitting across the table from the "three youngish women dressed like parrots," Haze meddles with their presumed faith: "'If you've been redeemed,' he said, 'I wouldn't want to be.'" It is a line that echoes Mark Twain's Huckleberry Finn, who declared that if Aunt Polly was going to heaven, he didn't want to have anything to do with it.[13] Laughter from one of the women follows. Haze presses the issue with a confrontational question, "Do you think I believe in Jesus?" His breathless speech insists that he would not believe "even if He existed. Even if He was on this train." O'Connor draws a deflating response from one of the women, "Who said you had to?" As the novel proceeds, it becomes obvious that Haze Motes lives in a post-Christian world despite the residue of religion.

The pattern of symbolism in *Wise Blood* parallels her second novel, *The Violent Bear It Away:* the central figure leaves the world of inherited Christian faith; he passes through complex stages of the journey away from faith; and at the end he returns to faith on another level. In making this claim, it is important to emphasize that the character does not return to faith at the original level but, as if in a spiral, arrives at "Christ-centered" faith on a higher plane.

HAZEL MOTES, PROTAGONIST

The name "Hazel Motes" symbolically suggests the character's identity. His eyes are hazel-pecan colored, reflecting the familiar Georgia pecans; more importantly he lives in a visual "haze"— and his nickname is "Haze." Even more telling is the surname, "Motes," because it conjures up the biblical saying: "Why look at the speck in your brother's eye when you miss the [mote] in your own? Remove the [mote] from your own eye first; then you will see clearly to take the speck from your brother's eye" (Matt 7:3–5). Haze is always trying to discredit or straighten out other people's beliefs. All the while, he reacts with his own "Christ-haunted" reflexes and denial of faith. Yet, there is a symbolic obstruction in his own eye. The dominant eye imagery in *Wise Blood* (and paralleled throughout O'Connor's fiction) serves to show us that Haze is the seeing unbeliever who, at the novel's end, ironically becomes the blind seer.

Before the first chapter concludes, one of the frequent death images of the "coffin" jogs Haze's memory while he is confined to the claustrophobic upper berth of the train's sleeping car, and we reenter the world of his childhood religious faith. "The first coffin he had seen with someone in it was his grandfather's," we are told, and Haze watched it "from a distance, thinking: he ain't going to let them shut it on him…" (9). We learn that Haze is the grandson of "a circuit preacher, a waspish old man who had ridden over three counties with Jesus hidden in his head like a stinger" (9–10). His daydream is interrupted but he continues to reminisce about being called up to the army at the age of eighteen. Haze's first thought is to maim himself by shooting his foot and avoid the military draft because he could be a preacher like his grandfather "without a foot." "A preacher's power is in his neck and tongue and arm," Haze explains. The first allusion to his grandfather's ministry, preaching from the hood of his Ford and shouting to the people gathered around that they were "like stones" (10) foreshadows Haze's actions. Then he remembers how his grandfather would point to him, acknowledging that he had "a particular respect for him because his own face was repeated almost exactly in the child's and seemed to mock him." The Calvinist doctrine of salvation and redemption that underlies his grandfather's preaching is evident in the irresistible grace of a "soul-hungry" Jesus:

> Did they know that even for that boy there, for that mean sinful unthinking boy standing there with his dirty hands clenching and unclenching at his sides, Jesus would die ten million deaths before He would let him lose his soul? He would chase him over the waters of sin! Did they doubt Jesus could walk on the waters of sin? That boy had been redeemed and Jesus wasn't going to leave him ever. Jesus would never let him forget he was redeemed. What did the sinner think there was to be gained? Jesus would have him in the end. (11)

Haze, however, places all his confidence in his human power to resist evil. O'Connor describes him as having inherited his grandfather's self-confidence when it came to resisting temptation: "...he trusted himself to get back [from the army] in a few months, uncorrupted." At the age of twelve he claims to know that "the way to avoid Jesus was to avoid sin." Flannery O'Connor deftly describes this as "a black wordless conviction" deep within Haze. Haze also knows at this same threshold of adolescence that "he was going to be a preacher." But O'Connor invites us inside Haze's self-consciousness:

> Later, he saw Jesus move from tree to tree in the back of his mind, a wild ragged figure motioning him to turn around and come off into the dark where he was not sure of his footing, where he might suddenly be walking on the water and not know it and then suddenly know it and drown. Where he wanted to stay was in Eastrod with his two eyes open, and his hands always handling the familiar thing, his feet on the known track, and his tongue not too loose. (11)

O'Connor calls attention to this "Christ-haunted" figure of Hazel Motes in her note appended to the tenth-anniversary edition of *Wise Blood*. The imagery of the two sentences just quoted foreshadows Haze's search for truth and his dramatic conversion. The "dark" way with unsure footing and the risk of drowning contrasts starkly with the open-eyed, familiar track of Eastrod. This symbolic imagery is as stark as the contrast between authentic faith—described by Paul as "seeing through a glass darkly" (1 Cor 13:12)—and the seemingly more reliable empirical certitude. There is also something of Peter's impulsiveness in the New Testament with the imagery of walking on water and suddenly becoming self-conscious and losing faith (Matt 14:22–33). Eastrod is abandoned so Haze cannot go back to the familiar "home." The only direction is to spiral upward toward the new plane of faith by first passing through intermediate stages of God-avoidance.

Haze's stages of life in *Wise Blood* recapitulate significant moments of Western religious culture. As we discover in chapter 3, at the age of ten Haze saw a naked woman in a coffinlike "box lined with black cloth" at the carnival. His mother's intuitive knowledge of his "guilt of the tent" gives way to "the nameless unplaced guilt that was in him." Attention to original sin and the inherited effects of Adam's fall dominates his consciousness. Haze places stones and small rocks in his shoes and walks as an act of penance. He walks a mile before easing "his feet in the wet sand," reflecting that "that ought to satisfy Him" (35–36). This first stage reflects a classic medieval spirituality: the human person got God off his mind and out of his conscience by penitential actions. In the wake of the Enlightenment, a second stage emerges with Romanticism in the nineteenth century. There is unparalleled optimism about humanity; philosophers convinced us that we are innately virtuous. It is this second stage that avoids sin and so comfortably avoids God in any meaningful sense. Haze rejects his army comrades' invitation to the brothel because he is avoiding sin and therefore avoiding evil, God, or the need to be redeemed. The third stage begins when Haze joins them at the brothel because he yields to their secular, post-Christian stance: "They told him he didn't have any soul...." O'Connor allows us to follow Haze's discovery that he is converted to philosophical Nothingness.

> He took a long time to believe them because he wanted to believe them. All he wanted was to believe them and get rid of it once and for all, and he saw the opportunity here to get rid of it without corruption, to be converted to nothingness instead of to evil....[During four years in the army h]e had all the time he could want to study his soul in and assure himself that it was not there. When he was thoroughly convinced, he saw that this was something that he had always known. The misery he had was a longing for home; it had nothing to do with Jesus. When the army finally let him go, he was pleased to think that he was still uncorrupted. (12–13)

When we meet Haze Motes in *Wise Blood,* he is at this third stage of philosophical nihilism. It becomes obvious in chapter 2 when he is en route to Leora Watt's "friendliest bed in town" to "do some things I never have done before" (5), as he cryptically phrases it for Mrs. Hitchcock early in chapter 1. His taxi driver mistakenly identifies him as a preacher because of his attire. Haze's curt rejoinder characterizes him: "'Listen,' he said, 'get this: I don't believe in anything.'" He adds a line that will unravel as the novel unfolds: "I don't have to say it but once to nobody." The driver's "look of disgust and righteousness" compounds the ironic humor of this situation when he adds (almost as an "aside"), "'That's the trouble with all you preachers,' he said. 'You've all got too good to believe in anything'"(17).

It is as an evangelist of twentieth-century nihilism or the philosophy of Nothingness that Haze stalks into Taulkinham. In one sense Hazel Motes is Flannery O'Connor's anti-evangelist who is intent upon denying religious faith. But in the broader course of *Wise Blood,* we discover the ruthless honesty that accompanies his philosophical quest and leads him up the spiral to reclaim Christian faith on a higher plane. He wants to see everything as it is, to give everyone his or her true identity. The porter on the train is a black man from Eastrod, a "Parrum nigger," as Haze calls him (8–9); yet the porter deceptively tells everyone that he comes from Chicago. This passion for exposing dishonesty echoes throughout the novel whenever Haze insists that something "ain't true." The second half of the novel accumulates episode after episode where Haze comes to recognize the truth by calling attention to whatever denies the truth. Perhaps the most evident examples are: rejecting Enoch Emery's "new jesus"; seeing behind the "blind" Asa Hawks's dark glasses; and encountering Onnie Jay Holy preaching the Church of Christ Without Christ. In the latter instance, Haze's immediate reaction is characteristically honest, "This man is not true" (86).

TAULKINHAM: ENOCH'S SECULAR CITY

To appreciate O'Connor's imaginative universe in this first novel and her fiction that follows it, the city of Taulkinham and its inhabitants, especially Enoch Emery, warrant attention. Haze carries two symbolic artifacts when he departs from the ruins of abandoned Eastrod: "a black bible and a pair of silver-rimmed spectacles that had belonged to his mother" (12). He leaves a note threatening lethal revenge on anyone who steals his mother's chifforobe, the only furniture that remains in the Eastrod house. Exiled, Haze arrives in Taulkinham "the next evening." In the second paragraph of chapter 2 O'Connor describes Haze's successful deception: "No one observing him would have known that he had no place to go" (15). The seductive lure of Leora Watts, however, invites him at the chapter's conclusion: "Make yourself at home" (18). There is no doubt that O'Connor portrays Leora Watts as the sex goddess of the secular city. Haze finds her address in the men's toilet at the train station. O'Connor parodies her and makes her look ridiculous, "cutting her toenails with a large pair of scissors," when Haze first observes her through the crack in the door. "She was a big woman with very yellow hair and white skin that glistened with a greasy preparation." At the opening of chapter 4, it is evident how he is repulsed by sex with Mrs. Watts. After his first night with a woman—"he had not been very successful with Mrs. Watts" (33)—the emptiness of Haze's endeavor is apparent: "When he finished, he was like something washed ashore on her..." (33). When he awakens on the second morning, he finds her arm flung over him. "He leaned up and lifted it off and eased it down by her side, but he didn't look at her....He got stealthily out of bed..." (37).

This behavior and repulsion compounds itself in Haze's would-be tryst with Sabbath Lily. He sees the seduction of a preacher's innocent daughter as the ultimate blasphemy, but as the truth unfolds about the bastard daughter of a dishonest preacher who pretends to have blinded himself, Haze's scheme collapses. Enoch

Emery's exposure of himself before the woman at the Rodemill Boys' Bible Academy affords O'Connor another incident of sexuality gone awry. Enoch is the premiere voyeur, spying on the woman at the swimming pool and uttering a blasphemous "King Jesus!" (48). His lust is evident in the description, "Enoch had watched her with pleasure on several occasions" (45). O'Connor's fellow novelist Walker Percy articulates best the predicament where, he says, only in a post-Christian society can people get this kick out of sex. Pagans simply enjoy it. The post-Christian doubly enjoys it because it is forbidden—or once was.[14]

But sex is only one of the meaning-of-life substitutes or religion surrogates that O'Connor unmasks in the secular city. It is a world where "enlightened" people believe in nothing. The symbolic action of the novel revolves around repeated episodes of ersatz religion. One of the first comes at the opening of the third chapter when a man sets up a card table and sells potato peelers in front of the department store. Next to sex, industrial gadgetry is the great satisfaction for people. When O'Connor describes, "The man stood in front of this altar..." (19), it becomes obvious. A more subtle suggestion comes when she shows us, "A few people gathered around." The "machine seller" (21) is one of the only persons capable of gathering people in an otherwise unfriendly and "almost deserted" (32) secular, or post-Christian, city. The Greek word in the New Testament first used by Paul to name the gathering of the early Christian community is *ekklesia,* the assembly of Christians (1 Thess 1:1). This *ekklesia*—church—is literally the community gathered at God's initiative, summoned by God's word. O'Connor ironically reminds her readers of the absence of the church in the secular city by dramatizing the salesman's patter, or sales pitch, and the action surrounding his "altar" stationed at the exit of the department store to intercept a "captive crowd."

This comic effect is magnified a few moments later when Sabbath Lily begins passing out her prayer tracts and Asa Hawks intrudes with his appeal: "Help a blind preacher. If you won't repent, give a nickel....Wouldn't you rather have me beg than preach?" The irony bristles in the dramatic scene O'Connor has created. "'What the hell you think you doing?' the man selling the peelers yelled. 'I got these people together, how you think you can horn in?'" When he concludes by calling them "These damn Jesus fanatics" and "These goddam Communist foreigners!" (21), O'Connor alertly feels the pulse of this era in American culture. The success of the salesman in gathering a crowd to hear his good news about this "bargain" and persuading people that they need his product ("You'll thank the day you ever stopped here...you'll never forget it") is parodied by O'Connor as the envy of many a church leader (20–21). She is prescient about the contemporary "church growth" phenomenon and the marketing of Christianity.

Hazel Motes's car is another symbol of the industrialized world and the new mobility made possible for the wandering "beat" generation that Jack Kerouac would immortalize in his 1957 novel *On the Road*. O'Connor presents the boy and his father at Slade's car lot in chapter 4 as a cameo of the post-Christian, secular city. The ritual of selecting a car and bargaining over the price replaces serious religious ritual. Car ownership symbolizes status, prestige, and power in American culture where the independence associated with private automobile travel gave rise to the demise of public transportation systems. The dialogue initiated by Haze's question, "How much is it?" and the boy's blasphemous response, "Jesus on the cross...Christ nailed," proves to be an ironic juxtaposition. When the boy proceeds to ask a question in response, "How much do you think it's worth?" O'Connor triggers a subtle repartee that mocks the crucifixion and Christ's redemptive act endowing every human person with inestimable dignity and worth. Haze's reply to the question of worth—"It ain't worth what it would take to cart it off. I wouldn't have it"—feigns the worthlessness of the automobile that is nonetheless desirable to him as both a vehicle and a house.

The truck driver's insult to Haze at the end of the chapter, declaring that his car is a "goddam outhouse" blocking the middle of the road (43), dramatizes Haze's misplaced values and the low threshold of violence when the truck driver threateningly places his hand on Haze's shoulder. O'Connor is brilliantly ironic when she has Haze later announce to Sabbath Lily, "Nobody with a good car needs to be justified" (64). Likewise, there is an important observation made earlier by Haze when he calls attention to the boy's repeated blaspheming, "Sweet Jesus, sweet Jesus, sweet Jesus." "What's he keep talking like that for?" Haze inquires. The father admits he does not know, echoing his remark moments earlier that "Something's wrong with him howcome [sic] he curses so much" (40–41). It is an early instance of Haze-the-philosophical-quester recognizing that someone is not true to his identity.

The character Enoch Emory is essential to O'Connor's symbolic action in *Wise Blood*. O'Connor creates him as a foil for Haze Motes. Enoch is neurotically friendly in a city where he claims, "I ain't never been in such a unfriendly place." O'Connor describes his behavior with a graphic image of Enoch's repulsiveness: "He was smiling. He looked like a friendly hound dog with a light mange" (23). In the context of his warning Haze about the unfriendly nature of Taulkinham, Enoch is jostled by "a little man lost in a pair of faded overalls" and growls back, "Whyn't you look wher [sic] you going?" The novel's short-fused violence explodes in a dogfight image: "The little man stopped and raised his arm in a vicious gesture and a nasty-doglook came on his face. 'Who you tellin' what?' he snarled" (25). This portrayal of Enoch dramatizes how people in the post-Christian world treat one another violently. Whereas our violence might be more hidden or unseen, O'Connor presents the violence as if it were on the surface. When Enoch first meets Haze in chapter 3 at the salesman's makeshift "altar," he punches Haze to call his attention to the fact that the "peeler man" is "talking to you!" It is an apt image of broken communication and the consequent violence circulating throughout the novel. Enoch's surname, "Emory," calls to mind the rough texture of an emery board used to file nails. Enoch is just such an abrasive personality, rubbing everyone the wrong way and presenting a gritty temperament.

Flannery O'Connor's imagination and her biblical literacy are apparent in the naming of Enoch Emery. In Genesis 4, Enoch is identified as the son of Cain, the son of Adam and Eve who killed his brother Abel. Cain founded a city in the name of Enoch; St. Augustine mentions Enoch and the secular city as opposed to the heavenly city. Enoch personifies for O'Connor the genius of the secular city. It is a place composed of country boys who have come to town; she anticipates the displacement that characterizes modern American metropolises where virtually everyone has come from somewhere else.[15] Enoch takes an interest in Haze when he sees him "thrust two dollars at the man selling potato peelers"—when the asking price was only a dollar and a half. He betrays a false motive when he then attempts to befriend Haze, volunteering as he pants, "I reckon you got a heap of money."

After Haze concurs with Enoch that he does not "go in for a lot of Jesus business" (23) like that displayed when Asa Hawks and his daughter interrupt the salesman, O'Connor presents a revealing scene at the corner. A policeman blows his whistle because Haze ignores the traffic signal. The comic exchange that follows comes at Haze's expense. He claims that he did not see the light—a statement laced with irony when readers discover how O'Connor will creatively use light and darkness imagery in the novel and ultimately show Haze embracing Christ, the light of the world (John 1:5). Likewise, as the agent of the law, the policeman personifies the antithesis of grace; the offer of divine grace ironically comes through Enoch's intercession as O'Connor later shows the violence that accompanies: "The [policeman], perceiving that Haze was conscious, hit him over the head with his new billy[club]" (131). This occasion also leads Enoch to claim, "I reckon I saved you that time," because he intervenes to extricate Haze from the crowd and the law enforcement officer. The small crowd gathered to watch the altercation reiterates O'Connor's ironic insistence that in the post-Christian world the only gatherings are for spectacle and not for the community of faith that defines the Church.

Enoch's repeated references to "my daddy" imaginatively return us to the Cain motif and lethal associations in his hereditary—but ironically dubbed—"wise" blood. He insists to Haze that "my daddy made me come" to the city of Taulkinham where "nobody here'll have nothing to do with nobody else" (32). After passing a church and other landmarks in the city, Haze resists Enoch's suggestion that they visit a house of prostitution. As Haze again attempts to depart from Enoch, the eighteen-year-old volunteers that he works at the zoo and guards a gate. It is O'Connor's comic revelation that "The park was the heart of the city." Enoch, the guardian of the zoo, presides as the priest of "a mystery" in the center of the post-Christian, secular city (45). As she unfolds her story, the irony compounds. Enoch hates the animals he guards at the zoo, yet he is obviously fascinated by them—as the extent of his later infatuation with the gorilla-celebrity at the movie house, Gonga, will dramatically demonstrate.

The plot turns back to Asa Hawks and his daughter when Enoch desperately reclaims Haze's attention. He divulges not only that he has their address but that the girl has given him the potato peeler that Haze presented to her. Moreover, Enoch reports with "his face stretched in an evil crooked grin": "She...ast [sic] me to visit them and bring you—not you bring me, me bring you—and it was you follerin' them." The scene collapses as Haze hurls the stack of evangelist's tracts at Enoch, who "tore off down the street" as Haze retires to Mrs. Watt's house (33).

The next morning as Haze purchases his car, Enoch plans his return to the mystery that he has discovered in a glass case in the museum at the center of the city. Before he arrives, Enoch performs his secular rituals: an afternoon mechanical drink from the Frosty Bottle and hotdog stand; his daily viewing ("full of awe and hate") of the caged animals; and finally to the bath house to lust after the woman at the swimming pool (46). Haze Motes appears in his Essex car and Enoch recognizes him. O'Connor has

Enoch "on all fours" in an animal parody as he looks across the pool toward Haze and the woman.

When Enoch pursues Haze, he ignores the question about Hawks's address and insists, "I got to show you something" (48). While Enoch foresees "a terrible struggle" to get Haze to the glass case, he persists in retracing the ritual stops at the Frosty Bottle and to see the animals. Haze's preoccupation as a "Christ-haunted" protagonist flares again in his exchange with Maude, the counter lady who "drank whisky [sic] all day from a fruit jar under the counter." At the same time that she denigrates Enoch by calling him a "son of a bitch," she dignifies Haze by calling him a "clean boy." Provoked by his "Christ-haunted" conscious-ness, Haze responds, "I AM clean," and adds, "If Jesus existed, I wouldn't be clean." When Haze visits the caged animals with Enoch, he squints at "an owl with one eye opened" in what appears to be an empty cage. "'I AM clean,' Haze said to the eye," echoing his earlier, self-conscious reaction. This eye imagery suggests a single-eyed vision that lacks any depth perception; and the symbolic emptiness of the cage happens again when "the eye shut softly and the owl turned its face to the wall" (54). O'Connor presents a stance of camouflaged silence not unlike the blinded Haze Motes at the end of the novel.

Their arrival at the column-framed MVSVEM where "there was an eyeless stone woman holding a pot on her head" links the two scenes through eye imagery. The classical image of Justice as blind may be an inherited symbol still standing at the heart of the post-Christian, secular city, but it is not the object of Enoch's attention. The pair of whispering interlopers sneak past the guard and tiptoe to the inner sanctum of the museum where Enoch guides Haze "into a dark room full of glass cases" toward three that are "coffin-like." O'Connor shows us Haze's reflection as his eyes are on the "shrunken man" in the glass case. "The reflection was pale and the eyes were like two clean bullet holes." It is a vivid and unmistakable foreshadowing of his forthcoming blind-ness. The woman with two boys (the same woman Enoch lusts after at the pool?) enters. Standing opposite Haze, their grinning faces are reflected along with his; together they mirror a mock family here at the heart of the secular city where Enoch's mysterious "shrunken man" is displayed for all gawkers. Haze's startled reaction is followed by his flight from the scene. Outside, when Haze remembers to badger Enoch for Hawks's address, violence erupts. A "wild"-faced Haze hurtles a rock toward Enoch and draws blood on his forehead beneath his eyes shut tight (56–57). There is something of a David and Goliath motif as Haze symbolically engages this guardian of the secular city and its zoo.

ASA HAWKS'S COUNTERFEIT RELIGION

Immediately following in chapter 6 Haze finds the blind man and child and follows them "on into a dark section" to the porch of the house where they stay. He notes the sign that advertises "ROOMS FOR RENT" and the address. Asa Hawks is no less dispensable to O'Connor's form for *Wise Blood* than the other major characters. She reconstructs Hawks's ministry as a sincere man of faith who attempted too much in its service. After Hawks failed to blind himself as a grotesque act of faith, he ceases to believe. The irony of his Promethean "will to power" serves O'Connor's larger purpose in the novel: she intends to expose all forms of pseudoreligion in the modern world. Since Hawks only pretends to have blinded himself, he has launched a career as the "blind man of faith" for his livelihood. "As a" predatory "hawk," he preys upon the sentiment of people who would be moved by this pretense but not engaged by genuine religion. Hawks operates by manipulating the guilt of people who know their own behavior deserves a punishment far worse than the presumed "man of faith's" self-blinding does. What is more, he falsely poses as the mendicant who begs in order to show a total dependence upon God's mercy and the mercy of others when we are first introduced to him in chapter 3: "Help a blind unemployed preacher. Wouldn't you rather have me beg than preach? Come on and give a nickel if you won't repent" (21). O'Connor offers Asa Hawks as a tragic figure of lost faith, the mock mendicant. He is the contrary of the higher plane where Haze Motes will arrive.

But O'Connor also presents Asa Hawks as a man capable of even greater evil as the abusive father of Sabbath Lily Hawks. In chapter 7, she stows away in Haze's car and introduces herself. It is not the fact that she then reveals—Hawks and Sabbath Lily's mother were unmarried—that makes him evil. The first glimpse of Hawks's abuse comes in his verbal exchange with her when Haze offers her the potato peeler in chapter 3 and she refuses it: "'You take it,' the blind man said. 'You put it in your sack and shut up before I hit you'" (27). Haze's motivation is complicated. On the one hand he wants somebody to try to convert him so he can demonstrate his nonbelief, or his belief in Nothingness; he directs his confrontation with Hawks and Sabbath Lily toward this purpose. Later, his intention clarifies. He decides the best way to prove he does not believe is to seduce the daughter of a holy man who blinded himself for Christ. But with typical O'Connor irony, Haze discovers that his intention is frustrated. Once he discovers the secret behind Hawks's dark glasses, he sees no blasphemy in seducing the bastard daughter of a phony "blind preacher" and abandons the scheme. The reversal of seductions becomes apparent early in chapter 9 when Sabbath Lily steals into Haze's room in the boarding house they share and he responds by raising a chair "as if he were going to bring it down on her." When she reports to Hawks about the episode and concludes that "nothing works," her father pressures his fifteen-year-old dependent: "'I'm leaving out of here in a couple of days,' Hawks said, 'you better make it work if you want to eat after I'm gone'" (82). His drunkenness does not hide his plan to abandon her. In the concluding chapter 14, we learn that after Haze's self-blinding her subsequent attempts at seduction are fruitless. "She hadn't counted on no honest-to-Jesus blind man and she was homesick for her papa," about whom the narrator tells us, "he had deserted her, gone off on a banana boat" (121).

The cover of Asa Hawks's biblical tract said, "Jesus Calls You." It is the standard proclamation of the street preacher, the vocation that Haze Motes intends to discredit. In chapter 3 he pursues both Hawks and his fifteen-year-old daughter outside the classical building with columns, a dome, stone lions on pedestals, and every parking place occupied. Enoch announces, "Ain't no church" (26); nonetheless, Hawks's purpose is to intercept his congregation when the "program" at the auditorium lets out. Once again, in the post-Christian, secular city other interests gather people instead of God's word or authentic religion. In their first real encounter, Haze stands silently before Hawks. The fraudulent evangelist declares, "I can smell the sin on your breath." When Haze accuses Sabbath of giving him "her fast eye," Hawks claims to hear "the urge for Jesus in [Haze's] voice." Hawks and Haze fence with words. The preacher insists that "you can't run away from Jesus. Jesus is a fact." But Haze is unmoved, in part because Hawks's mouthing of formulas does not move beyond the claims of fact in order to arrive at faith in what is unseen. Hawks perceives that "some preacher has left his mark on you." The command to "Repent" receives Haze's rejoinder, "I'm as clean as you are." When Hawks ups the ante in this game of words (Haze says that fornication and blasphemy "ain't nothing but words") by telling him that "Jesus loves you," Haze blunts the claim: "Nothing matters but that Jesus don't exist" (31).

When Hawks finally attempts to engage Haze publicly before the crowd of onlookers, Haze disclaims that he has "followed" the preacher in any religious sense. "I wouldn't follow a blind fool like that. My Jesus," he announces. And suddenly, in a dramatic irony, Haze claims, "Listenhere [sic], I'm a preacher myself and I preach the truth"—"the church of truth without Jesus Christ Crucified" which "won't cost you nothing to join" (30–31).[16] Haze carefully makes a distinction in keeping with his identity as the philosopher in quest of the truth. He insists that the people are "clean" from sin, but not "because of Jesus Christ Crucified." "I don't say he wasn't crucified but I say it wasn't for you," Haze concludes, in a retreat from his absolute denial moments earlier. The admission of the historical fact of Christ's crucifixion is easy for the reader to miss; but again it evidences the ruthless honesty of this philosophical quester in search of the truth. O'Connor deepens the integrity of her character Hazel Motes in this scene when she has him volunteer this subtle gesture of truth finding. In a final effort, he asserts: "I don't need Jesus....What do I need with Jesus? I got Leora Watts" (31). The question rebounds on Haze as subsequent chapters ironically show. The drama reaches a turning point in Enoch's presentation of the "new jesus" and Haze's rejection of him.

REJECTING THE "NEW JESUS"

Enoch fixates upon the "shrunken man" in the glass case at the museum. It is a fitting pose because Enoch personifies his biblical ancestor's identity: the city and humanity are his entire universe and only concern. Earlier in the novel O'Connor has the novel's omniscient narrator describe how the collective "city" of Taulkinham is oblivious to the sky and the transcendent mystery it symbolizes:

> The black sky was underpinned with long silver streaks that looked like scaffolding and depth on depth behind it were thousands of stars that all seemed to be moving very slowly as if they were about some vast construction work that involved the whole order of the universe and would take all time to complete. No one was paying any attention to the sky. (19)

Enoch's "man" is shrunken; and the fact that he sees this mummified figure as a fascinating mystery that his "wise blood" tells him is the center of the universe is O'Connor's symbolic way of being sardonic about every aspect of secular humanism. Enoch personifies the misplaced worship of the human as its own god. He succeeds in drawing Haze to the heart of his city and the shrine.

O'Connor describes Enoch looking at the shrunken man whose "eyes were drawn almost shut as if a giant block of steel were falling down on top of him." The violent metaphors in both the reference to Haze's eyes as "clean bullet holes" and the grimace of the mummy coincide. The truth-seeking philosophical quest for Nothingness forces Haze to recognize that Enoch's humanism only offers him a purely secular religion. Haze's eyes pass right through this empty fossil (the mummy) because he sees it as counterfeit. It will become even more evident in chapter 11 when Haze violently rejects the shrunken man that Enoch steals and presents as the "new jesus" whom Haze preaches.

There is a subtle but telling coda added to this scene when the woman with her two boys approaches the glass case, snickering. "When Haze saw her face on the glass, his neck jerked back and he made a noise. It might have come from the man inside the case" (56). Of all the gospel stories leading to the passion and death of Jesus, the climactic story is the raising of Lazarus just prior to Jesus' reentering Jerusalem for the Passover festival. Upon Jesus' arrival at Bethany, he meets Mary, the sister of Lazarus. The narrative in John's gospel (11:1–44) is unique in the New Testament. "When Jesus saw her weeping and the Jews who had come with her weeping, he became perturbed and deeply troubled." When he asks where Lazarus has been laid, they invite him to "come and see." John's gospel tells us, "And Jesus wept." Biblical scholars note the startling phrase in the Greek text of John's gospel, "he became perturbed," and translate this literally as "he snorted in spirit," explaining how this response manifests Jesus' anger at the presence of evil or death. It carries connotations and echoes of Jesus' exorcisms—the driving out of the devil as well. The ambiguity about the source of the "noise" (coming from Haze or the man inside the case) and the reflex jerking of Haze's head are rendered comic. Enoch mistakenly reacts with panic and flight when he interprets it as emanating from the shrunken man. But at a more symbolic level, O'Connor draws a startling image of Haze's new life beyond nihilism and secular humanism by the mirror image of his own reflection in the coffin-like glass case. It is an even more compelling interpretation vis-à-vis this biblical text that continues with the Jews' exclamation about Jesus weeping: "See how he loved him." Immediately, in counterpoint, John's gospel describes, "But some of the Jews said, 'Could not the one who opened the eyes of the blind man have done something so that this man would not have died.'" Suddenly all the imagery and symbolism of *Wise Blood* converges with the resurrection mystery writ large in the raising of Lazarus–Haze Motes. Haze himself employs the same question in confronting Hawks: "If Jesus cured blind men, howcome [sic] you don't get Him to cure you?" (63).

Throughout the novel Haze Motes blasphemes. In chapter 4 he encounters the son of Slade, the used car salesman. The boy's father complains to Haze that he does not know "what ails him." The boy continuously utters phrases: "Jesus on the cross"; "Christ nailed" (38); "Sweet Jesus, Sweet Jesus" (41). They are the familiar proclamations of evangelical Christianity mistaken for a disturbed mind. Haze drives out of town in his newly purchased car and a slowly driving truck forces him to slow down. A boulder bearing a sign in white letters catches his attention: "WOE TO THE BLASPHEMER AND WHOREMONGER! WILL HELL SWALLOW YOU UP?" At the bottom of the sign "in small letters" is the good news of Christian faith: "Jesus saves." Haze lingers and looks at the sign. Suddenly a huge oil truck blares its horn. But Haze is so absorbed that he does not hear the horn and is interrupted only when the "red square face" of the driver confronts him at his car window. O'Connor signals Haze's vulnerability to truth as a philosophical quester by describing him: "Haze turned his fragile placed[sic]-looking face toward him" (42). The driver disputes the message of the sign and counters, "That's not the sin, nor blasphemy. The sin came before them." Haze's reflex response mixes blasphemy with racism, "Jesus is a trick on niggers" (43). Once again Haze protests his nihilism. He asks directions toward the zoo. He literally turns around and heads back to the city where his quest leads him to encounter again Enoch's "new jesus."

In chapter 6 Haze moves on to the movie house, another gathering place in the secular city. He intercepts the captive crowd and, raising his hands in an evangelist's pose, cries out to three boys, "Where has the blood you think you been redeemed by touched you?" When one boy tells Haze that he belongs to the Church of Christ, Haze blasphemously declares, "Well, I preach the Church of Christ Without Christ....[I]t's the church that the blood of Jesus don't foul with redemption." He claims that there was "no Fall and no Redemption and no Judgment." "Nothing matters but that Jesus was a liar," blasphemes Haze (59).

The next morning Haze rents a room at the boarding house where Asa Hawks and his daughter, Sabbath Lily, live. After announcing his residence in the building, Haze drives off. Sabbath Lily unwittingly describes the deeper symbolism of Haze when she remarks to her father, "'I like his eyes....They don't look like they see what he's looking at but they keep on looking'" (61). It is an apt description of his philosophical quest and a prescient remark about his eventual self-blinding, in contrast to Hawks's failure in self-blinding and in faith. Hawks replies to Sabbath Lily that Haze is a "Goddam Jesus-hog" (64). When Haze returns, he confronts Hawks and the fake blind man hands him the news clipping with the headline "EVANGELIST PROMISES TO BLIND SELF." Hazel Motes responds to Sabbath Lily's explanation that her father blinded himself "for justification": "Nobody with a good car needs to be justified" (64). The chapter ironically ends with the mechanic at the garage honestly telling Haze that his car cannot be repaired. He leaves his car at another shop where he is reassured that he has a good car and that it is in superlative hands at a superlative garage. O'Connor plays the metaphor of America's post–World War II love affair with the automobile for great comedy. For all his ability to recognize what "ain't true," Haze moves closer to the midpoint of the novel, the victim of a multitude of deceptions.

SABBATH LILY, THE SECULAR CITY'S SEDUCTRESS

Chapter 7 opens with the next morning's drive into the country in Haze's repaired car. The seductive Sabbath Lily has stowed away in the back seat of the car, "a bunch of dandelions in her hair and a wide red mouth on her pale face" (66). For the first time she tells him her name and reveals that she is the bastard child of Hawks and her unnamed mother. Even though Haze tells her that he has business to attend to and no time for "foolishness," Sabbath Lily makes conversation. She mentions a letter she wrote to the newspaper columnist Mary Brittle.[17] The all-knowing advice columnist emerges as another of the substitutes for religion in the secular city. O'Connor deftly allows Sabbath Lily to proclaim the ersatz "religion" that is evident in the response to her letter about whether "I should neck or not?" She reports to Haze that Mary Brittle advised her: "Light necking is acceptable, but I think your real problem is one of adjustment to the modern world. Perhaps you ought to re-examine your religious values to see if they meet your needs in Life. A religious experience can be a beautiful addition to living if you put it in the proper perspective and do not let it warp you. Read some books on Ethical Culture" (67).

O'Connor mocks the modern accommodation that reduces religious experience to an "addition" rather than the foundation of life. (There is wonderful irony in the name "Brittle" because the advice columnist is unashamedly "flexible.") Sabbath Lily and her father, Asa Hawks, personify the emptiness that results. When Mary Brittle recommends some reading on "Ethical Culture," an alert reader thinks of Søren Kierkegaard's distinction between the ethical and religious person. There is little chance of the "leap of faith" when a flexible ethic preempts it. And even the ethical stance is endangered when the etiquette and conventions of the advice columnist displace the mystery of the human person.

Haze turns the conversation to a pair of questions about Hawks, "How did he come to believe?" "What changed him into a preacher for Jesus?" Coming at the midpoint of the novel, these queries foreshadow the action of the second half of *Wise Blood* and Haze's conversion. Sabbath Lily proceeds to seduce Haze by taking off her shoes and stockings and inviting him to walk in the field. Her rejoinder to his interest in Hawks is to claim, "I can save you....I got a church in my heart where Jesus is King" (68). Haze claims that he believes "in a new kind of Jesus...because he's all man and ain't got any God in him" (69). It is a proclamation of purely secular humanism. Sabbath Lily persists in the seduction. O'Connor plays the action for all the burlesque it offers. Sabbath Lily is virtually oblivious to the serious conversation Haze has initiated. Her shallowness is unmistakable when she offers, "It don't make any difference to me how much you like me" (70). Sex without love is her goal. She demonstrably shows us the results of Mary Brittle's "religion."

Haze's reaction is swift and direct. "'Git away!' he said, jumping violently." He retreats to the car only to panic when it fails to start. He accuses Sabbath Lily of doing something to the car. On foot, he walks back to the fork in the road in search of the gasoline station he had seen. Haze will literally and symbolically begin to retrace his steps at this juncture and take different turns in the second half of the novel. It is appropriate that O'Connor describes the store on the dirt road as "deserted" because Haze has encountered several temptations and devils (Matt 4:1–11) in this episode. He notices the cage beside the shack when Sabbath Lily approaches it. The sign reads, "TWO DEADLY ENEMIES. HAVE A LOOK FREE" (71). The one-eyed bear and the small tailless chicken hawk are a startling reminder of violence in nature. But their caged captivity and exploitation by the owners of the store give evidence of humans wounding these creatures. The freedom to be voyeurs only adds to the violence.

The man who fills the gas tank of Haze's car is a third victim of some unnamed violence, "a one-armed man" with "eyes that were slate-blue and thoughtful" (71). Both chapters 6 and 7 conclude with a car repair scene. In the former Haze is deceived when he thinks that he is leaving the car "in honest hands." In the latter, the mechanic does not touch anything on the car; he does not say anything until Haze mentions payment for service. When Haze asks what he owes, the man replies, "Nothing, not a thing." Taken aback, the ungrateful Haze shuns the act of mercy: "I don't need no favors from him." Haze resists anything that suggests grace or gratuity.

A whole complex of symbols converges in this scene. Haze's xenophobia escalates as he claims that his car was not built by "foreigners or niggers or one-arm men" but "by people with their eyes open that knew where they were at." The boast brims with pride. The one-armed man simply replies in a paradox, "Some things'll get some folks somewheres." The secular humanism of Haze's philosophic quest does get him to a termination point— and to a disappointing one. To underscore her irony, O'Connor concludes the chapter with a reference to the same cloud remarked at the beginning. There is little doubt that Haze Motes is headed in the wrong direction as he drives back into town. "The blinding white cloud had turned into a bird with long thin wings and was disappearing in the opposite direction." This symbol of transcendence and Haze's failure to see or to heed it prepares us for his inevitable conversion—although it does not prepare us for the surprising turn of events that O'Connor unfolds in the second half of the novel.

ENOCH SETTING
"THE HAVOC IN MOTION"

In chapter 8, the reader discovers Enoch Emery's identity as priest of the secular city. O'Connor creates Enoch, a character she describes as "a moron,"[18] to make Haze's eventual acceptance of grace more credible. They are at opposite poles of reality. She explains this comic character in the context of her comments on "the devil's territory." And she orients her readers: "In my stories a reader will find that the devil accomplishes a good deal of groundwork that seems to be necessary before grace is effective." O'Connor explains, "[T]he more a writer wishes to make the supernatural apparent, the more real he has to be able to make the natural world...."[19] Enoch's ritual washing of furnishings in his "mummified"-looking residence shows him inclined to fool's gold because the layer of gilt easily fades after a second washing. The cabinet's "tabernacle-like" compartment is meant to hold a slop jar. After painting "the inside of it with the gilt," Enoch comes to realize that it was meant to be "used FOR something" (76). But he ironically reverses the sense of the sacred into life's banalities. The painting from the Hilltop Funeral Home depicted a small boy praying, "And bless daddy" (75). Realizing that the father of the biblical Enoch was Cain, Enoch's claim that this is "his favorite" proves ironic. Enoch awaits some revelation. The title of the novel plays out comically in Enoch's anticipation: "Then for about a week his blood was in secret conference with itself every day, only stopping now and then to shout some order to him" (76). Following a visit to two horror movies, Enoch realizes the object of his vision and exclaims "Hazel Motes" as "his heart began to slam from side to side like a wild bell clapper" (79). O'Connor sets in motion Haze's encounter with the secret mystery to be revealed by the priest Enoch at the heart of the secular city.

Haze happens to be preaching his Church Without Christ that evening when Enoch meets him for the second time. The coincidence propels Enoch to set in motion his decision to break the law and steal the museum mummy. He interprets Haze's search for a "new jesus" who is "all man, without any blood to waste,...one that don't look like no other man" as a mandate for his mission. "Give me this new jesus, somebody," shouts Haze, "so we'll all be saved by the sight of him!" (80). Enoch the moron serves O'Connor well as one of the characters she describes in a 1961 letter: "I am much interested in this sort of innocent character who sets the havoc in motion" (1147).

In chapter 9 the novel's reversals begin to confront Haze. "Nothing was working the way Haze had expected it to" (83). Despite his preaching there were no new members of his church. Enoch, we discover, is a "Lapsed Catholic" (an ironic twist by O'Connor directed at smug Catholics), and claims that he cannot join. A new character appears at all four picture shows where Haze preaches one night. Onnie Jay Holy repeatedly winks at Haze. Her description of him bristles with ironic images of deception: "He looked like an ex-preacher turned cowboy, or an ex-cowboy turned mortician. He was not handsome but under his smile, there was an honest look that fitted into his face like a set of false teeth" (83). Onnie Jay interrupts as two men and a woman walk away from Haze's preaching. His claim that he needs his guitar to talk about Jesus because "I just somehow can say sweet things to music bettern [sic] plain" is punctuated by a patronizing address of everyone as "friends." There is a distinct barb aimed by O'Connor at the Dale Carnegie salesmanship made famous in the best-seller of 1937, *How to Win Friends and Influence People*.[20]

This former radio evangelist (his program aptly named "Soulease") preys upon an unsuspecting audience by insisting, "I don't tell you any lie." Not only does he promise to be "giving something away," but also he assures them, "I wouldn't have you believe nothing you can't feel in your own hearts." Flannery O'Connor introduces us to another substitute for religion in the secular city with Onnie Jay Holy's sentimentality. The claim of this new secular humanism—that we are "all sweetness inside"—

competes with Christian grace. But without the mystery of the cross and a recognition of evil, Onnie Jay Holy's new secular humanism is a poor substitute for Christian faith. This smiling preacher will later complain to Haze that "we just lost ten dollars." Moments earlier Hazel Motes boldly states, "This man is not true" (86). When Onnie Jay Holy was preaching at the previous picture show, Haze asked, "Do you people care anything about the truth?" He unconsciously describes his own path: "The only way to the truth is through blasphemy, but do you care?" (84). Like Paul, who blasphemed and persecuted Christ in the Christians, Haze will pass through the stage of blasphemy to recover faith on a higher plane.

Onnie Jay Holy tugs at people's emotions, asking if they know what it's like not to have a friend in the world; what it's like to be lonesome; what it's like to be perplexed, miserable, and in despair. There is a telling gesture of his sales pitch when he invites everyone who wants to "take advantage of this church" (87) to sign their names on a pad and give a dollar. It is Onnie Jay who takes advantage of the hearers. To Haze's credit, he repeatedly counters the smiling stranger's lies ("Onnie Jay Holy's face showed a great strain;...the only way he could keep his smile on was to hold it"). When he claims that the first time he met Haze, he thought of "Jesus Christ and Abraham Lincoln," O'Connor describes Haze's face as "suddenly swamped with outrage." "You ain't true," he repeats (88). Onnie Jay's interest in Haze's Church Without Christ is purely a matter of greed. He claims that he is no amateur. "If you want to get anywheres [sic] in religion, you got to keep it sweet." When Onnie Jay volunteers to "pay you a little something" to see the "new jesus," Haze chases him away and reorients readers to his philosophical quest with a revealing remark about his own metaphorical language: "There's no such thing as any new jesus. That ain't nothing but a way of saying something" (90).

Onnie Jay departs with the threat of "a little competition" after revealing his name, "Hoover Shoats." The symbolism is appropriate because he literally "sucks up" everything in his path (especially money) like a Hoover vacuum cleaner. He is equally well named as a "shoat," a young, well-fed pig. After Haze falls asleep in his car, he awakens at midnight and mistakes the hour for morning. Upon returning to the house he dares to enter Hawks's room and light a match to startle him. The discovery that Hawks is not blind but sighted ("The two sets of eyes looked at each other for as long as the match lasted") compounds this chapter's early signal that nothing was working the way Haze expected. O'Connor's use of eye imagery brilliantly symbolizes an inner experience: "Haze's expression seemed to open onto a deeper blankness and reflect something and then close again" (92). The "deeper blankness" is not just Haze's quest for Nothingness but an awakening to the possibility of real faith as he eliminates, one after the other, false substitutes for religion and his own empty nihilism.

The shortest chapter in the novel is chapter 11, three and a half pages in length. Its brevity nonetheless holds one of *Wise Blood*'s most powerful revelations for Haze Motes. Another night of street preaching outside the Odeon Theater and we find Haze announcing his nihilism: "No truth behind all truths is what I and this church preach!" (93). He echoes his earlier doctrines when he reminds the "trickle of people" exiting the movie that "Your conscience is a trick" that should be hunted down and killed. Your conscience, he concludes, is "no more than your face in the mirror is or your shadow behind you" (94). The metaphor foreshadows the action of the chapter as Hoover Shoats returns with a Haze Motes look-alike, preaching his Church Without Christ. O'Connor describes the scene: "He was so struck with how gaunt and thin he looked in the illusion that he stopped preaching. He had never pictured himself that way before" (94). The mirror image presented in the appearance of Solace Layfield forces Haze to recognize the illusion in his nihilism. Once again, Haze's own words foreshadow his hunting and killing the mock apparition as part of his quest for the truth. This encounter becomes an authentically contemplative experience for Haze.

But before that action, Haze returns to his room and finds the seductive Sabbath Lily waiting for him. Asa Hawks has abandoned her in the wake of Haze's discovery of his deception about self-blinding. Her invitation to be "pure filthy" meets approval from Haze who undresses and joins her in bed. "Take off your hat, king of the beasts" (96), she says. And Haze succumbs to the pleasures of passion (different from his experience with Leora Watts) en route to his return to faith.

Enoch Emery meanwhile will have his own encounter with the "king of the beasts" in chapter 11. First, in a scene marked by comedy, he has to steal the mummy from the museum case. Disguised, with his face darkened by shoe polish and wearing a black beard and dark glasses, Enoch could only be more conspicuous in the tiny town. He brings the mummy to his room and squeezes its head into the "tabernacle" of his washstand. It dawns upon him that he has committed a crime. Despite his priestly role, Enoch sullenly decides that "one jesus was as bad as another" (99). So he hurries to Haze's room to deliver the mummy and minimize his responsibility for the robbery from the museum. En route, he spies a life-size color picture advertising that Gonga the gorilla will appear "in person" at noon in front of the movie theater. Enoch sees it as "an opportunity to insult a successful ape" and a providential gift from the new jesus. His reverence restored, Enoch waits in line with the children. O'Connor's hand at comedy plays well in this scene. Enoch is "terrified" and takes courage from the children who surround him. The idea of an adult (Enoch is eighteen years old) being deceived by a man in a gorilla costume is ludicrous. Even children see through the hoax. But Gonga is a "successful" gorilla and Enoch, the zooworker, seeks revenge by insulting him.

Enoch struggles to think of "an obscene remark" (102) to insult Gonga. When his turn comes to meet Gonga, the ape extends a hand "with an automatic motion." However, "It was the first hand that had been extended to Enoch since he had come to the city. It was warm and soft." Enoch stammers his name and begins to tell his life's story. The surly voice is joined to human eyes behind the ape suit, "You go to hell," and jerks the hand away. It is a violent act. But at a deeper level, the violence comes in the "humiliation...so sharp and painful" that it leaves Enoch disoriented. Running to Haze's rooming house to deliver the new jesus, Enoch unburdens himself of the "urgent need to insult somebody" by telling Sabbath Lily that he is surprised Haze has anything to do with her.

The chapter comes to a climax when Sabbath Lily unwraps the package Enoch leaves for Haze. "For a while her face had an empty look" as she gazes at the new jesus. "[T]here was something in him of everyone she had ever known, as if they had all been rolled into one person and killed and shrunk and dried." From this grotesque image Sabbath Lily moves to a maternal pose, cradling the mummy in the crook of her arm and saying, "...you're right cute, ain't you" (104). Flannery O'Connor offers us the ironic, grotesque portrait of the Madonna of the secular city. Sabbath Lily decides to give Haze "a jolt" by presenting the new jesus. Haze has already awakened at the noise of Enoch slamming the door. He is intent upon making a new start in a new city with his preaching the Church Without Christ. He finds in his duffel bag his mother's glasses, puts them on, and looks at himself in the mirror. The reader recalls that Haze's mother intuited his sin at the carnival. Now, as Sabbath Lily intrudes and exclaims, "Call me Momma now," Haze sees with his mother's eyes. He snatches the mummy and throws it against the wall. He flings the skin out the upstairs door where the fire escape once stood. Haze responds to her claim that he wants nothing but Jesus by saying, "I've seen the only truth there is!" But a telltale cough escapes from Haze. The image of "a little yell for help at the bottom of a canyon" describes Haze's cough. His colorless and expressionless face, "blank as the rain falling down behind him" (107), ends the chapter on an ominous note.

Enoch returns as chapter 12 opens, seeking revenge for his humiliation by Gonga "the gorilla." Hope for Enoch is "two parts suspicion and one part lust"—a secular surrogate for religious hope. This young man's only ambition is to be accepted and respected in a purely superficial way—seeing "a line of people waiting to shake his hand" (108). By the chapter's end, however, Enoch wears the gorilla outfit and his appearance causes a man and woman to flee—not together, but in opposite directions: one toward the woods and the other down the highway. It is the supreme irony that his envy of Gonga and the scheme for celebrity and acknowledgment end in repulsing people and dividing them. But even more importantly, the "look of awakening" (109)—when Enoch gets the idea to attack the man wearing the gorilla suit and steal it for himself—leads to his ultimate dehumanization. This would-be priest of the secular city reverses the evolutionary plan and makes himself into a gorilla. He tells the waitress at the restaurant, "You may not see me again—the way I am" (110). This language that suggests on one level a conversion experience turns out to be the language of a superficial (and misguided) acting out of jealousy, Enoch's manifest dissatisfaction with his very self. O'Connor adds comedy and sorrow to this scene as Enoch ritually folds his clothes and then buries them. Under the moonlight, we recognize Enoch as the victim of violence inflicted by the man from whom he stole the ape's costume: "His natural appearance was marred by a gash that ran from the corner of his lip to his collarbone and by a lump under his eye that gave him a dulled insensitive look." He resembles the creatures caged beside the store earlier in the novel, the one-eyed bear and the tailless chicken hawk.

Lest a reader mistake Enoch's shallowness, the narrator points out, "Burying his clothes was not a symbol to him of burying his former self; he only knew he wouldn't need them any more" (111). Enoch is light-years away from the kind of religious conversion that Haze Motes approaches. In the splendor of his gorilla suit, reverting to bestial identity, we are told: "No gorilla in existence...was happier at that moment than this one, whose god had finally rewarded it." Ephemeral happiness quickly gives way to disappointment when the frightened couple flees. "The gorilla stood as though surprised and presently its arms fell to its side" (112). We leave Enoch in his lonely posture, staring over the valley and the skyline of the secular city.

HAZE AT THE ABYSS: A REVELATION

In the penultimate chapter 13 O'Connor presages the grace of Haze's conversion with unmistakable violence. Haze observes Onnie Jay Holy's hired Prophet preaching the next night. He is described spying on the scene, "watching him with the kind of intensity that means something is going to happen no matter what is done to keep it from happening" (113). It is the same expression he wore when he left Leora Watts's bed after his first night with her and set out to buy a car: "...his face had a fragile look...like a gun no one knows is loaded" (37). Solace Layfield's name connotes both a "sweetness inside" spirituality (solace) and a "priesthood of all believers" church order (the laity as distinct from any ordained minister or priestly ministry). At the end of the evening, Haze follows Solace's car outside town and rams the back end. Haze protests to the man dressed like him, "You ain't true." Haze interrogates him about impersonating him as the Prophet for the Church Without Christ. In keeping with his philosophic quest for truth, he confronts Solace Layfield: "What do you get up on top of a car and say you don't believe in what you do believe in for?" (114). He forces him to remove his clothes, knocks him down by driving his car over him, and backs over the body once again. "Two things I can't stand," Haze announces, "a man that ain't true and one that mocks what is" (115). The dying man makes a confession of sins (he had stolen a car, never told the truth to his father, took a fee for turning in Henry's still) and wheezes out his dying words, "Jesus hep [sic] me" (115). It is questionable contrition because nowhere does Solace Layfield acknowledge his role as an accomplice to Hoover Shoats's scam.

This scene and the violence demand interpretation. It offers a compelling symbolic action in Haze Motes's destruction of his own false self mirrored in the person of the man ironically identified as "the Prophet" and recognized by Haze as the "illusion."

At the filling station the next morning Haze tells the boy attendant that he is going to a new city to preach. His rational, secular humanism reaches a crescendo in the monologue he delivers to the boy. "He said it was not right to believe anything you couldn't see or hold in your hands or test with your teeth." Even blasphemy is discounted by Haze "because then you were believing in something to blaspheme." Nevertheless, Haze curses and blasphemes "in a quiet intense way" that causes the boy to stop working and listen. The boy objectively advises Haze that there is one gas tank leak, two radiator leaks, and a tire that would only go twenty miles. Haze's pride inflates just before his downfall. He claims that the car "is just beginning its life. A lightening bolt couldn't stop it" (116). The allusion to Paul's being struck on the road to Damascus (Acts 9:1–19) and the conversion that follows is the paradigm for Haze, the modern Saul.[21] Within moments a highway patrolman pursues his car and pulls him over. When Haze protests that he was not speeding, the officer replies, "No, you wasn't." He also agrees that Haze was driving on the correct side of the road. "What you want with me?" Haze asks. The patrolman tells him, "I just don't like your face," and asks for his license. Haze returns the insult and admits that he does not have a license. O'Connor creates a symbolic encounter with the Law in this scene. The arbitrary action of the Law (in the person of the patrolman) compromises Haze's rational and humanist path to truth. The officer orders Haze to drive his car to the top of the next hill, coaxing him with the view—"puttiest [sic] view you ever did see" (117). He coaxes Haze, saying that he can see better if he gets out of the car. As he gazes thirty feet down the sheer embankment, the patrolman pushes the Essex car over the precipice. "Them that don't have a car, don't need a license," he asserts. By a shocking symbolic action, the capricious destruction of Haze's automobile precipitates his religious conversion. Haze himself has asserted that "Nobody with a good car needs to be justified" (64); and "This car'll get me anywhere I want to go. It may stop here and there but it won't stop permanent" (72). Now he faces the implications.

The scene of Haze staring off into the distance between his eyes and "the blank gray sky that went on, depth after depth, into space" marks his moment of conversion. (The scene is the inverse of Enoch in his lonely posture, staring over the valley and the skyline of the secular city but totally unaware of any transcendence.) Haze's knees buckle and he sits on the edge of the abyss with his feet dangling—the very figure of pride deflated and humbled. He responds to the patrolman's invitation to give him a ride ("Was you going anywheres?"), with the monosyllable "No." Hazel Motes faces the abyss and recognizes for the first time that he has avoided the *invisible* truth. Now his philosophical quest moves to the plane of faith, but a faith more mature and trusting than childhood faith born of guilt and fear.

Thomas Merton's insights about the abyss as a symbol of annihilation and nothingness lend insight to O'Connor's climax of the novel. Early in his autobiography, *The Seven Storey Mountain*, Merton recollects his days as a Columbia University graduate student. He uses the archetypal metaphor of the abyss to describe his own and his classmates' spiritual alienation: "In those days one of the things we had most in common, although perhaps we did not talk about it so much, was the abyss that walked in front of our feet everywhere we went."[22] As World War II brewed and the Third Reich wreaked chaos throughout Europe, Merton and his peers experienced the existential threat. A few pages earlier in his autobiography, Merton ventures a truth that resonates with Hazel Motes. He penetrates the spiritual vacuum and the illusion of well-being. Merton's story of conversion, replete with what he later described as living under "the name of a fictitious character occupied in a very active self-impersonation,"[23] recounts the pride before his fall. "The wounds within me were, I suppose, enough....[T]he very anguish and helplessness of my position was something to which I rapidly succumbed. And it was my defeat that was to be the occasion of my rescue."[24] Merton's introduction to his translations of the Desert Fathers captures this quest for authentic conversion: "What can we gain by sailing to the moon if we are not able to cross the abyss that separates us from ourselves? This is the most important of all voyages of discovery."[25]

In her 5 July 1958 letter to "A," O'Connor elaborates upon this contemplative undertaking. She reminds her most important correspondent that "the setting in which most fiction takes place is exactly a setting in which nothing is so little felt to be true as a faith in Christ." She insists that the challenge of the author is "to succeed in making the divinity of Christ seem consistent with the structure of all reality. This has got to be got across implicitly in spite of a world that doesn't feel it, in spite of characters who don't live it."[26] We remember how Haze insisted that his Church Without Christ would offer "a new jesus" who is "all man, without any blood to waste,...one that don't look like no other man" (80). She describes in this letter the ethos of *Wise Blood* and its protagonist, Hazel Motes. She proceeds to fault "A" for saying that Catholic fiction writers must write about their religious faith "as though anyone who questioned it would obviously be utterly foolish and irrelevant...perhaps even a little insane."[27] O'Connor continues, emphasizing the potential she holds for both her characters and her audience:

> What the Catholic fiction writer must realize is that those who question [the faith] are not insane at all, they are not utterly foolish and irrelevant, they are for the most part acting according to their lights. What he must get over is that they don't have the complete light....It is a matter of getting across the reality of grace, or as you say later on "in examining the relationship of human beings to their God," plus making FIRST their God believable. To, as I have said before, an audience not adequately equipped to believe anything.[28]

Merton demonstrates the same respect for the philosophical quest of nonbelievers like Hazel Motes. A pair of essays in his collection aptly titled *Faith and Violence* informs an interpretation of O'Connor's novel. Reading Martin Marty's *Varieties of Unbelief*[29] stimulates Merton's reflections. The monk is taken by Marty's concern with "the real unbelief of apparent believers" and their idolatry in Romantic individualism, nationalism, progress, and hope. "In a word," Merton agrees, "Dr. Marty suggests that what passes for Christian faith among many Americans is perhaps less respectable, intellectually and spiritually, than the concerned atheism of those whose unbelief implies the courageous assumption of loneliness, dread and risk." He concludes that obedience to the imperatives of marketing and an affluent society is not obedience to God and deserves to be called "bad faith."[30]

Merton's second essay opens with a note of gratitude to the "nonbeliever" who refuses to accept "the inadequacy and impertinence of so much of what is inflicted on you in the name of religion." His description fits perfectly the character of Hazel Motes, refusing to patronize the nonbeliever: "The militant Unbeliever is, in fact, a Believer—though perhaps a Believer-in-reverse." On the other hand, Merton takes direct aim (as does O'Connor) at the surrogates for religion: "Where authentic religious concern degenerates into salesmanship it becomes an affront to the honest perplexities of the vast majority of men. I think, frankly, that you are entitled to be left unbothered by the sheer triviality of so much religious vaudeville."[31] Could there be a more devastating indictment of Asa Hawks or Hoover Shoats?

The imagery and metaphors of vision in *Wise Blood* coincide with Merton's interpretation of the unbeliever's integrity. He reminds his readers that "clear insight is a matter of intelligence and reasonable judgment, not emotion. Yet such insights are not the fruit of argument and cannot be pounded into another by debate."[32] He ushers us into the world of Hazel Motes with a penetrating reflection:

...Faith comes by hearing, says St. Paul: but by hearing *what?* The cries of the snake-handlers? The soothing platitudes of the religious operator? One must first be able to listen to the inscrutable ground of his own being, and who am I to say that your reservations about religious commitment do not protect, in you, this kind of listening?

The "absence of God" and the "silence of God" in the modern world are not only evident, but they are facts of profound *religious* significance....We keep insisting that God and we deal with each other morning, noon and night over closed circuit TV. These pious metaphors are permissible with certain reservations, but to try to force them on you can border on blasphemous idiocy. Thus our very language itself (to many of us still adequate) has tended to become an important element in the absence and the silence of God. Does it occur to us that instead of revealing him we are hiding him? As a matter of fact, the Second Vatican Council admitted this. In the Constitution on the Church in the Modern World we read that "Believers can have more than a little to do with the birth of atheism" when by their deficiencies "they must be said to conceal rather than reveal the authentic face of God and religion."[33]

Merton succeeds in identifying blasphemy not with the nonbeliever but with the believer! This is the very irony that informs O'Connor's Catholic imagination in *Wise Blood*. The two Catholic writers share a contemplative perspective that penetrates illusion, unmasks the disguise, and touches the deeper reality. So it is that Merton can speak of his own role as a "solitary explorer" for whom "faith sometimes mysteriously takes on the aspect of doubt when, in fact, one has to doubt and reject conventional faith and superstitious surrogates that have taken the place of faith." He implicitly identifies with Hazel Motes by admitting that "*all* are bound to seek in honest perplexity. Everybody is an Unbeliever more or less." But Merton goes on to insist (as does O'Connor) that only when this fact is "fully experienced, accepted, and lived with does one become fit to hear the simple message of the Gospel—or of any other religious teaching."[34] The abyss is both the dead end of Haze's quest for truth in humanistic categories ("He said it was not right to believe anything you couldn't see or hold in your hands or test with your teeth" [116]); and a place in which Haze comes to terms with his potential to believe—a Jungian symbol of admitting and then emerging from failure and woundedness into new life.

The concluding paragraph of chapter 13 in *Wise Blood* gathers the imagery and metaphor of vision through the character of Mrs. Flood. She is described ironically: "A woman like her, who was so clear-sighted, could never stand to be blind" (119). She thanks "her stars" that she is not "religious or morbid." The fact that she equates these terms exposes the same predicament that Merton points out—religion has ironically become the midwife of modern atheism. She explains Haze's self-blinding to religious people being "a little off in their heads." Mrs. Flood's perplexity insists upon a reason to explain his behavior and his sacrifice of the pleasure of his sight. In the final chapter of *Wise Blood* O'Connor ventures to show that Haze's unexpected action is not irrational but suprarational. She admits to "A" in a letter three years after the novel's publication that the symbolic blinding is problematic because her protagonist does not seem human enough (963).

Whatever the dramatic limitations of the character Hazel Motes, O'Connor's final chapter makes his conversion unmistakable. In the opening paragraph, the ubiquitous Mrs. Flood finds herself staring at "the mess he had made in his eye sockets" and expecting "to see something she hadn't seen before." The fact that she feels he is "cheating" her out of something in "some secret way" tells us volumes about the manipulative, greedy Mrs. Flood. It was her type, who fashioned in her heart nothing but wickedness all day long (Gen 6:5–6), who occasioned the great deluge in which the upright Noah and his family were spared. Mrs. Flood is well named. Her designs upon more and more of Haze's military disability check for rent and board, and her attempt to marry him in order to gain a widow's benefits, confirm her identity.

When she cautions him that Sabbath Lily is "only after your money" (121), she is all the more despicable. She shares with Enoch an appetite for "secret knowledge"[35] (50), a Gnostic paranoia about their own lack of self-esteem. Mrs. Flood intuits the fact that Haze is "seeing something" with his "peculiar pushing look" on his face. O'Connor punctuates this chapter with image after image of the "distance" that Haze discovered before he collapses before the abyss. His posture ("knees bent" and "on the edge of the embankment with his feet hanging over") connotes the experience of hierophany, some manifestation or epiphany of the sacred. Mrs. Flood perceives that he is "straining toward something" and the imagery takes on specific content when she tries to imagine "the whole black world in his head." She sees her own head as "a switchbox where she controlled from"; the image conforms to her own secular humanism and mechanical rationalism:

> She imagined it was like you were walking in a tunnel and all you could see was a pinpoint of light. She had to imagine the pinpoint of light; she couldn't think of it at all without that. She saw it as some kind of a star, like the star on Christmas cards. She saw him going backwards to Bethlehem and she had to laugh. (123)

O'Connor's choice of imagery proves fertile for her theological imagination. She has already suggested through Mrs. Flood's descriptions of Haze's vision—seeing something, the pushing look on his face, and his straining toward something—that he is blessed with revelation. The association of the "star" of Bethlehem with Haze's coming-to-believe makes his embracing of the Christian faith all the more obvious. The Christmas mystery claims the incarnation of the Son of God. Christ is born into humanity, fully human and fully divine. The imagery and symbolism are apt in subtle ways.

Matthew's gospel is unique in the mention of the Magi and the star at Bethlehem. He constantly challenges his largely Jewish-Christian audience (and the Jews he seeks to convert) to be more inclusive in understanding the universal salvific will of God. It is apparent in the genealogy that opens Matthew's gospel and includes the foreigners Rahab and Ruth in the ancestry of Jesus. No surprise that the xenophobia of Matthew's audience should also be challenged by the privilege of the "pagan" astrologers from the East who seek the newborn king. In the Book of Numbers (chapter 24) Balak, king of the Moabites, consults his *magus* (seer) for an oracle when the Israelites on Exodus request safe passage across his country. Balaam's oracle is retrieved by Matthew at Jesus' birth and the symbol employed as the fulfillment of the Messianic prophecy: "I see him—but not now, I behold him—but not close at hand: a star shall rise from Jacob, a scepter arises from Israel" (Num 24:17). Like the Magi of old, Haze follows the pinpoint of light, a star that also leads him to pay homage and to recognize Christ as king, priest, and prophet—identities symbolized by the Magi's gifts of gold, frankincense, and myrrh. That Mrs. Flood sees Haze "going backwards to Bethlehem" confirms his conversion to the all-inclusive Christ of faith, whose epiphany begins there.

In Luke's infancy narrative we find another Christmas symbol that explains even more cogently Haze's journey to faith. Three times in Luke's story he mentions the "manger" where Christ lies and is to be found by the shepherds (Luke 2:7; 2:12; 2:16). The source of this powerful symbol, of course, is the Hebrew prophet Isaiah. The opening of Isaiah's prophecy employs the manger as a central image: "Listen, you heavens; earth, attend for Yahweh speaks: 'Sons have I raised and reared, but they have disowned me! The ox knows its owner, and an ass its owner's manger; but Israel does not know, my people has not understood'" (Isa 1:2–3). This image embedded in the Christmas story fits perfectly with Hazel Motes's pilgrimage. Like the once rebellious and unfaithful Israelites, he now returns to the manger of the Lord, to faith.

Every serious commentator on *Wise Blood* alludes to the date of Asa Hawks's counterfeit self-blinding scene. The newspaper clipping which he shows Haze is dated ten years earlier, October 4.

Because this is the only date to appear in any of O'Connor's fiction, the coincidence of its being the feast of St. Francis of Assisi bears scrutiny. No saint in the Roman Catholic Church is more universally beloved than the friar of Assisi. Revered as *Il Povrello,* the mendicant who begged and served especially the poor, Francis is the antithesis of Asa Hawks's mendacity and his charlatan preying upon would-be believers. Had Francis's thirteenth-century reforms of the Catholic Church succeeded, then the fifteenth-century Reformation might not have been needed. In some ways, Francis's steadfast witness amid the scandals of medieval Christendom makes him an apt patron saint for the post-Christian world. Blind preceding his death (although suffering an infirmity and not self-inflicted blindness), Saint Francis, who bears the scars of the crucifixion on his own body, ironically becomes the imaginative ideal for O'Connor's Hazel Motes.

Chapter Three

The Christic Imagination: Creative Gestures of a Humble God

Of course I do not connect the Church exclusively with the Patriarchal Ideal. The death of such would not be the death of the Church, which is only now a seed and a Divine one....In the end we visualize the same thing but I see it as happening through Christ and His Church.
                    —Letter to "A," 6 September 1955

In the wake of *Wise Blood*'s publication in 1952, Flannery O'Connor would discover additional theological catalysts for her Catholic imagination. This chapter assesses how Romano Guardini and William F. Lynch served as implicit dialogue partners to deepen her understanding of the mystery of Christ.[1] She would transform such christological insights into the uniquely imaginative expressions of her fiction. For O'Connor, it would not be a matter of forcing theological formulas into her stories.

Instead, her Catholic Christian realism worked itself out in the very form and drama of her mature fiction. Flannery O'Connor's theological importance originates in a distinctively christological aesthetics. She enacts stories of a humble God's creative gestures of redemption through her "Christic imagination."

Roberta Bondi, a theologian at Emory University's Candler School of Theology, has reflected with exceptional insight upon a teaching experience with a graduate class studying the early Church's views of Christ. She admitted to a certain ambivalence, in part because of the admixture of Christology texts that are both "subtle and intricate" and "frequently bombastic and often boring." Moreover, she anticipated a hostile response because for the first time in her twenty-eight years of teaching graduate students, this class was comprised exclusively of women she knew to be feminists. Her curiosity piqued, Bondi was prepared to disarm their "feminist mistrust" of these classic Christian texts. She was convinced that they would discover an affinity for the Christology of Antioch, emphasizing the humanity of Jesus in the incarnation and cautioning against forcing human attributes, especially male imagery, onto our image of God. She was surprised at their attraction to the Christology of the Alexandrian tradition—Christ is the Word of God—and the particular insights of Cyril of Alexandria. Bondi quotes her students:

> Look at what it means to women and men, too, if Jesus is not just some innocent human victim God has set up to die, but rather is God's own self, the powerful God who created us and gives shape to our universe and loves us intimately—who for our sake chooses to be emptied of the divine power and shares in real human suffering and dies for the sake of the resurrection. Don't you see? What we have right here in the tradition are some real resources for a strong feminist Christology.

When she pressed the students about whether or not Christ's humanity is lost in this Divine Word, they insisted that Christ's humanity is not "lost." "Cyril never denies Jesus' humanity; it's just that, like Athanasius, he sees that there is no human being on earth who can set right what is broken in human life—including the effects of sexism. That is why he argues for the natural union of humanity and divinity in Christ. Of course, we can be saved only by sharing life with God in Christ!"[2]

Virtually all commentators remark that O'Connor's writing predates the feminist movement and fails to show elements of feminist consciousness. However, in a September 1955 letter to "A" she ventures what, in retrospect, is a bold feminist assertion: "Of course I do not connect the Church exclusively with the Patriarchal Ideal. The death of such would not be the death of the Church, which is only now a seed and a Divine one" (952). This insight adds to her sober appreciation of the Church's historic foibles and failures. O'Connor's ecclesiology anticipated the Second Vatican Council's insistence upon the fact that the Church is an *ecclesia semper reformanda* ("a church always being reformed"). Her ecclesiology rests upon foundations that include a carefully considered Christology.

Flannery O'Connor's attraction to the Church's classical Christology is evident through her correspondence, essays, and personal library. In a 1956 letter to "A" she writes: "The other day I ran up on a wonderful quotation: 'The dragon is at the side of the road watching those who pass. Take care lest he devour you! You are going to the Father of souls, but it is necessary to pass by the dragon.' That is Cyril of Jerusalem instructing cate-chumens" (978). She employs this same excerpt to conclude her essay "The Fiction Writer and His Country." In that context, she interprets for the reader: "No matter what form the dragon may take, it is of this mysterious passage past him, or into his jaws, that stories of any depth will always be concerned to tell, and this being the case, it requires considerable courage at any time, in any country, not to turn away from the storyteller" (806). O'Connor's longtime friend and junior, William Sessions, recalls how she often repeated this passage, which she had found in Romano

Guardini's book on prayer. Sessions insists that it means that "the story better be well made, whatever its ideology, and work toward that single purpose of getting past the dragon."[3] In other words, the story must "enable the reader-passerby to survive" the journey, from which there is no escaping. And an invariable part of the journey was the omnipresence of evil, "the jaws of the dragon."

Among the many meanings of the fiction writer's "country," ranging from an actual landscape to a geographical region or nation's character, or ethos, O'Connor adds the category of the literary artist's "true country." She insists that the Christian writer understands it to be "what is eternal and absolute" (801). The mystery of Christ reminds O'Connor that our humanity is not lost. Her stories continually awaken us to recognize the union of the human and the divine. Her memorable characters discover their own "true country." What Roberta Bondi's students discovered in the Church's ancient texts, Flannery O'Connor had discovered and then explored more deeply through the writings of two gifted guides, Romano Guardini and William F. Lynch.

ROMANO GUARDINI

O'Connor's first letter to "A" (dated 20 July 1955) complimented this new correspondent for her initiative in writing. She remarked how startling it was "to find someone who recognizes my work for what I try to make it," adding, "I would like to know who this is who understands my stories" (942–43). This inaugural letter to "A" proceeds immediately to focus upon her understanding of Christ—her christological concerns. O'Connor accepts "A's" reference to her as a "God-conscious writer" and exclaims, "I write the way I do because (not though) I am a Catholic." While she admits that she is a Catholic with "a modern consciousness," she recognizes that such a perspective is "a necessary burden for the conscious Catholic." She refers to Carl Jung's definition of the modern consciousness as "unhistorical, solitary, and guilty" to clarify her meaning. At this point she volunteers her own commitment to the Church but adds a subtle insight:

> I think that the Church is the only thing that is going to make the terrible world we are coming to endurable; the only thing that makes the Church endurable is that it is somehow the body of Christ and that on this we are fed. It seems to be a fact that you have to suffer as much from the Church as for it but if you believe in the divinity of Christ, you have to cherish the world at the same time that you struggle to endure it. This may explain the lack of bitterness in the stories. (942)

Attention then shifts to her collection of short stories, *A Good Man Is Hard to Find,* published six weeks earlier. O'Connor confesses to "A" that she is "mighty tired of reading reviews that call 'A Good Man' brutal and sarcastic." She explains that those stories are "hard but they are hard because there is nothing harder or less sentimental than Christian realism." W. B. Yeats's poem "The Second Coming" affords her a ready metaphor as she speaks ironically of her grotesque stories: "I believe that there are many rough beasts now slouching toward Bethlehem to be born and that I have reported the progress of a few of them, and when I see these stories described as horror stories I am always amused because the reviewer always has hold of the wrong horror" (942).

In the second paragraph of her second letter to "A," less than two weeks later, O'Connor again gravitates to the mystery of Christ. She explains how countercultural this mystery proves to be for her modern audience.

> I believe too that there is only one Reality and that this is the end of it, but the term, "Christian Realism," has become necessary for me, perhaps in a purely academic way, because I find myself in a world where everybody has his compartment, puts you in yours, shuts the door and departs. One of

the awful things about writing when you are a Christian is that for you the ultimate reality is the Incarnation, the present reality is the Incarnation, and nobody believes in the Incarnation. That is, nobody in your audience....

As for Jesus' being a realist: if He was not God, He was no realist, only a liar, and the crucifixtion [sic] an act of justice. (943)

That last sentence borders on brash overstatement as O'Connor insists upon the divinity of Christ. But lest her readers accuse her of insisting upon the divinity of Christ at the expense of Christ's humanity, her sixth letter to "A" (6 September 1955) articulates a balanced grasp of the underlying theology: "To see Christ as God and man is probably no more difficult today than it has always been, even if today there seem to be more reasons to doubt" (953). In this same context O'Connor compares Bishop Fulton J. Sheen to German theologian Romano Guardini. While she pleads that she is not one of the American bishop's detractors, she suggests, "If Msgr. Sheen would conceive of wanting to be what Msgr. Guardini is, then that prelate would go up in my estimation" (953). Her complaint about Sheen is the "vulgarity" with which he carried out his ministry. This comparison helps us to understand why O'Connor would find an important alternative in the theological stimulus of Guardini.

Romano Guardini's *The Lord* was published in Germany in 1937 and translated into English in 1954. O'Connor first mentions having read it in a December 1954 letter to Sally Fitzgerald, describing it as "very fine" and noting, "I am reading everything I can of Romano Guardini's" (928). In her fifth letter to "A" (28 August 1955), O'Connor chronicles a comic account of "the embarrassing subject of what I have not read and been influenced by." She continues with a catalogue of authors that she discovered while she attended graduate school in Iowa. The letter concludes with a reminder that she has "more to say about the figure of Christ as merely human." But because she realizes this letter has already been long, she promises to "save it." There is, however, a telling connection when she immediately adds, "Have you read Romano Guardini? A German of Italian descent. His master work is something called *The Lord* which in my opinion there is nothing like, anywhere, certainly not in this country" (951).

Kerygmatic Theology:
A Christocentric Worldview

While commentators make passing acknowledgment that O'Connor had praised Guardini's writings, they fail to fathom the depth of her attraction to his work. Robert Kreig's recent study of Guardini as one of the most creative theologians of the twentieth century facilitates this task of discovery. Moreover, because he rescues Guardini from efforts to portray him as a reactionary Catholic theologian, Krieg's study indirectly strengthens our appreciation of O'Connor as a theologically progressive, creative Catholic literary artist. Guardini's pastoral leadership with the Catholic liturgical and youth movements in Germany, along with his acceptance of the modern world, anticipated the Second Vatican Council's 1965 Pastoral Constitution on the Church in the Modern World *(Gaudium et spes)*, which insisted that the church read "the signs of the times" in its dialogue with culture. This theologian's themes of divine revelation as God's self-disclosure, Jesus Christ as mediator, and literature as the expression of religious experience provided O'Connor with rich coordinates for her imagination. Guardini's kerygmatic theology—a theology that *proclaims* the mystery of salvation in Christ's birth, death, and resurrection—sees revelation as God's self-disclosure in Jesus Christ, God desiring and seeking to enter into an "I-Thou" relationship with all human persons.

With respect to his identity as a kerygmatic theologian, Guardini has often been compared to Karl Barth, the great twentieth-century Reformation theologian who grounded himself in biblical theology. Barth's concerns were formulated as kerygmatic presentations that gave modern readers access to the living Christ. In Protestant circles Paul Tillich coined the term "method of correlation"[4] to characterize this neo-orthodox method of beginning with existential questions and then reformulating the answers found in the biblical revelation in light of those lively and often novel modern questions.

Guardini's existential theology relies upon an inductive method of inquiry. It contrasts starkly with the dry Scholastic and Neoscholastic formulas and deductive methods of official Roman Catholic theology from the late nineteenth century until the reformulations of the Second Vatican Council. Krieg points to Guardini's own adult religious conversion (although he was baptized as an infant) in 1905 to illustrate the inductive method. Guardini's autobiographical reflections acknowledge a number of factors that brought about his "encounter" with the living God. His studies in chemistry and economics resulted in failure and frustration. His interaction with atheistic and agnostic university fellow students in Tubingen, Munich, and Berlin brought him to doubt God's existence. Conversations with his friend Karl Neundorfer during a vacation in the Bavarian Alps led him to realize vicariously a new understanding of Christian faith. Krieg describes Guardini's simultaneously reading Houston Stuart Chamberlain's *The Foundations of the Nineteenth Century* (1899) and feeling God's nearness awaken within him. Guardini's autobiographical remembrance of this event rivets the reader's attention: "The sense of a supreme presence remained with me, a presence weaving behind everything and caring [for us]—a presence about which however one can say nothing."[5]

Upon his return home to Mainz in August 1905 Guardini met again with Neundorfer; in recalling their meeting he recollects how Matthew 10:39, "Those who find their life will lose it, and those who lose their life for my sake will find it," would provide the key. Guardini asked himself, to whom would he relinquish his life? He answers:

Not simply to God for if a person means only God, then he can say "God" and mean himself. There must be an objective reference....There is however only one: the Catholic Church in its authority and certainty....For [my friend Neundorfer] the quest had been, where is the way of love, and the answer had come: in the church. During the following days I was very happy, [filled with] a peaceful and calm happiness.[6]

When one recalls O'Connor's conviction "All good stories are about conversion" (1067), the origins of Guardini's mature faith coincide with her own imaginative efforts. In fact, in a review of Guardini's 1960 study, *The Conversion of Augustine,* O'Connor credits him with avoiding two extreme approaches: conversion stories that end with theoretical interests, ignore psychology, and omit "hesitations along the way"; or the "case study" approach that "makes psychology and the living process everything." She applauds Guardini's "interpretation of Augustine's spiritual drama" as "a psychological study well-informed on spiritual realities....The result is as penetrating a study of the saint as we are liable to get."[7] A line from Guardini's book on Augustine gauges the conversion event from the perspective of kerygmatic theology and evokes the response of the total person: "[Conversion] can only be something that seizes a man with a life-or-death grip: total orientation to the all-demanding God, to Jesus Christ."

It becomes more and more apparent that O'Connor's attraction to Guardini's theology reveals how her own insights and reflections resonate with his kerygmatic presentations. But something more happens. Since the beginning of the twentieth century, Catholic theologians such as Maurice Blondel had searched for an alternative philosophical basis for religious thought. The seeds of the inductive method in Catholic theology can be found in Blondel's "turn to the subject." His emphasis upon the will did not result in a purely subjectivist theology, but in an understanding of the person as a subject (with a will that makes meaningful choices) and revelation as an objective reality. The Augustinian dynamism of restlessly seeking God was integral to discovering the transcendent God's objective self-disclosure.

Krieg's careful historical research revisits Guardini's 1923 inaugural lecture when he assumed the academic chair for the Philosophy of Religion and Catholic *Weltanschauung* at the University of Berlin. Guardini articulated some foundational ideas on revelation in this lecture entitled "On the Essence of the Catholic Worldview." Another professor at the University of Berlin, William Dilthey, was writing extensively on "worldview" in light of the ongoing human search for meaning in life. It was an important topic for German scholars after World War I. In the wake of the eighteenth-century Enlightenment, many westerners developed a philosophy of life independent of explicit religious belief. The philosophical and historical background for *Wise Blood* is evident in this German academic discourse about modern secularization and a post-Christian culture.[8] Dilthey's definition is central: "...a worldview is the frame of reference in which, on the basis of a perception of the world, questions concerning the meaning and significance of the world are resolved and the ideal, the good, and the most important standards by which one conducts one's life are derived."[9] Krieg summarizes succinctly Guardini's theological point of departure:

> According to Guardini, a *Weltanschauung* is the point of view from which a person describes the whole of reality as well as each of its elements and their interconnectedness. It involves both the perspective of seeing and also what is seen. The knower seeks to bring into congruence his or her vantage point and the deepest dimensions of life so that what results is not the knower's subjective apprehension but the knower's conformity of heart and mind to objective reality, the truth....This kind of viewing involves insight, including "intuition" *(Anschauung)* which permits the knower to detect inner relationships and the heart of reality....
>
> ...One must build a worldview on the basis of God's word in Jesus Christ. Such an understanding of life presupposes

Christian faith, for "[f]aith means stepping to Christ, to the standpoint where he stands [and] to see out of his eyes."[10]

Although Flannery O'Connor would never read this text of the lecture, it manifests a theology of revelation that reverberates throughout Guardini's theological writings and that is central to O'Connor's own christocentric worldview. As Krieg describes it, Guardini had staked out a position distinct from the two prevalent philosophies of the day. First, he refused to embrace neo-Kantianism because it located Christian belief in the realm of purely subjective feelings; neo-Kantianism also excluded any consideration of belief's objective referent, God. Second, he criticized the antimetaphysical forms of "philosophy of life" *(Lebensphilosophie)* represented by Nietzsche, Dilthey, and Henri Bergson as too nonrational and too Romantic—"they accentuate the emotive and volitional aspects of personal existence but neglect both our use of reason and the rational order of objective reality."[11]

Guardini's alternative was to follow a philosophical trajectory of idealism from Plato through Christian thinkers like Augustine, Anselm of Canterbury, Bonaventure, Søren Kierkegaard, and Fyodor Dostoevsky. (It comes as no surprise that Flannery O'Connor's intellectual resources include these same thinkers.) In Germany, this movement under Edmund Husserl and Martin Heidegger came to be known as phenomenology. Krieg offers a reliable summary: "[I]t analyzes personal existence in such a manner as to go beneath the empirical aspects of reality in order to penetrate to the 'essence' *(Wesen)* of human life. Thus it treats such topics as the reality of being a person and the character of love....In short, it intends to inquire into objective reality."[12] O'Connor's stories evidence the same phenomenological preoccupation with attention to detail and dramatic action leading to universal and abiding truths about human existence and love. We cannot absolutely know to what extent O'Connor simply reinforced her own insights by reading Guardini, or to what extent she drew new insights from his work. Nor will we know the real extent of his influence upon her Catholic imagination and fiction. In my judgment, however, the latter has been ignored. One illustration offers a compelling argument for Guardini's role as a primary catalyst for deepening O'Connor's christological understanding.

Christ as God's Humility

Only two and a half months after her first letter to "A," O'Connor protests that her new correspondent exaggerates her as a Thomist and Aristotelian when it comes to philosophy. "I am one, of course, who believes that man is created in the image and likeness of God," Flannery insists in a 24 September 1955 letter. "I believe that all creation is good but that what has free choice is more completely God's image than what does not have it." Then O'Connor introduces a key term: "...also I define humility differently from you. Msgr. Guardini can explain that" (957). A reading of Guardini's *The Lord,* the book that O'Connor repeatedly praises, bears out her reference. The third chapter is entitled "God's Humility." I demonstrate in the following chapters how Flannery O'Connor's enthusiasm for Guardini's work is ultimately rooted in the Christology that Guardini presents in those pages. (She explicitly credits his 1956 essay on Dostoevsky as a direct influence upon her second novel, *The Violent Bear It Away.*)[13] It is a Christology that already animates O'Connor's imagination. But the clarity of Guardini's kerygmatic theology contributes to her understanding and stimulates her creative imagination. The worldview and the aesthetics of her fiction evidence a distinct debt to this German theologian's creative reinterpretation of the Christ mystery.

As Guardini begins the chapter "God's Humility," he acknowledges that millions of contemporaries reject Christ and "the conception of man drawn by Christ." He admits an ever-deepening opposition (even violence) against this essence of Christianity—in both nonbelievers and in Christians themselves. He distinguishes between accepting Christ and his "radically new conception of man" by an act of will or blind loyalty on the one hand and, on the other, the "vital conviction" demanded by a kerygmatic theology.[14] Guardini contrasts how the ancient world emulated the traits of the will-to-greatness, -wealth, -power, and -fame, with the fact that "Jesus is poor...in the sense of absence of needs." He describes Jesus as a "failure" whose teachings take root nowhere, even among his followers. Guardini reminds readers that the Eucharist is the central Christian mystery, that Christ's death is humanity's healing event, and that the resurrection is history's all-transforming power.

Guardini's understanding of Christ focuses through a question: What is the true nature of man and how may it be realized? Antiquity, he observes, answers, "By a life of grandeur." In contrast, Guardini sees Christianity's reply as distinct: "Anything is possible." He elaborates, "Everything, the noblest and the basest, receives from Christ new significance, for in everything lies the 'seed' of new beginning." Guardini admits that this conception is no longer generally accepted in the culture-at-large.

Then Guardini ventures his most creative christological insight. "Not only our idea of man has been modified by Christ," he says, but "also our idea of God." New questions flow: "What message is there for us in the life of Jesus?" "What kind of Father becomes apparent in this Son who is so lamentably 'unsuccessful'?"—that is, arrested, liquidated as dangerous. Guardini recognizes that something within us revolts at the implications:

> We forget, in the Incarnation, God did not merely fill a human being with his light, or carry him away in a surge of divine enthusiasm, [God] himself "came"—*in person* (John 1:11). What Christ did, God did. What Christ suffered, God suffered....Never again is God to brush off the handful of finite being that was Jesus of Nazareth. Henceforth and to all eternity God remains the God who became man.[15]

Here is the fullest affirmation of the humanity of Christ. Guardini emphasizes that "the brief life of God on earth is no episode ending with Jesus' death; the bond that connects him with humanity continues through the resurrection and ascension into all time." The God revealed in Jesus "must be one who loves," concludes Guardini. "Love does such things."

But Guardini ventures further, convinced that "there must be something else in God that the word love does not cover. It seems that we must say, God is humble." Not "humble" in the sense of bowing to another person's grandeur or esteeming another's greater talent or appreciating without envy another's merit. Guardini insists, "That is not humility but honesty…simple intellectual integrity." He points out that respecting the importance of inferiors, being touched by weakness, and defending the weak, these are actions comprehensible without Christianity. "But [Christian] humility begins only where greatness *reverently* bows before one who is not great."

Guardini uses the example of Francis of Assisi, a story that penetrates into the world of history and experience. He observes that when Saint Francis knelt before the pope, it was not humility but an act of "verity" since he believed in the papal dignity. Francis was *humble,* Guardini reminds us, when he bowed to the poor. "Not as one who condescends to help them, or whose humanitarian instinct sees in every beggar a remnant of human dignity, but as one whose heart has been instructed by God flings himself to the ground before the mystery of paltriness as before that of majesty," he explains. Francis, he says, "was only reproducing in himself the secret of Jesus." Guardini points to Matthew 11:29: "…learn from me for I am meek and humble of heart," and to Jesus' action at the last supper when the love command is made manifest when he washes the disciples' feet. He describes Jesus' kneeling before the disciples and washing their feet "not to debase himself, but to reveal to them the divine mystery of humility (John 13:4)."

The conclusion that "God himself must be humble" leads Guardini to present the christological mystery in strikingly fresh imagery: "In all reverence, it must be mysteriously blissful for [God] to refind himself in the flesh-and-blood heart of the Nazarene. Here is a bliss the sense of which outstrips all measure, this assuming the responsibility for, experiencing the fate of, such an abandoned and questioned human life." Guardini cites Paul's text from Philippians 2:6–9, the famous hymn that says of Jesus, "...who though he was by nature God, did not consider being equal to God a thing to be clung to, but emptied himself, taking the nature of a slave and being made like unto men....Therefore God has exalted him and has bestowed upon him the name that is above every name...." As the contemporary Christologian Jean-Marc Laporte states this mystery, "...out of strength which abides, [God] chooses to be weak."[16] The fullness of Jesus' divinity and the fullness of Jesus' humanity are not compromised; the mystery of the God-man is kept in full tension.

In Guardini's reflection upon the mystery of Christ I find the same matrix from which O'Connor's imagination creates stories touching this mystery. One of her essays in *Mystery and Manners* describes her understanding of "what makes a story work" or "hold up as a story." She reports that it is "some action, some gesture of a character that is unlike any other in the story, one which indicates where the real heart of the story lies."

> This would have to be an action or a gesture which was both totally right and totally unexpected; it would have to be one that was both in character and beyond character; it would have to suggest both the world and eternity. The action or gesture I'm talking about would have to be on the anagogical level, that is, the level which has to do with the Divine life and our participation in it. It would be a gesture that transcended any neat allegory that might have been intended or any pat moral categories a reader could make. It would be a gesture which somehow made contact with mystery.[17]

O'Connor uses the example from her story "A Good Man Is Hard to Find" to illustrate how such a gesture occurs. At the conclusion of this story the grandmother reaches out to touch The Misfit and calls him "one of my children." It is a gesture of compassion fulfilling O'Connor's demand that it be "both totally right and totally unexpected." But it is more. It centers on what O'Connor calls the reader's feeling that the hypocritical old grandmother "has a special kind of triumph in this story." As the grandmother is alone, facing The Misfit, O'Connor describes the old lady's head clearing "for an instant and she realizes, even in her limited way, that she is responsible for the man before her and joined to him by ties of kinship which have their roots deep in the mystery she has been merely prattling about so far." She reminds her readers that "in this story you should be on the lookout for such things as the action of grace in the grandmother's soul, and not for the dead bodies." She prefers to think "the old lady's gesture, like the mustard-seed, will grow to be a great crow-filled tree in The Misfit's heart, and will be enough of a pain to him there to turn him into the prophet he was meant to be."[18]

O'Connor then catches herself and reminds us that such a turn would involve another story, a new story. The grandmother's gesture in this story orients us to the redemptive moment she embraces by this gesture, "both totally right and totally unexpected." The year before O'Connor read Guardini's *The Lord*, she published her short story "A Good Man Is Hard to Find." In it she offers her readers a character who intuitively enacts humility—it is the humility that she discovers Guardini cogently describing and reflecting upon in his description of St. Francis. The grandmother's reaching out and touching The Misfit on the shoulder at the moment she admits her ties of kinship ("Why you're one of my babies") is not unlike Francis of Assisi's reverently kneeling before the poor man—in Guardini's interpretation of the christological mystery, "as one whose heart has been instructed by God flings himself to the ground before the mystery of paltriness as before that of majesty." Jesus' secret of God's humility is revealed in the action of grace in the grandmother's soul as she humbly *reverences* The Misfit.

In her reflective comments upon this story O'Connor admits once again, "Our age not only does not have a very sharp eye for the almost imperceptible intrusions of grace, it no longer has much feeling for the nature of the violences which precede and follow them."[19] Perhaps it is in light of her reading of Guardini that her retrospect on "A Good Man Is Hard to Find" speaks of her stories' violence being "strangely capable of returning my characters to reality and preparing them to accept their moment of grace." She alertly points out that the return is costly and seldom understood by casual readers—"but it is one which is implicit in the Christian view of the world."[20]

This insistence coincides with the conclusion of Guardini's chapter on "God's Humility" in *The Lord*. He describes Christ reversing all human values. The humility of God destroys the pride of revolt. We are tempted to refuse to accept a humble God. When we protest that such a God is not to our proud taste, Guardini reminds us of the fuller mystery of Christ:

> Humility means the breaking of this satanic taste-reaction, and bowing deeply, not only before God's majesty, but even more deeply before his humility: obeisance of all that is deemed great in the world before him whom the world despised. It means that as a natural human being conscious of health, beauty, strength, talent, intelligence and culture, he submits to him who from these familiar standards seems so questionable: Christ under the cross. To him who says of himself: "But I am a worm and no man: the reproach of men and the outcast of the people" (Psalm 21:7). This is the foundation and point of departure of Christian humility, never to be confused with the weakness of self-surrender or with the ruse that purposely makes itself less than it is; still less with an inferiority complex. Humility and love are not virtues of degeneracy. They spring from that creative gesture of God which ignores all that is purely natural and are directed towards the new world in the process of creation. Thus a man can practice humility only to the extent that he is con-

scious of the grandeur, both actual and latent, that God has planted in him.[21]

Such an insight tells us much about O'Connor's character of the grandmother—her own potential for grace and her recognition of the latent potential of The Misfit who wrestles conscientiously with the fact that "Jesus thown [sic] everything off balance" (151). The grandmother finds her own goodness by offering the gesture of reverence toward The Misfit. But she likewise glimpses the goodness of The Misfit in a manner that reminds the reader of "Christ under the cross," welcoming the good thief into paradise. The image of the dead grandmother ("who half sat and half lay in a puddle of blood with her legs crossed under her like a child's and her face smiling up at the cloudless sky") unmistakably mirrors the crucifixion. It makes all the more plausible the christological intuition that O'Connor shares with Guardini: "Humility and love are not virtues of degeneracy." In this moment we know the grandmother as a person who finally practices humility and is ironically awakened to the grandeur latent in The Misfit's honest wrestling with the mystery of Christ.

Robert Krieg's appreciation of Guardini's work is not without a realization of the celebrated German theologian's shortcomings. He is quick to point out that the starting point of *The Lord* differs markedly from Karl Rahner and Edward Schillebeeckx's contemporary approaches. A generation of Catholic theologians has since reinterpreted Christ's incarnation in terms of a "Christology from below," or an "ascending Christology." Rahner especially systematized a transcendental theology that restored a balanced appreciation of Christ the God-man because he feared the heresies of Docetism and Monophysitism—the denial of the humanity of Christ and the swallowing of the humanity of Christ by an overemphasis upon divinity.[22] Krieg also faults Guardini for neglecting the important new historical-critical study of biblical texts—a criticism of him that O'Connor herself made.[23]

Nonetheless, Monika Hellwig credits Guardini's *The Lord* as an early attempt at a Christology "from below" (i.e., placing the emphasis upon "grounding Christology more intensively, extensively, and attentively in the full humanity and historical reality of Jesus"). Her appraisal of his work points to his early awareness of how the timeless, detached classic Christology that eclipsed Jesus' humanity and inflated his divinity is an irrelevant Christology. Hellwig reminds us that a preoccupation with Christ's divinity causes us to understand him as the mediator of "that other, eternal realm...the realm of the spirit." As a consequence, she cautions, "Risen bodies are quite awkwardly located there, and mortal bodies not at all." Hellwig has also recognized Guardini's creative use of linguistic categories from existentialist philosophy.[24]

We dare not overlook the historical context in which Guardini wrote and published *The Lord*. The year 1937 proved a crucial moment in the rise to power of Adolf Hitler. Krieg reminds us that in this book "Romano Guardini fashioned a Christology for Germans living in the Third Reich, most of whom judged that they had little choice but to endure Hitler's tyranny." Guardini indeed anticipates the way in which a Christology "from below" will challenge the structures of oppression and injustice in light of the spiritual integrity of Christians committed to "Jesus as Lord." It is for this reason that Krieg points to Guardini's success in promoting awareness that Christology is "self-involving" as a hallmark of the more recent liberation theologies of the Third World. Such Christian witness flows from a kerygmatic theology.[25] There is no better description of the religious importance of Flannery O'Connor's fiction.

William F. Lynch

Flannery O'Connor could be a disarmingly objective and honest critic of her shortcomings as a fiction writer. In an October 1955 letter to "A" she looked back at *Wise Blood* and criticized

her treatment of the protagonist, Hazel Motes. The criticism orig-
inated with another correspondent's remarks. George Clay had
written an appreciative letter about her short story "Good
Country People," which he applauded as "successful." However,
when O'Connor asked him to "read the rest" of her work, she
records for "A" his sobering verdict on *Wise Blood:*

> He said WB bored and exasperated him because H. Motes
> was not human enough to sustain his interest....About WB I
> think he is in a sense correct....He points out, correctly that
> it is hard to sustain the reader's interest in a character like
> that unless he is very human. I am trying to make this new
> novel *[The Violent Bear It Away]* more human, less farcical.
> A great strain for me. (963)

Three weeks later she writes again to "A" about her correspondent George Clay. "A" must have read his short story,
"We're All Guests," that Flannery sent her. "I don't agree with
you that he has no talent," O'Connor writes back. She goes on to
repeat Clay's remark, "...he believes that the highest thing the
writer can do is to explain the reasonable man to himself." A year
in law school had primed George Clay to appreciate this legal
concept of "the reasonable man" and apply it to his own writing
and to his criticism of O'Connor's. It occasions a significant
reflection in O'Connor's letters:

> He [Clay] went on to admit that H. Motes might ultimately
> be found to be more reasonable than the legal reasonable
> man....
> Mine is certainly something else—God's reasonable man,
> the prototype of whom must be Abraham, willing to sacrifice
> his son and thereby show that he is in the image of God Who
> sacrifices His Son. All H. Motes had to sacrifice was his sight
> but then (you are right) he was a mystic and he did it. The
> failure of the novel seems to be that he is not believable
> enough as a human being to make his blinding himself believ-
> able for the reasons that he did it. For the things that I want

them to do, my characters apparently will have to seem twice as human as humans. Well, it's a problem not solved by the will; if I am able to do anything about it, it will simply be something given. (968)

Another critical assessment of her characters' humanity came almost simultaneously from Mercer University professor Ben C. Griffith, about whom O'Connor—ever attentive to detail—wrote to "A" at the end of November 1955: "Mr. Griffith is a nice man anyway, with a slight stutter. I have never met anybody with a stutter who was not nice." His observations raised another critical concern and credited her with creating very human characters:

> He [Griffith] remarked that in these stories there was usually a strong kind of sexual potential that was always turned aside and that this gave the stories some of their tension—as for instance in A Circle in the Fire where there is a strong possibility that the child in the woods with the boys may be attacked—but the attack takes another form. I really hadn't thought of it until he pointed it out but I believe it is a very perceptive comment. (971–72)

In the next line of this letter, O'Connor mentions her regular reading of the journal *Thought,* published by Fordham University in New York City and edited by Jesuit William F. Lynch. She comments with an enthusiasm equal to her regard for Guardini and recommends Lynch's work when comparing his latest essay to Elizabeth Sewell's essay in the current issue: "A much better piece is the one following by Fr. [William F.] Lynch, one of the most learned priests in this country I think." Although there are only five additional references to this scholar-priest in O'Connor's published letters, his influence warrants special scrutiny for an adequate appreciation of her fiction. Flannery O'Connor was no pushover when it came to the Catholic clergy. Her respect for the christological reflections of Guardini and Lynch is all the more compelling in light of her opinion about the failure of the

Church—its priests in particular—in the modern world. She agrees with Charles Peguy and quotes his low opinion of the clergy in *Temporal and Eternal* for a 1959 book review:

> It is no longer a secret, even in the schools, and it can no longer be concealed, except perhaps in the seminaries, that the de-Christianization stems from the clergy. The shrinking, the withering of the trunk of the spiritual city, temporally founded, eternally promised, does not come from the laity, it comes from the clerks.[26]

All the more impressive that Flannery uses a metaphor of excellence when she inserts into a May 1959 letter to "A," "I am reading a corker called The Image Industries by William Lynch SJ" (1097). Four years later she writes to Janet McKane and remarks particularly about *Thought,* "Fr. Lynch was editor for many years and much of Christ & Apollo appeared there" (1188).[27]

WILLIAM F. LYNCH, S.J.

If Romano Guardini clarifies and deepens the mystery of Christ in O'Connor's understanding of a kerygmatic theology, then William F. Lynch integrates for her the mystery of Christ and the literary imagination. (Chapters 4, 5, and 6 of this book analyze the ways in which the last decade of her mature fiction writing yields evidence of Lynch's impact upon the Christian realism of her imaginative fiction.) A natural place to begin is her August 1959 review of *The Image Industries,* her first published comment on Lynch's contribution. O'Connor's unvarnished diction and style (and the Cold War context of her time) are evident in her opening sentence that describes the thesis of "this fine book": "...the trash put out by the mass media industries is causing the American imagination to rot and...this is as dangerous for the life of the nation as any of the external threats to our security." She focuses upon Lynch's conclusion that "life ordered on a basis of unreality" will destroy our underlying "moral fiber." Lynch was pioneering the cooperation of artists and theologians as "natural allies." O'Connor endorses his effort. In fact, she readily admits that the Catholic Church has been especially guilty of reducing the role of the theologian to that of a censor of books, "usually to the detriment of future cooperation with the artist." She agrees with Lynch that their collaboration will provide "a theology of creativity." A succinct quotation from *The Image Industries* concludes O'Connor's enthusiastic review of the book.

> The matter of style is a great theological question, but the theologian, the moralist, and the censor will recognize that it is not their competence, but the competence of art, to destroy the phony, to laugh it out of court, and to create the true. Our [the theologians'] task is to encourage them, to raise them up among us, and on our knees to beg them to accomplish this task: the task of reality against fantasy.[28]

O'Connor's annotated copy of the spring 1954 issue of *Thought* contains Lynch's seminal essay, "Theology and the Imagination." He auditions themes that O'Connor would find developed in his subsequent books, *The Image Industries, Christ and Apollo: The Dimensions of the Literary Imagination,* and *The Integrating Mind: An Exploration into Western Thought.*

O'Connor claims that she cut her fiction writer's teeth on Jacques Maritain's aesthetics.[29] But William F. Lynch's wrestling with new *theological* questions vis-à-vis the literary imagination in the later modern context engages O'Connor as she further develops her own aesthetic sensibility. As early as May 1953 she mentions in a letter to Sally and Robert Fitzgerald that she has met a Danish man who studied at Fordham and there knew Lynch, who was editing the university's journal *Thought* from 1950 to 1956.[30] The encounter with Lynch's work—two years after the publication of *Wise Blood*[31]—virtually forces her to reflect upon her own vocation as an unashamedly Catholic fiction writer. It proves a revealing exercise to read Lynch's 1954 essay,

"Theology and Imagination," because he anchors it in Christology as the source of the literary artist's sacramental imagination. The second paragraph of the essay declares:

> It will be clearer later that when I use the word "theology" I am thinking pre-eminently of Christology. The whole theology of the fact and mystery of Christ...can be summed up under the terms of total and actual, positive and "athletic" penetration of the finite....As such, Christology stands as the model and enduring act of the healthy and successful imagination.[32]

Lynch effectively frames the essay in terms of two contradictory theologies: (1) the christological, as expressed in the "Christic" imagination; or (2) the Manichaean, or "non-Christic" imagination. He insists that theology is a legitimate part of literary and cultural life because "these two theologies [the Christological and the Manichaean] lie, one or the other, at the very heart and internal structure of the image, of our imaginative life!"[33] For Lynch, Christology illuminates the imagination; Manichaean theology distorts the imagination. The former is healthy and the latter is pathological. If the Christic imagination is absent, then Manichaean theology will invariably fill its place. The scholarly Jesuit, Lynch, diagnoses our cultural predicament: "Our fundamental failure comes from a loss of faith in the limited image or thing, from a lack of patience for the staying with it as a path to the infinite."[34]

The Analogical Imagination

Lynch carefully defines these two mutually exclusive theologies and analyzes their effect upon the imagination. He follows the Catholic tradition and uses the "analogy of being" to speak of the analogical imagination. The "analogy of being" addresses the fact that all things that exist possess what Thomistic philosophers called an analogical structure: they participate in both "being" and "nonbeing." They contain "the same" [associate] and "the different" [dissociate] within their very structure. This "double participation" means that things have their own reality but also participate in the larger community of being. Nonetheless, these existents also claim to be unique. The conclusion is that each creature represents a new act of existence. Lynch outlines major qualities of the analogical imagination—"taking these as a set of human addenda to the major meaning of Christology"[35]—and contrasts it with Manichaean theology's adverse effects upon the imagination. The result is quite striking.

> For our present purposes, we may roughly and initially describe the analogical as that habit of perception which sees that different levels of being are also somehow one and can therefore be *associated in the same image,* in the same and single act of perception.

And,

> We may lump together under the word "manichaean" all those habits of perception which instinctively *dissociate,* which dispose levels of being in a relationship of hostility or complete otherness.[36]

In the second installment of his essay, Lynch employs the contrasting pair of persons, Christ and Apollo, to illustrate his point. (His 1960 volume, *Christ and Apollo: The Dimensions of the Literary Imagination,* gives full expression to this treatment.) He points to thirteenth-century changes in biblical exegesis as the initial ground on which the contemporary crisis of the human imagination was anticipated and resolved. Instead of replacing the literal meaning or the actual historical events in the scriptural narrative with some allegorical or symbolic meaning, theologians of this late medieval period, such as Hugh of St. Victor, returned to "the dense and precise reality" of actual human situations to interpret texts.

> With Christ Himself [the thirteenth-century commentators] had, of course, a preeminent theological warrant for not leaping too quickly (and magically!) out of the facts of His life and personality to grasp some vague Godhead. No one had ever cared much about the precise details of the life of Apollo (who was indeed entirely symbol) but Christian spirituality doted on every detail, in all its density, of the life and passion of Christ, where the actuality and the thing signified were so completely one.[37]

Lynch reminds us that "nobody is asked to love Apollo, and nobody has the slightest interest in his cousins—or any other part of his 'actuality.'" He insists that Christian spirituality tells the scholar something quite different: "...it pours endlessly over the concretions of Palestine, every step, every word, every limited movement of the Hero. The [abstract] love of love is over with. The question Christ asks Peter is 'Lovest thou *me*?'" Lynch insists that the imagination enters into an exploration of the finite, the limited, and the historical as "the necessary condition of a higher freedom"[38] because Christ's patient movement through the "human mysteries"[39] is the model of a healthy and successful imagination.

An example from Lynch's general remarks at the beginning of the essay illustrates his insight about Christology. He uses the metaphor of a fish, struggling to breathe out of water. If we let the water represent "the finite" and the air represent "the infinite," the power of the metaphor for understanding our human existence becomes apparent. The fish out of water opens its mouth and with torment and anguish tries to take in the air. But the fish is created to take in air through the water. "Any attempt to make the process more immediate," Lynch points out, "produces terrible distortions in his nature."[40] As the fish lives and breathes air *in* water, so human persons live in the finite and only *through* the finite do we arrive at the infinite.

This leads to Lynch's recapitulation of the three primary Manichaean cultural forms: (1) rebellion; (2) dissociation; and (3) flight. He identifies the most obvious personality exhibiting the Manichaean tendency as the Romantic hero, who distorts (and frustrates) modern and contemporary attempts at authentic dramatic tragedy. Insecurity gives rise to "angelism" and various forms of release from the human; alienation replaces our confidence in the capacity of the finite to lead us to the infinite. Lynch describes one such expression of the Romantic hero as the "challenger of God" who abandons "the human confrontation with the finite and human finitude, to ignore the true and historical and evidential image of death, and instead to invent a non-human, non-evidential and purely mystical thrust into a vague infinite."[41] He points to Sartre and Camus as examples of such empty gestures of a rebellion that shies away from "the ultimate moment of human contingency."[42] Lynch contrasts their rebellious gestures with Sophocles' *Oedipus* where he finds that "there is a complete collapse of human energy, and a paradoxical exaltation, but not by way of exaltation. The face of the finite is seen as deep and terrible; the last artistic step is taken, the price is paid."[43]

It becomes more apparent how Lynch's understanding of theology as preeminently the mystery of Christ, or Christology, undergirds his theory of the Christian imagination. His emphatic endorsement of Oedipus also bears upon my interpretation of *Wise Blood* and its climactic scene of self-blinding as the dramatic gesture that ironically identifies Hazel Motes as the blind seer by way of faith. As Lynch outlines in the second installment of this essay, "Theology and Imagination," there is a Manichaean temptation for the imagination "to win its freedom by seeking quick infinities through the rapid and clever manipulation of the finite" instead of passing through "all the rigors, densities, limitations, and decisions of the actual."[44] Here are the makings of an ascetic identity that O'Connor will employ in creating her characters.

Dissociation is evident in the two poles (or dichotomy) of mind and body, "the one no longer penetrating the other"; in such literary artists, mind and body regard each other with hostility.

Lynch sees that a culture that dissociates also distrusts the intellect. The language of the spirit deteriorates into a language of "self-salvation": "integrity, purity, freedom, sincerity, autonomy." It is drawn away from realities into "an artificially concocted world of cheap mysticisms and false heavens and overly quick infinities." The attitude of flight or evasion betrays a negative stance toward the body and the reality of whatever is limited. Lynch concludes that flights into pure mind or a pure infinite "will always be a desert"—the very kind of direct (and *un*-mediated) confrontation of God and the life of the spirit (mind) that he finds both the Reformers of the sixteenth century and the followers of Descartes—and their cultural descendents—have taken. These same coordinates figure prominently whenever O'Connor relies upon eucharistic symbols in her stories or whenever her characters personify the Cartesian passion for rationalism and abstractions. She touches upon these issues in a June 1962 letter to Alfred Corn:

> One of the effects of modern liberal Protestantism has been to turn religion into poetry and therapy, to make truth vaguer and vaguer and more and more relative, to banish intellectual distinctions, to depend upon feeling instead of thought, and gradually to come to believe that God has no power, that he cannot communicate with us, cannot reveal himself to us, indeed has not done so, and that religion is our own sweet invention....

> Of course, I am a Catholic and I believe the opposite of all this. I believe what the Church teaches—that God has given us reason to use and that it can lead us toward a knowledge of him, through analogy; that he has revealed himself in history and continues to do so through the Church, and that he is present (not just symbolically) in the Eucharist on our altars. To believe this I don't take any leap into the absurd. I find it reasonable to believe, even though these beliefs are beyond reason. (1166)

Much as Robert Krieg interprets the theology of Romano Guardini, Gerald J. Bednar systematically analyzes and interprets William F. Lynch's theology in dialogue with the literary imagination. Already in his 1954 *Thought* essay, Lynch points to *The Spiritual Exercises* of the Jesuits' founder, Ignatius of Loyola, as a study of "the art and power of the limited image and experience" practiced in meditations on the incidents in the life of Christ. He wonders if theorists of the imagination would not benefit from carefully exploring this text because it recommends that each meditation be "bounded off with patience from that which is to come." Similarly, Lynch suggests that the Ignatian "composition of place" reflects Gerard Manley Hopkins's "inscape art," with its emphasis upon the particular, the definite, and the uniqueness of each created being. Bednar is quick to pick this Ignatian spirituality as a foundation of Lynch's method: "...the deepest dimension of reality is its ability to communicate the infinite."[45]

Contraries: Interpenetration of the Finite and the Infinite

Bednar also shows how Lynch supports this understanding through Plato's theory of "the unification of contraries." Here again, the vocabulary and terminology is precise and bears special scrutiny: "By 'contrary,' Lynch means that any finite entity is composed of certain 'opposites' that contribute to the making of the thing. Those opposites are always found together in the thing." Lynch uses the example of "left" and "right" as opposing features in any physical reality, hence "contraries." Distinct from these are what we name "contradictories." They are found separated because they cancel out one another, such as "good" and "evil." Contradictories are mutually exclusive.

Lynch enumerates pairs of opposites that are contraries: the one and the many; the finite and the infinite; the immanent and the transcendent; the sacred and the secular; fear and trust. It is all too common for people to mistake these contraries as contradictories. Bednar alertly reports, "Lynch's insight is that a person does not have to worry about putting together contraries that were never separated in the first place." Contraries become "interpenetrating realities." Lynch has moved from Plato's *Parmenides* and its understanding—that the one cannot exist without the many—to the realization that the finite cannot exist without the infinite, as interpenetrating realities.[46]

Bednar offers another insight developed when Lynch relies upon Plato. The principle of intelligibility in Plato is unity. In this sense, Lynch agrees with Plato that God is not "the Other" (as so commonly stated in modern philosophies and theologies), but that we creatures are the "other" of God insofar as we are God's self-communication beyond God's self. Speaking philosophically, even if we are "removed" or estranged from God, God is not removed or estranged from us. Bednar borrows an analogy from music to make this point clear. Aaron Copland's *Appalachian Spring* could be described as an "other" of Copland. It is one more instance of the "many" that participates in Copland's creation. "Being part of a whole does not diminish the [single] note [of music]. It enhances it." Consequently, whenever one produces an "other," this active dynamic set in motion between the "one" and the "other" produces what Lynch calls "an augmentation of reality." So God is manifest in the interpenetrating of the finite and the infinite, in God's "creation moments." The fullest or highest expression of this creation is Jesus the Christ, "the moment of perfect interpenetration of the infinite and finite."[47] We see more clearly how nature and the supernatural are contraries—distinguishable but not separate. Lynch's task is identified: to show the inwardness and identity of God through the finite nature of each human being. In other words, how do we discover the "grace of inwardness"? In *Christ and Apollo* Lynch succinctly phrases this mystery: "If the 'Infinite-One' is truly a constitutive aspect of the finite, then there is no need to go beyond the finite, limited Christ to arrive at infinite 'meaning, joy or illumination.'"[48]

In this theological system, grace and nature are not seen as contraries. The supernatural and the natural are the contraries. Lynch tells us that grace designates the proper relationship between the two contraries, the natural and the supernatural. Grace has no contraries. Grace describes the dynamic relationship between the One and the many, between God and creation, between the natural and the supernatural, between the divine and the human.

Grace does have a contradictory which is called sin: the disordered relationship between the One and the many, between God and creation, between the natural and the supernatural, between the human and the divine. Lynch describes sin as the attempt of the "many" to organize the whole; in other words, sin is "rebellion against the One." As Bednar paraphrases Lynch's conclusion, reality is filled with contraries that belong together—Lynch's "both-and"; and reality is *not* filled with an "either-or" conflict.[49]

Any reader of Flannery O'Connor will recognize that here is the storm center of her fictional universe. What is more, Lynch's understanding of analogy as "to exist according to a proportion" clarifies the task of the analogical imagination. It is a matter of holding together in proper proportion the various components (i.e., the contraries) that make up reality. Lynch's earlier illustration of the fish serves as an appropriate example. Water and oxygen are structurally integrated. The water needs the oxygen to be what it is. Yet the two are distinct but not separate. The relationship of the finite to the infinite is like that of the fish in water that derives its oxygen from the water itself. "To the extent that we attempt to leave the finite, we are like fish out of water."[50]

Flannery O'Connor the literary artist knew that the contraries of life could not be ignored or diminished. Nor can they be confused with contradictories that exclude their opposite. Her fiction leads to a fuller and more fertile interpretation of what she herself understood and endorsed in Lynch's Christic imagination and the emphasis upon lively contraries.

Soon after William Lynch refined and expanded this pair of essays and kindred reflections into his 1960 book, *Christ and*

Apollo: The Dimensions of the Literary Imagination, Flannery O'Connor reviewed it. She voices the desire that "a wide Catholic audience" will read Lynch's book in America, and especially in the colleges. She credits Lynch with ultimately helping "in the formidable task of raising our level of literary appreciation." *Time* magazine heralded Lynch's contribution in *Christ and Apollo,* naming him "one of the most incisive Catholic intellectuals in the U.S."[51]—a compliment all the more important, coming from the secular press in the days before the Second Vatican Council. O'Connor's brief review is a model for economy of phrasing. She once described her numerous reviews for the local Catholic press as "Church Prose (from Church Mouse)—lean spare poor and hungry!" (1001). With *Christ and Apollo* she exhibits a succinct grasp of the contents of Lynch's explorations:

> Fr. Lynch describes the true nature of the literary imagination as founded on a penetration of the finite and limited. The opposition here is between Christ, who stands for reality, in all its definiteness, and Apollo who stands for the indefinite, the romantic, the endless. It is again the opposition between the Hebraic imagination, always concrete, and the agnostic imagination, which is dreamlike. In genuine tragedy and comedy, the definite is explored to its extremity and man is shown to be the limited creature he is, and it is at this point of greatest penetration of the limited that the artist finds insight. Much modern so-called tragedy avoids this penetration and makes a leap toward transcendence, resulting in an unearned and spacious [sic] resolution of the work.[52]

A distinction central to Lynch's insight lies behind O'Connor's abbreviated review. In the 1954 essay he twice mentions the "univocal" imagination. He discredits it as "bruising its own power." He also gives examples where both Graham Greene and T. S. Eliot fail to penetrate fully the human and end up in evasion and loneliness because they prefer "the compulsions of a univocal pity for our state."

Christ and Apollo multiplies such examples. Chapter 5 elaborates on "the univocal and the equivocal" imagination and clearly contrasts them with the analogical imagination. Lynch insists that he cannot give clear definitions although he knows what each type is about. He again identifies the univocal imagination with our aspiration to be angels, the act of rebellion that leads us to seek what he calls "quick infinities" without passing through all the rigors, densities, limitations, and decisions of actual human life. The attitudes of the univocal imagination are "a leveling of the real, a manipulation of it in the interests of the One, and a foreshortening of the insights that can come only from a richer penetration into the more complicated materials present in actuality itself."[53] At the other extreme is the equivocal imagination with equally disastrous results. Lynch describes the equivocal as "the love of the darkness and pain that is present to some minds in the fact that no one thing seems to be truly connected with anything else." The resulting dilemma is one of absolute autonomy. "It is a mentality which believes that in the whole world of reality and being no two things *are* in the same sense; everything is completely diverse from everything else....Everything is a private world; everything is solipsism. All is absurd, lonely, a private hell."

Lynch breaks the impasse with a chapter of *Christ and Apollo* devoted to the analogical imagination—again elaborating on his 1954 essay. Here he elaborates on Plato's theory of the unification of contraries. He names the predicament with an apt metaphor: "There are people who are afraid that the pattern...will suffer from the emergence of the detail...There are those, reversely, who are afraid the detail...of the world and of the imagination will suffer from the pattern."[54] We have traced, above, his remedy of "interpenetrating realities" by way of the analogical imagination.

While O'Connor avoids Lynch's technical language of Manichaean theology or the Christic (or analogical) imagination, she calls attention to Lynch's supplementary essays on medieval exegesis of scripture. "The principle of this thorough penetration of the limited," she adds in the review, "is best exemplified in medieval scriptural exegesis, in which three kinds of meaning were found in the literal level of the sacred text: the moral, the allegorical, and the anagogical. This is the Catholic way of reading nature as well as scripture, and it is a way which leaves open the most possibilities to be found in the actual."[55]

O'Connor's fiction reinterprets this distinctively Catholic way of reading in her second novel, *The Violent Bear It Away*, and in her two collections of short stories. Her confidence in the human as the epiphany of the divine had gained new momentum through the christological insights of Romano Guardini and William F. Lynch. Her fiction opens new possibilities in the actual, the possibilities that Lynch had invited her to create by acts of Christic imagination—"to destroy the phony, to laugh it out of court, and to create the true."

Chapter Four

The Good
under Construction:
A Good Man Is Hard to Find

*The serious writer has always taken the flaw in
human nature for his starting point, usually the flaw
in an otherwise admirable character. Drama usually
bases itself on the bedrock of original sin, whether
the writer thinks in theological terms or not.*
—From *Mystery and Manners*, 167

Shortly after Flannery O'Connor completed her 1955 first collection of short stories, *A Good Man Is Hard to Find*, she
described them in a letter to Sally Fitzgerald as "nine stories about
original sin" (927). The collection grew to ten stories with the late
insertion of her most recent creation, "Good Country People."
O'Connor's enthusiasm shows in a letter to publisher Robert
Giroux, where she exclaims that it "is really a story that would
set the whole collection on its feet" (929). One early reviewer,
however, burst the bubble with a damning conclusion: "These

stories are technically excellent; spiritually empty" (960). The fact that O'Connor records and discounts this slight in a September 1955 letter to "A" resurrects the critical issue of her imagination as religiously grounded.

O'Connor gives significant evidence of her affinity for William F. Lynch's Christic imagination and its discovery of the infinite through the finite by contrasting two characters in "Good Country People," Mrs. Hopewell and Hulga. Again writing to "A" in December 1955, Flannery responds to her friend's apparent inquiry about the story and "the woman who is the Realist." She describes it as "a complicated subject." O'Connor throws light on the question by reminding her correspondent "that Poetry is always dependent upon Realism, that you have to be a realist to be a poet." She points out that Mrs. Hopewell is a realist yet not a poet; Hulga, on the other hand, "has tried to be a poet without being a realist." She concludes by reminding "A" that the realist is not "the ogre" (975).

This realism at the heart of *A Good Man Is Hard to Find* revolves around her characters' recognition of their flawed human nature and their innate attraction to an *apparent* good that is chosen selfishly. The Catholic tradition has a name for this universal human condition of being deprived of the capacity to choose the authentic good: *original sin*. Concupiscence (a result of original sin) is the orientation or inclination of the lower human faculties toward some created good without respect for the higher faculties. O'Connor's collection of short stories dramatizes this human mystery by grounding the protagonists in haunting exposés of pride. In some instances the pride takes the form of betrayal, lies, or deceit. In others, pride is manifest as vanity or possessiveness. These characters are captive to multiple forms of illusion when it comes to freely choosing "the good," and they tenaciously resist recognizing or letting go of their darker dispositions.

Throughout this collection of short stories, we detect O'Connor's ironic voice dramatizing the universal effects of

Adam's loss through original sin. But she also reminds us of an alternative horizon of redemptive grace and fulfillment in the mystery of Christ, the second Adam. Even when the reminder comes only by way of O'Connor's irony, the stories can transform the obvious absence of grace into a powerful presence to the imagination. Some stories are more successful than others, whether aesthetically, dramatically, or religiously speaking. The emphasis in these early imaginative efforts falls upon O'Connor's conviction that she had to bring her audience first to recognize sin in order to make grace believable. She writes in her essay "Novelist and Believer": "I think that if writers with a religious view of the world excel these days in the depiction of evil, it is because they have to make its nature unmistakable to their particular audience." Ever attentive to the limits and the potential of her audience, O'Connor admits to the absence of a "believing society." She names well the effort she undertakes in *A Good Man Is Hard to Find* and her own task as a believing artist writing for unbelieving readers:

> ...[T]he artist will have to do the best he can in travail with the world he has. He may find in the end that instead of reflecting the image at the heart of things, he has only reflected our broken condition and, through it, the face of the devil we are possessed by. This is a modest achievement, but perhaps a necessary one.[1]

The Catholic doctrine of original sin affords O'Connor the complex of symbols to translate "our broken condition" into the fiction in *A Good Man Is Hard to Find*. She was then writing in response to a *Life* magazine editorial "[a] few seasons back" in which Henry Luce charged that novelists today do not speak for America because their fiction lacks "the joy of life" and "the redeeming quality of spiritual purpose." O'Connor exhibits a highly charged reaction to what she calls the "stridency"[2] of Luce's demands for literature in a prosperous and optimistic

America during the early 1950s. In one such draft of the essay ("The Fiction Writer and His Country"), she speaks bluntly:

> What these editorial writers fail to realize is that the writer who emphasizes spiritual values is very likely to take the darkest view of what he sees in this country today. For him, the fact that we are the most powerful and the wealthiest nation in the world doesn't mean a thing in any positive sense. The sharper the light of faith, the more glaring are apt to be the distortions the writer sees in the life around him.[3]

In a September 1956 letter to "A," Flannery elaborates on her imaginative enterprise and alludes to the *Life* editorial. She argues that the artist cannot be asked to be "affirmative" any more than she can be asked to be "negative." It is noteworthy that O'Connor refers to Romano Guardini as her authority that "The human condition includes both states [the affirmative and the negative]." She quotes him, saying, "Art fastens onto one aspect of the world, works through to its essence, to some essential thing in it, and presents it in the unreal arena of the performance." This echoes the insight she was simultaneously gleaning from William Lynch's critical theory of the religious imagination. "I mortally and strongly defend," she insists, "the right of the artist to select a negative aspect of the world to portray and as the world gets more materialistic there will be more such to select from." She adds that the "light [the artist] sees by may be altogether outside of the work itself." But the greater imaginative question for her "is not is this negative or positive but is it believable." O'Connor refuses to yield her artist's eye for "the particular" to Dr. Charles E. Kinsey's and Dr. George Gallup's new polling techniques on sexuality, politics, and social issues and the resulting statistics. "If you are too cavalier about particulars," she complains, "you will find yourself a Manichean without knowing how it happened" (1002). *A Good Man Is Hard to Find* is a collection of stories that serve as an imaginative Catholic antidote to the Manichean toxins of the time.

"A GOOD MAN IS HARD TO FIND"

The title story of the collection is the most often anthologized of all the work in O'Connor's canon. Because it has become such a signature story—with violence, the grotesque, and two prototypical characters (The Misfit, who evidences an intense struggle with faith in Jesus the Christ; and the grandmother, who personifies a transforming conversion experience)—it warrants careful attention.

The fundamental stance of the grandmother is evident in the opening line of the story, where she objects to plans for the family's Florida vacation. Her negative temperament this time has been ignited by the newspaper story alarming readers about the Florida whereabouts of an escaped convict calling himself The Misfit. Her overreaction and crisis mentality are gauged early in the story when she shanghais her cat into the car because she fears the risk of leaving him to be asphyxiated by accidentally brushing against one of the gas burners. This prim, properly dressed old lady anticipates the worst possibilities. Her vanity guards her social standing: "In case of an accident anyone seeing her dead on the highway would know at once that she was a lady" (138). But appearances and reality diverge sharply in this story that splinters around fault lines of betrayal.

Upon their arrival at a roadside barbecue restaurant named The Tower, the proprietor, Red Sammy Butts, and his wife receive the rude remarks of granddaughter June Star about the "broken down place." The story's deceptions gallop along with Sammy's wife replying, "Ain't she cute," and the grandmother perfunctorily scolding, "Arn't [sic] you ashamed?" Red Sammy unfolds the very kind of negative happening that only confirms the grandmother's worst fears: "These days you don't know who to trust." A week ago he had let two strangers charge the gasoline they bought. The grandmother spontaneously judges him as "a good man" and explains that his trusting nature made him do it, though underneath her praise lies a tacit disapproval of his vulnerability.

No sooner does she flatter him than Red Sammy's wife compounds the lament about suspicion by agreeing, "It isn't a soul in this green world of God's that you can trust"—including Red Sammy at whom she looks directly and says, "I don't count nobody out." Whether she alludes to a marital infidelity or financial matter is unclear, but betrayal of trust includes the present company. Sammy offers the title line of the story at this juncture while he bemoans the spiraling crisis: "A good man is hard to find...Everything is getting terrible..." (141–43).

As the family's journey to Florida continues, the grandmother launches into reminiscences about having visited a plantation in the vicinity when she was a young lady. She whets her own appetite to return for a visit and proceeds to fabricate a story about its "secret panels." The children's vivid imaginations are recruited and they persuade Bailey to turn around and take the dirt road she had remembered. O'Connor is a master storyteller at this point. She describes the grandmother having an unspecified "thought so embarrassing" that she blushes, her eyes dilate, and her feet jump, upsetting the valise and literally letting her cat out of the bag. As a result, an automobile accident throws the family around the car and outside the vehicle. The cat clings "like a caterpillar" around Bailey's neck. Only in the aftermath do we learn that the grandmother had misspoken. The plantation was not in Georgia but in Tennessee. Her willful selfishness has taken them down both the literal and symbolic wrong path. And their encounter with The Misfit and his gang ironically comes not from Bailey's designs for a Florida vacation but from the grandmother's mischief and selfish desires.

When the ominous "hearse-like vehicle" of the escaped prisoners approaches, there is no escaping fear. The mention of The Misfit's being at large in the first paragraph (as well as the grandmother's preoccupation with an "accident") guarantees that we will see him again in O'Connor's story; it is not unlike the principle in the theatre that if you see a gun on the wall in the opening scene of a play, it had better be fired before the end. Again, to make matters worse, it is the grandmother, the reader of the *Journal* newspaper account of the escape from the federal penitentiary, who now shrieks with recognition when she surmises and blurts out, "You're The Misfit!...I recognized you at once." The irony is that her unthinking action, speaking the truth as it turns out, absolutely jeopardizes the family. She now has literally "betrayed" her family to murderers. When Bailey then "said something to his mother that shocked even the children," the strained family relationships become even more evident. The appearance of a picturesque family vacation fades and the ugly reality of their quarrelsome habits and neglect of affection is evident. In a telling reply The Misfit blushes while the grandmother cries at her son's words. "Sometimes a man says things he don't mean," says The Misfit. "I don't reckon he meant to talk to you thataway" (147). He calls attention to the discrepancy between words and intentions. At another level, it is ironically The Misfit who summons the best possible interpretation and makes generous allowances for personal shortcomings.

The grandmother's self-interest returns us to the story's title. "'Listen,' the grandmother almost screamed, 'I know you are a good man. You don't look a bit like you have common blood. I know you must come from nice people.'" Her insincerity repeats in a distracted moment when the two remark about the weather and she comments ironically, "Yes, it's a beautiful day." Her flattery in calling him "a good man at heart" gets nowhere. Goodness does not lend itself to the kind of superficial "sizing up" of appearances ("I can just look at you and tell") that the grandmother utters. The Misfit eventually confronts her manipulation and reacts, "Nome, I ain't a good man...but I ain't the worst in the world neither." O'Connor's artistry in dramatizing original sin focuses sharply at this point in the story. Pistol shots in the woods unmistakably evidence her family members' fate. The grandmother denies the inevitable, even in the face of this concrete evil. She suggests that Bailey might have an extra shirt for The Misfit to wear. And she patronizes him with a moralism:

"You could be honest too if you'd only try." But original sin at the core of her human nature proves an obstacle to such a sheer act of will. O'Connor's "A Good Man Is Hard to Find" explores another reality, the sheer gratuity of grace and the human person's transformation in the presence of grace.

In her final manipulative effort, the grandmother asks The Misfit, "Do you ever pray?" His "Nome" [No, ma'am] is followed by the revelation that he once was a gospel singer—so he is no stranger to the Christian story. He continues with the story of his wrongdoing and the prison sentence. "I was buried alive," he announces. The narrator tells us that The Misfit "held her attention with a steady stare." When she interrupts with a pious remark about that being the time to start praying, The Misfit speaks of "a wall" to the left and to the right; a ceiling and a floor confining him. It was not a theft, and not a murder (despite the prison psychiatrist's suggestion of an Oedipal desire!)—nothing The Misfit can remember explains his incarceration and loss of freedom (149–50).

The Misfit deflects the grandmother's final question about prayer and volunteers, "I don't want no hep [sic]...I'm doing all right by myself." His pride confirms original sin in his life. His mind is locked in an argument about punishments fitting the crimes. But he does not have Dostoevsky's wisdom to deal with the mystery. There is a Job-like passion and misguided effort to argue the merits of his legal case before God. And so The Misfit determines that "because they had the papers on me" this one time, he will resolve to place his signature on everything from now on and to "keep a copy of it" so that he can prove his unjust treatment and undeserved punishment. He wants to merit what he deserves. He wants the right to appeal any undeserved suffering. He seems most in search of mercy, learned during his gospel-singing days.

The Misfit recalls Jesus because he also was punished—even though Jesus did not commit any crime. "Jesus thown [sic] everything off balance," he concludes. The Misfit names well his own predicament: "I can't make what all I done wrong fit what all I gone through in punishment." When The Misfit exclaims that "Jesus thown [sic] everything off balance" (151), he unwittingly names the truth of faith but wrongly interprets it. For him, the equity between crime and punishment became unbalanced when the innocent Jesus suffered and died; in effect, he argues that Jesus' undeserved suffering became the warrant for endless occasions of innocent suffering. But The Misfit misses a deeper theological mystery that O'Connor ironically presents through "A Good Man Is Hard to Find" and its companion stories. It is The Misfit's pride that blinds him to the redemptive mystery of Jesus.

Only when the grandmother reaches out to The Misfit—in what O'Connor describes as her short story's paradigm of a gesture that is "both totally right and totally unexpected; it would have to be one that was both in character and beyond character"[4]—that grace becomes visible and the deeper meaning of Jesus' redemptive life and death becomes clear. Where there is sin, grace abounds. God's mercy became disproportionately gratuitous in the Christ event. Such grace cannot be earned. It cannot be coerced. There is no calculus to compute the terms for reconciliation beyond God's own initiative and immeasurable compassion. The sin of Adam's pride and selfishness, inherited original sin, is reversed by the second Adam's perfectly unselfish love. What Adam lost is restored and the new creation now claims even greater possibilities in this pattern of redemptive suffering.

The Misfit elaborates on how Jesus "thown everything off balance" by saying that Jesus ought not to have raised the dead. When the grandmother falters and mumbles in a selfishly patronizing moment that "maybe Jesus didn't raise the dead," the criminal introduces a rationalistic, empirical criterion: "I wasn't there so I can't say He didn't." But he insists that if he had been there, "I would of known" (152). Such a passion for certitude is not unlike Hazel Mote's early philosophical quest for truth. However, as with Haze, O'Connor portrays The Misfit as a character struggling with faith and capable of further progress. It is not along the path of Cartesian "clear and distinct ideas" but by way of what

O'Connor describes as faith—"It's TRUST, not certainty" (1110)—by which any person comes to believe. So O'Connor ends her story not by the grandmother's telling The Misfit, but by her showing him the fullness of the Christian mystery.

When the grandmother's head "cleared for an instant" during his passionate plea for certain knowledge, she calls him "one of my babies...one of my own children" and reaches out to touch him on the shoulder. It is unmistakably an act of unconditional love. Even though The Misfit "sprang back as if a snake had bitten him" (152) and fatally shoots her three times, her gesture is nonetheless effective. For one, the grandmother's own transformation is evident. She is no longer the controlling and manipulative woman whose religion has evaporated into social prestige and self-righteous judgment of others. The alienation of original sin in her life is ultimately overcome. In the first paragraph of the story she claims that "I couldn't answer my conscience" (137) if she allowed Bailey to take the children to Florida while The Misfit is on the loose. But we know from a sequence of betrayals and deceits throughout the story that this is not a woman whose conscience easily comes into play. The sudden maternal instinct and affective gesture toward this otherwise despicable criminal proves all the more compelling as grace because he has just murdered her son and his family. The story's mention of the snakebite is reminiscent of the story of the serpent in the Garden of Eden and the temptation to disobey and "become like God" (Gen 3:5) by pride. The grandmother's open gesture of inclusive love is a maternal gesture that associates her with Mary the mother of Jesus, whose heel crushes the serpent, a creature of the underworld's waters of chaos and darkness threatening death and annihilation (Gen 3:15). Catholic tradition points to Mary's being free from original sin (her immaculate conception) because she is to be the mother of God incarnate, Jesus the Christ. Mary's *fiat* ("let it be done to me according to your word"—Luke 1:38) symbolizes her part in Christ's victory over evil and his conquering the effects of original sin on all humankind. The grandmother's reaching out to touch

The Misfit symbolizes that she has found the goodness God gave her, goodness that original sin had eclipsed.

The beatific description of the grandmother at the end of the story shows her childlike, "her face smiling up at the cloudless sky." It is a portrait of the once wizened and fearfully selfish old lady born again through the mystery of a faith that has transformed her pessimism and pride into the capacity to find goodness in those rejected or excluded, even those marginalized for a just cause like crime. In this instance the grandmother's gesture is not unlike Christ's promise to the good thief crucified beside him on Calvary: "This day you will be with me in Paradise" (Luke 25:38). The Misfit himself is described at the story's end as "defenseless-looking" after killing the grandmother. It is as if her cat takes up the task of coaxing him to accept such grace by "rubbing itself against his leg" in another gesture of playful affection.

The compound mystery of O'Connor's story becomes clear in the final lines when The Misfit tells his fellow escapee, Bobby, "She would have been a good woman...if it had been somebody there to shoot her every minute of her life." Lacking such a conscience to monitor and guide her decisions between the good and the apparent good, the grandmother had succumbed to the effects of original sin. But in her dying moments she not only accepts grace but also offers grace to the despised murderer. He himself gives evidence of a subtle conversion, moving from the assertion, "No pleasure but meanness," to a final line exclaiming the emptiness of his futile ways: "It's no pleasure in life"—not even in meanness.

O'Connor thus opens the door for The Misfit's pilgrimage to a fuller appreciation of the grace that has been extended to him. He may have recoiled from the grandmother's touch but O'Connor subtly suggests how he has already been changed. Meanness is no longer a pleasure. He has laid down his gun. He is now "defenseless-looking" and, in reality, vulnerable to the mystery that he has confronted in the story's final scene vis-à-vis the dying grandmother. O'Connor's omnipresent eye imagery implies that he is on the brink of a new view of reality as The Misfit removes his glasses "to clean them."

"THE RIVER"

This story of the baptism of the young boy Harry Ashfield by the fundamentalist preacher bespeaks the mystery of original sin and the human desire to overcome alienation and selfish betrayal. O'Connor offers one of her familiar ironies in the first paragraph when Mrs. Connin the babysitter comes to take Harry for the day. In the early morning chaos the boy's mother clumsily struggles to finish dressing him while Mrs. Connin smells the cigarettes from the previous night's revelry. The boy's father hurries her, "Well then for Christ's sake fix him" (154). The utterance is not intended to be blasphemous because the language of faith has no currency in this family. As the boy will say later when the sitter introduces him to the heirloom children's book about the carpenter named Jesus, "If he had thought about it before, he would have thought Jesus Christ was a word like 'oh' or 'damn' or 'God,' or maybe somebody who had cheated them out of something sometime" (160). The fact that the father speaks of the boy's need to be fixed, and do it "for Christ's sake" (154), inadvertently alerts us to the levels of human brokenness the story will unfold.

The watercolor that Mrs. Connin studies while she waits for the boy offers a subtle symbol of Harry's world. Its "black lines crossing into broken panes of violent colors" reinforces the chaos of the home itself. In contrast, her house is filled with pictures and calendars, including the colored picture of the children watching the carpenter Jesus, who we then discover is a stranger to Harry. Mrs. Connin overhears the mother's parting plea to the father, "Bring me an icepack," and her first question to Harry is forthright, "What's her trouble?" (155). It is only later when Harry is baptized in the river and the preacher is reminded to pray for the boy's sick mother that he answers the question about the nature of her sickness: "She has a hangover" (165). The innocent child has knowledge of good and evil. Moreover, he has been the victim of neglect and psychological, if not also physical, abuse.

Mrs. Connin asks the boy his name after leaving his house, and it dawns upon the reader how impersonally his parents have entrusted him to the new babysitter. The fact that Harry gives his name as "Bevel," the name of her preacher which she just mentioned, suggests the boy's playfulness and the urgency of his trying a new identity. It also reminds us of the initiatory rite of taking a name in baptism to symbolize the new identity in Christ.

As the pair wait at the railroad tracks, Bevel listens to her report on Mr. Connin's surgery and hospitalization. Even though the preacher was unable to heal him because he lacked faith, Bevel asks her, "Will he heal me?" The boy's woundedness becomes more and more evident. Bevel immediately identifies what needs healing when he says, "I'm hungry" (156). Mrs. Connin takes his request literally and promises to feed him breakfast when they arrive at her house. But the deeper hungers of the boy's heart will eventuate in his appeal for baptism and the promises he discovers in it.

Three boys at her home mischievously lure Bevel to the pig pen and the ensuing chaos as the long-legged and humpbacked pig escapes. The meanness of children toward another child presents a stark image of humanity deprived of the capacity for hospitality and grace. The presence of pigs, shoats, and hogs in O'Connor's stories evoke memories of Jesus' casting out the tormented man's devils into a herd of swine who stampede into the Sea of Galilee (Mark 5:1–17); later in the story Bevel remembers a picture of the carpenter driving a crowd of "sour-looking" pigs out of a man (160). It foreshadows the preacher's scrutiny at the point of baptism, the ultimate question: "Jesus or the devil?...Testify to one or the other!" O'Connor playfully uses Bevel's name as she describes him walking on "the outside edge" of the highway toward the river and the preacher. Bevel is about to leave the edge of one world and step into another. When he enters the woods for the first time, Bevel looks from side to side "as if he were entering a strange country." The colorful scene of the pasture and river bank on the other side of the woods climaxes with a description of the "orange stream where the reflection of the sun was set like a diamond." The unmistakable value associated with this river and the baptism about to take place there radiates O'Connor's deeper symbolism.

The youthful preacher's message is directed toward the mystery of suffering. He reminds them that "You can't leave your pain in the river." He goes on to distinguish another river, "the River of Life, made out of Jesus' blood," where you "lay your pain in, in the River of Faith,...in the rich red river of Jesus' Blood." And ultimately the preacher reveals that "you can lay your pain in that River and get rid of it because that's the River that was made to carry sin" (162). The healing of baptism is clearly the antidote to original sin in O'Connor's imagination, even though this theology is foreign to her fundamentalist characters. A pair of symbols immediately indicates how O'Connor anticipates Bevel's spiritual hunger. The boy watches "two silent birds revolving high in the air." They are a symbol of transcendence but also reminiscent of the wind that swept over the surface of the waters of chaos at creation (Gen 1:2) and the dove who appears at Jesus' baptism in the Jordan River (Mark 1:10). In the distance the city is described as rising "like a cluster of warts on the side of the mountain" (162). It is a perfect symbol of the ugly life the boy has known and from which he seeks to escape.

Bevel hears that the "River of Life" is for people with trouble and that it slowly goes to the "Kingdom of Christ." When the preacher asks if Bevel wants this, the boy replies: "I won't go back to the apartment then, I'll go under the river." The preacher adds two striking reminders: (1) "You won't be the same again"; and (2) "You count now....You didn't even count before" (165). Together these mysteries touch the woundedness of Bevel.

Upon his return to the apartment Mrs. Connin discovers from his mother that the child's name is Harry. And she informs her that he was baptized that morning. Harry's mother learns that the preacher has also prayed for her own healing and she asks in a startled voice, "Healed of what?" Although Mrs. Connin has heard Harry name it as a hangover, she diplomatically calls it "your affliction." When Harry's father urges her to say more, he volunteers, "The exact nature of it has escaped me..." (167). Here is another subtle exchange in O'Connor's story. At a deeper level these parents are oblivious to the pain of their son, and to their own anesthetized existence in their chaotic home. They prefer the chemically induced illusion of the moment to the change that Bevel seeks, a life where he "counts" and is not ignored or treated as a burden.

The next morning Harry is described twice as "wandering" through the apartment while his parents sleep. We learn that he has to destroy his old books in order to get new ones. His theft of the colored handkerchief and the book, "The Life of Jesus Christ for Readers Under Twelve," gauges how starved he is for beauty and meaning. When the parents discover the book he has taken, they value it because of its age—an 1832 "collector's item"—not because of the mystery of faith that it proclaims. In his final moments as he attempts to immerse himself permanently in the river, Harry discovers his own buoyancy and fears that "the river wouldn't have him." When he thinks, "it's another joke, it's just another joke," we touch a reflex reaction in a boy who has been abused by one domestic rejection after another. In a final betrayal, the unbelieving Mr. Paradise pursues the boy. He is not trying to rescue him but to lure him into another ugly form of abuse, sexual abuse, with a "red and white" peppermint stick. It is an ominous climax to the story of original sin. O'Connor's metaphor to describe the ironically named Mr. Paradise links him unmistakably with the image of the devil from earlier in the story: "like a giant pig bounding after him" (171).

The tragedy of "The River" is not only the death of a child but the greater tragedy that he has suffered in a world mired in the effects of original sin. Harry-Bevel is offered no alternatives. The child's faith takes literally the salvation story offered, but it is a symbolic awakening to the spiritual. He sees death as a way out and becomes another of the rebels described by William Lynch, unable to penetrate the finite world, a victim of the Manichaean imagination that distorts and destroys.

"THE LIFE YOU SAVE MAY BE YOUR OWN"

The juxtaposition of strange characters in this story includes an old country woman and her mentally challenged daughter who share the same name, Lucynell Crater and Lucynell Crater, and the one-armed "tramp"-carpenter, Tom Shiftlet. O'Connor immediately offers a character sketch of the two major protagonists. The old lady only rises from her porch chair when Mr. Shiftlet gets to her yard and then she stands authoritatively "with one hand fisted on her hip." She is a striking contrast to the jumping, stamping figure of her daughter, whose "excited speechless sounds" begin as soon as she sees him. The omniscient narrator introduces Mr. Shiftlet with what we will later learn is pure irony: "He seemed to be a young man but he had the look of composed dissatisfaction as if he understood life thoroughly" (172). The initial exchange of polite greetings—her "Good evening" and his tipping his hat and then swinging it all the way off for the old lady—disguises their eventual testing of wills.

It is also ironic on O'Connor's part that Mr. Shiftlet's first remark is how he would "give a fortune to live where I could see me a sun do that every evening." We have just been told that the old woman stands with her arms folded across her chest "as if she were the owner of the sun." The terms of their commerce will indeed involve high stakes, for both protagonists have met their match in each other. Mr. Shiftlet continues the conversation with his opinion that "The world is almost rotten," anchoring this story in the mystery of original sin. The old woman concurs and asks where he comes from. He volunteers his name, Tom Shiftlet.

He ignores a second time her inquiry about his whereabouts. This pattern of indirect response repeats throughout the short story. Once Mr. Shiftlet volunteers that he comes from Tarwater, Tennessee, then he ushers us into the real drama by asking, "[H]ow you know I ain't lying?" When the old lady replies, "irked," that "I don't know nothing about you," O'Connor deftly reminds us that both characters share a damaged human nature. He soon follows with a declaration, "Lady...people don't care how they lie" (174).

The old woman probes his marital status. Her preoccupation with marrying her daughter erupts. Tom Shiftlet's response reminds us of the loss of innocence and the reality of adultery, promiscuity, and the fragile nature of modern marriage. But underneath this sad fact lies a comic allusion to Eve the temptress: "Lady...where would you find you an innocent woman today?" Mrs. Crater's possessive pose (and it is only a pose, the appearance of maternal protection) comes forth when she describes Lucynell as "My only,...and she's the sweetest girl in the world." The sparring by two equally formidable brokers is evident in the reverse psychology the old woman employs: "I would give her up for nothing on earth. She's smart too. She can sweep the floor, cook, wash, feed the chickens, and hoe. I wouldn't give her up for a casket of jewels" (176).

When Mr. Shiftlet volunteers that there isn't "a broken thing on this plantation" that he can't fix, we are also in the precincts of pride and possessiveness. His wandering eye has already spied an automobile bumper, and he lusts after their car. The "personal interest" he takes in repairing the car sets in motion the spiral of deceptions. When the old woman provides the money for a fan belt so that he can make the car run, she points to Lucynell and begins to barter about a husband for her nearly thirty-year-old daughter, who looks "Fifteen, sixteen" because of her innocence. The catch comes when she insists that the girl not be taken away. A husband for her daughter will also be a guarantee of the old lady's security.

Once the car is repaired and running—O'Connor tells us of Mr. Shiftlet's pride ("serious modesty") when he resurrects ("raised the dead") the abandoned automobile—the old woman makes her possessiveness clear. "Saturday...you and her and me can drive into town and get married." There are three partners in this strange marriage arrangement. When Mr. Shiftlet bargains for money to take his bride on a honeymoon trip to a hotel "like she was somebody," the old woman counteroffers. She reminds him in a condescending tone that "there ain't any place in the world for a poor disabled friendless drifting man" (179). These "ugly words" reach his ears "like a group of buzzards." He counters that our spirit is like an automobile, "always on the move." Finally, the old lady "laid the bait carefully" and offers to have the car painted. Her offer of fifteen dollars for the trip desperately increases fivefold to seventy-five dollars as the price of this arranged marriage.

After the courthouse marriage Mr. Shiftlet is described as looking "bitter and morose." He complains that the law does not satisfy him. When the newlyweds return the old lady to the farm and depart for the honeymoon trip, Mrs. Crater cries tears at the separation. But this maternal instinct for an especially vulnerable daughter is betrayed by her own self-interest in being disencumbered of her retarded adult daughter. "I wouldn't let no man have her but you because I see you would do right," she declares. But the reader's suspicion is otherwise; this is probably not the first (or final) attempt she will make to find a man to take her bait for Lucynell's hand in marriage. Mr. Shiftlet is excited about driving the car on the open road to the point that he "forgot his morning bitterness." Yet quickly he "became depressed in spite of the car" and sets in motion his abandonment of Lucynell at the roadside diner. Mr. Shiftlet betrays Lucynell and makes a mockery of their marriage by identifying her to the counter boy as a hitchhiker. The young man looks at the sleeping girl and exclaims, "She looks like an angel of Gawd" (181).

No sooner is Mr. Shiftlet on the road, "more depressed than ever," than he comes upon an actual hitchhiker. His arrogance and self-righteousness are evident again when the narrator tells us that he kept an eye out for hitchhikers because having a car brings "a responsibility to others." On the heels of his abandoning Lucynell, this claim exposes a predatory personality. When the young boy accepts the ride, his suitcase indicates he is a runaway. Mr. Shiftlet's surmise that the boy is running away from home triggers a saccharine homily about mothers. Coming from the scheming and immoral Mr. Shiftlet, it is an incongruous appeal; in the wake of his recent transaction with Mrs. Crater it proves deadly ironic. O'Connor compounds the irony when the boy is totally unmoved by the one-armed man's description of his own mother as "a angel of Gawd." Mr. Shiftlet's tears have no positive effect on the boy. To the contrary, the boy turns on him and tells him to "go to the devil." He calls his own mother a "flea bag" and Mr. Shiftlet's "a stinking pole cat" before he leaps from the car.

The scene of the stunned Mr. Shiftlet in the wake of this eruption mirrors the storm that brews overhead. His telltale attitude, feeling "that the rottenness of the world was about to engulf him" (183), triggers a final, proud act of defiance. "'Oh Lord,' he prayed. 'Break forth and wash the slime from this earth!'" Two references that Mr. Shiftlet has made to the human heart in the story shed important light upon this reprobate O'Connor character. For no apparent reason he describes to Mrs. Crater how surgeons in Atlanta have removed the human heart—but he insists that even if the doctor cut it into pieces, "he wouldn't know no more than you or me." He is correct on at least one level. The heart as symbol of personal intimacy is unfamiliar to Mr. Shiftlet—and to the old woman. The adulterated heart of sinners is the classic image of the Hebrew Prophets. It is an even more telling image of humanity alienated from intimacy with both God and the deepest self because of original sin. The effects of such alienation are all too evident in this story of multiple betrayals and abandonment, possessiveness and arrogant pride. Mr. Shiftlet proves ironically right when he repeats at the courthouse wedding, "If they was to take my heart and cut it out...they wouldn't know a thing about me" (180). There is little that can be known by examining a stony heart—"This people's heart is far from me" (Matt 15:8; Isa 29:13; Ps 78:36f.). The covenant once struck with the Israelites and now renewed in the Christ event is a circumcision of the heart, not the external sign of circumcision, which Paul argues is no longer necessary for salvation (Rom 2:28–29).

The story's title, taken from the roadside sign, "The Life You Save May Be Your Own," ironically takes on a clear meaning by the final page of O'Connor's text. The hitchhiker boy foreshadows O'Connor's young girl, Mary Grace, in "Revelation." When he tells Tom Shiftlet, "You go to the devil," he confronts him with a truth that the one-armed carpenter refuses to admit. Mr. Shiftlet's attitude about the rottenness of the world, his deceit and betrayal of Lucynell Crater, and now his patronizing attitude toward the boy, all give evidence of his failure to see himself as sinful. Unlike Ruby Turpin in "Revelation," Mr. Shiftlet lacks the vision to recognize how he is deprived of grace. But the story ends on an unmistakable note of original sin as this man with scars of violence and calluses of sin self-righteously condemns the world that he has helped to corrupt.

"A STROKE OF GOOD FORTUNE"

Flannery O'Connor writes to Sally and Robert Fitzgerald about "A Stroke of Good Fortune": "It don't appeal to me either and I really didn't want it there but Giroux thought it ought to be." Her critical judgment proves accurate because the story fails to hold a reader's attention. Her intent, however, was to write a story that shows how the imagination theologizes: "It is, in its way, Catholic, being about the rejection of life at the source, but too much of a farce to bear the weight" (939). Nonetheless, the story warrants a brief critical assessment in light of the collection's focus on original sin.

A trademark O'Connor symbol of vision, the mirror, is found in the first paragraph of the story when Ruby, the protagonist, "gazed with stony unrecognition at the face that confronted her." Her self-alienation is an index of the reality of sin—as it is with a chorus of O'Connor characters. Ruby is described as "shaped nearly like a funeral urn" and the symbolism immediately connotes death.. Another lethal note is struck when the narrator tells us that a statement of Ruby's was spit out "as if it were a poisonous seed" (184). It is not a stretch of the imagination to recall that Augustine describes original sin as being transmitted by conception—the poisonous seed of concupiscence.

Ruby's five-year-old marriage to Bill Hill is now preoccupied with the prospect of moving up to a new house, the duplex bungalow "with yellow awnings" in Meadowcrest Heights. She lusts after the prestige it symbolizes. The revelation that Ruby is "sick" and that she has consulted not a doctor but instead the palmist Madam Zoleeda tells us volumes about her. She is oblivious to the literal facts of her fortune telling: "A long illness...[that] will bring you a stroke of good fortune" (185). O'Connor's reservations about the farce quality of the story are accurate. When Ruby quickly shifts to a comparison with her mother, the attention focuses upon her mother's eight children and how childbearing left her "a puckered-up old yellow apple, sour....Her mother had gotten deader with every one of them. And all for what? Because she hadn't known any better. Pure ignorance. The purest of downright ignorance" (186). Ruby's possessiveness and vanity contrast with her mother's sacrificial life. She describes Rufus, the brother who has just returned from military service to live with the mother, as "good for absolutely nothing" (185). She remembers fleeing the house to avoid her mother's screams when he was born. Ruby's selfish attitude and the motive for a marriage regulated by birth control becomes evident: "All that misery for Rufus! And him turned out now to have no more charge than a dish rag" (186). Her disappointment in her brother exposes Ruby's propensity to judge others. She boasts of marrying better than her sisters. She is blind, however, to her own barren life and prefers the self-deception that at the age of thirty-four she is "extremely young looking."

When Ruby identifies the six-year-old Hartley Gilfeet with his pistol as a nuisance who leaves treacherous messes on the stairs, her selfish attitude toward children is clear. It is an ironic moment when O'Connor has Hartley's mother refer to him as "Little Mister Good Fortune" and claim that he is the only thing of value that his dying father left her. She sees with very different eyes than Ruby. We learn more about Ruby when she tells of her self-doctoring and its effects: "no bad sick spells, no teeth out, no children, all that by herself." The parallel between these desired effects tells all. That Ruby self-sufficiently regulates her life only sets the stage for the unexpected pregnancy that is about to be revealed by her friend Laverne's comic dance and song that shocks her to recognize her unplanned pregnancy. Ruby prefers to attribute her breathlessness on the stairs to heart trouble—which can be treated. On one level it is a problem of the heart, but not a physical ailment. Ruby lacks the compassion and redemptive suffering that identify a nurturing mother. Her insistence that "There was nothing permanent wrong with her" is another of O'Connor's indirect allusions to Ruby's denial of original sin. She is mired deep in selfish illusions. She persists in denial even after Laverne's outburst. No doubt Ruby is "swollen all over"(194)—not only four or five months into her pregnancy, but swollen with pride.

By the time Ruby has climbed the stairs, she has endured "gasping and feeling as if her knees were full of fizz" (190), and breathlessness after "the stairs stopped seesawing" (196). When she speaks the words that echo in the cavern of the stairwell, they echo back the revelation that is not unlike the echo Ruby Turpin will hear in "Revelation": "Good Fortune, Baby." In the final paragraph O'Connor tells us, "Then she recognized the feeling again, a little roll." What she recognizes is not confined to her stomach, the pregnancy. Instead O'Connor speaks metaphorically: "It was as if it were out nowhere in nothing, out nowhere, resting and waiting, with plenty of time" (196). If we interpret the story at this serious moment of conclusion in an analogical sense, then Ruby stands on the brink of recognizing an unmerited, surprising grace in both her conception of a child and imminent motherhood. She also stands to be healed of her pride and selfish disposition, her original sin that robs her of fruitfulness and love. She is on the verge of being asked to accept the "misery" of motherhood (by her redemptive suffering) *and* the surprising fullness of grace.

"A TEMPLE OF THE HOLY GHOST"

O'Connor's Catholic culture plays a major role in understanding this story of convent boarding schools, purity, and the rite of Benediction. In contrast to the explicitly secular context of the vast majority of her stories, readers will fathom the meaning of "A Temple of the Holy Ghost" only if they appreciate the symbols and ethos of twentieth-century American Catholicism before the Second Vatican Council.

The story centers upon the sexual rites of passage for Susan and Joanne, two fourteen-year-old girls who visit cousins on the farm for a week away from their convent school. The confining discipline of the nuns relaxes when the girls toss aside their brown school uniforms and try on womanly identities with lipstick, red skirts, loud blouses, and heels. Despite the reputation of the nuns for keeping "a grip on their necks" (197) when it came to boys, this pair is preoccupied with the prospect of dates and the bodily desires awakened with puberty. Sister Perpetua, the senior nun at Mayville, recently lectured the girls on what to do if a young man behaved "in an ungentlemanly manner." The girls only ridicule and mock her advice to halt and say, "I am a Temple of the Holy Ghost" (199). They have no intention of stifling either their own raging hormones or the attentions of young, sexually stirred males. O'Connor presents another generation of teens who arrogantly act as if they are the first to discover sexuality.

Their unnamed second cousin, a twelve-year-old who lives on the farm, serves as a foil to the older girls. Her awkward, prepubescent age is evident by the braces on her teeth ("her mouth glared like the sun" [198]). She looks suspiciously upon the cousins—only two years older than herself, but quickly changing in striking ways—as they approach the house; she concludes that their preoccupaton with boys renders them "practically morons" (197). Her own naiveté about sexuality becomes more apparent later in the story when she innocently describes her imagined version of the rabbit giving birth through its mouth.

The twelve-year-old irritates and teases the girls by suggesting that the local teacher's admirer and the two-hundred-and-fifty-pound black taxi driver show them around town. She misrepresents Wendell and Cory Wilkins as attractively tall and driving a sports car. No sooner do the boys arrive than they offer a medley of gospel music. The two girls reciprocate with a song, "Tantum Ergo," familiar to them from the ritual of Benediction at the convent school. It is apparent that they know neither the translation of the words nor the meaning of this eucharistic devotion. When the Protestant boys respond that this must be "Jew singing" because it is unfamiliar, the girls "giggled idiotically" with adolescent nervousness and anxiety. The twelve-year-old, however, bursts out with the insult, "You big dumb Church of God ox!" and flees (202). The cook, an objective, unrestrained observer, confronts the girl, "Howcome [sic] you be so ugly sometime?"

When the two teenage couples depart for the fair, the twelve-year-old retreats to her dark bedroom. She momentarily recalls visiting the fair the year before but being unable to enter some of the tents reserved for grown-ups. When she imagines the tents had something to do with medicine, her reverie carries her to imagining herself as a doctor, only to recall that she has since reconsidered her vocation and wants to be an engineer. More seriously, she considers the occupation of saint; but concedes in a moment of self-scrutiny that she lies, is slothful, sasses, and is ugly to everybody. "She was eaten up with the sin of Pride, the worst one." A martyr's life appeals to her—if she could be killed quickly and not be burned in oil. But her romantic notion of taming lions in the arena only exposes her spiritual naiveté. Her rote and perfunctory prayers and momentary sentimental fervor over Jesus' crucifixion dissolve into emptiness. When she does fix her consciousness upon the Church of God boys, she prays thankfully that she is not like them—a perfect parallel to the Pharisee's self-righteousness (Luke 18:9–14).

When the visiting girls return from the fair just before midnight, the twelve-year-old's inquiries are met with the reply that they saw "all kinds of freaks." It is the mysterious "you know what" freak who upset Joanne. There is a comic moment when they reveal that they have seen the hermaphrodite—"a freak with a particular name but they couldn't remember the name" and "a man and a woman both"—and the farm girl mistakenly tries to perceive a creature with two heads. She imagines the crowd in this tent at the fair: the men are more solemn than they were in church; and the women are "standing as if they were waiting for the first note of the piano to begin the hymn." Then, a striking coincidence. The hermaphrodite reminds these voyeurs of the sacredness of her abnormal circumstance: "If anybody desecrates the temple of God, God will bring him to ruin and if you laugh, He may strike you thisaway. A temple of God is a holy thing. Amen" (207). Sister Perpetua's formula for girls to ward off unwanted sexual advances from boys is exactly congruent: "I am a temple of the Holy Ghost."

The cast of O'Connor freaks includes not only the slow-witted, the deformed, and those rejected by society on mental, ethnic, or racial criteria, but now the sexual aberration of the hermaphrodite and the freakish teenagers themselves. The story concludes with the drive back to the convent school and their arrival just as Benediction has begun. The child's "frigid frown" and escape from a kiss symbolizes her proud resistance to the nun's welcome as they speed down the hallway to the chapel. During the "Tantum Ergo," her "ugly thoughts" halt and she suddenly realizes that she was

"in the presence of God" (208). The experience evokes a spontaneous confession of her sins of contempt and meanness toward
others. No sooner does she rest in peaceful contemplation than
the priest raises the monstrance holding the consecrated Host
from the Eucharist. She has been thinking of the hermaphrodite's
claim, "This is the way He wanted me to be," just as "the Host
shining ivory-colored" (209) like the sun in the center of the monstrance is raised. O'Connor juxtaposes the hermaphrodite's suffering indignities as a freak at the fair with the mystery of the
incarnate Christ and the Eucharist. The twelve-year-old comes to
fathom the mystery of the former in terms of the latter. When the
nun "mischievously" swoops down on her at the end of the story,
"mashing the side of her face into the crucifix hitched onto her
belt," the mark of the cross appears in her own flesh—just as it
appears in the flesh of the hermaphrodite. It symbolizes how the
hermaphrodite and the young girl are both loved by the compassionate God revealed in Jesus' redemptive suffering.

In a letter to "A" just two years before her death, O'Connor
wrote of how odd it was that nobody noticed "A Temple of the
Holy Ghost" and that it was never anthologized (1172). But
seven years earlier she had written to "A" about the intent of the
symbolic climax of the story:

> ...[R]emember that when the nun hugged the child, the cru-
> cifix on her belt was mashed into the side of the child's face,
> so that that one accepted embrace was marked with the ulti-
> mate, all-inclusive symbol of love, and that when the child
> saw the sun again, it was a red ball, like an elevated Host
> drenched in blood and it left a line like a red clay road in the
> sky. Now here the martyrdom that she had thought about in
> a childhood way (which turned into a happy sleeping with
> the lions) is shown in the final way that it has to be for us
> all—an acceptance of the Crucifixtion [sic], Christ's own and
> our own. As near as I get to saying what purity is in this story
> is saying that it is an acceptance of what God wills for us, an
> acceptance of our own individual circumstances. (976)

The child's vision at the story's end confirms her new understanding of faith in these Christian mysteries. But the depth of symbolism resonates with the appropriation of layers of meaning found in the "Pange Lingua," written in the late thirteenth century by Thomas Aquinas. The "Tantum Ergo" used in the Benediction comprises the final two stanzas of that hymn. The larger hymn opens with a proclamation of incarnation: "I shall praise the Savior's glory,/Of his flesh the mystery sing,/...God made man for our salvation...." The fullness of Christ's humanity is affirmed along with the mystery of his humility and vulnerability to suffering and death: "Suffering bitter death unflinching,/And immortal love did show." The hymn celebrates Christ's gift of the Eucharist: "Word made flesh, true bread of heaven,/By his word made flesh to be...." The final two stanzas open with a summons to reverence before the Eucharist, the action of the Spirit transforming bread and wine into Christ's body and blood. O'Connor recognizes, with an uncanny ability, the hermaphrodite's experience of symbolic martyrdom in the form of her own flesh. Hers is an affirmation of faith, the fullest perception of the "Tantum Ergo's" revelation given now to the child: "Ancient forms are now departed,/For new acts of grace are here,/Faith our feeble senses aiding,/Makes the Savior's presence clear."[5]

"THE ARTIFICIAL NIGGER"

Few of O'Connor's stories have been as controversial as this archetypal story of the journey of an old man and his grandson to the city. Not only does O'Connor dare to employ a vulgar word of derision in the title; she actually transforms it by the end of the story into a sublime symbol to identify the suffering of African Americans with Christ's passion. She writes to Caroline Gordon that her rewriting of the story for *The Kenyon Review* still left it without "beautiful sentences" and "it may be too long" (926); O'Connor simultaneously writes to Ben Griffith in May of 1955 and reports that she has read "The Artificial Nigger" several times since its publication, "enjoying it each time as if I had had nothing to do with it" (932). By September of that year she writes to "A" that "I suppose The Artificial Nigger is my favorite" (953). Six months later she writes to Maryat Lee that this story "is probably the best thing I'll ever write" (1027). While several critics have criticized the moralizing tone of the story's conclusion as an aesthetic and dramatic flaw,[6] O'Connor nevertheless achieves something unique in her imaginative effort with this story.

When Mr. Head, one of the pair of protagonists, "awakened" to discover the room full of moonlight in the first line of the story, O'Connor's choice of the verb "awaken" anticipates the ultimate action of the story. "The Artificial Nigger" is about Mr. Head and Nelson's awakening to recognize the harrowing experience of betrayal and the need for forgiveness. And for Mr. Head there is the humbling horror of his sinfulness and the wonder of "the action of mercy" that he is learning late in life. As the first sentence ends, the moon pauses "as if it were waiting for his permission to enter." We are told that it "cast a dignifying light on everything." There is a premonition of grace in this personification of the moon whose silver light transfigures things: the straight chair into a "stiff and attentive" military figure "awaiting an order"; or Mr. Head's trousers into "the garment of some great man" who gives them "an almost noble air." Even more, the moon is described in the first paragraph as appearing "to contemplate itself with the look of a young man who sees his old age before him." Mr. Head and Nelson mirror each other in ways that will become evident by the story's end. But even before they depart for the city, the narrator emphasizes their deeper kinship in a striking image:

> They were grandfather and grandson but they looked enough
> alike to be brothers and brothers not too far apart in age, for

> Mr. Head had a youthful expression by daylight, while the
> boy's look was ancient, as if he knew everything already and
> would be pleased to forget it. (212)

Nelson's journey with his grandfather will include a contemplative experience that penetrates powerful illusions and touches the reality of betrayal as an integral part of his initiation. O'Connor ironically introduces the sixty-year-old Mr. Head as the possessor of "that calm understanding of life that makes him a suitable guide for the young." She compares him in his pride to a Virgil guiding Dante or a Raphael assisting Tobias. Like in the great festivals in all world religions, their journey to the city will begin in the darkness of night to avoid the intense heat of the sun and to give them the benefit of the lunar cycle's full light for the journey. They will need the moon's light and more to guide them to the "homecoming" at the end of this story. It will not be just a return to a literal place but a recovery from the depths of spiritual alienation—what O'Connor signals by calling these stories about original sin.

A Test of Wills

The habitual rivalry between Mr. Head and Nelson emerges when the boy reminds his grandfather that although this will be the old man's third trip to the city, it has been fifteen years since his last visit. Mr. Head's proud reply, "Have you ever seen me lost?" ironically foreshadows not only their later confusion over street directions but his admitting to a deeper spiritual disorientation. The two characters trade insults throughout the story. The test of wills comes easily because, living together, each knows the other's habits and regularly evokes a hair-trigger response from his counterpart. Mr. Head chides the boy, but his own words will eventually rebound and pierce his own proud attitude. "'The day is going to come,' Mr. Head prophesied, 'when you'll find you ain't as smart as you think you are.'" The remark aims to remind the boy that his having been born in the city is "no cause for pride" (211).

Mr. Head has arranged for the train to make a special stop for them. His insecurity mounts as they await the "apparition" of the train. In a defiant stance of pride, they "were prepared to ignore the train if it passed them by" (213). Upon boarding the train the pair continue their verbal and psychological sparring. Mr. Head patronizes the boy by telling the man across the aisle that Nelson has never seen anything before and is "as ignorant as the day he was born." There is an ironic twist when O'Connor has Mr. Head boast that the only thing to do for such a boy is "to show him all it is to show. Don't hold nothing back." The mystery of pride will climax in a moment of betrayal and the revelatory encounter with the lawn statue. O'Connor writes to "A" about this central symbol in the story and remarks that "there is nothing that screams out the tragedy of the South like what my uncle calls 'nigger statuary'" (954).

The appearance of a "huge coffee-colored man" at the far end of the train car causes Mr. Head's expression to change from serene to "fierce and cautious both." He grips the boy's arm and the procession of the man and two women—all well dressed—passes. Mr. Head asks the boy what he has just seen. He replies, "A man," but he is indignant because he feels once again insulted at having his intelligence tested. The addition of the adjectives "old" and "fat" does not suffice to answer his grandfather's question. In condescending fashion the old man announces, "That was a nigger," and then sits back in all-knowing satisfaction. Nelson protests that his grandfather had told him they were "black." In a comic twist, O'Connor has the boy interpret the Negro's passing by as a deliberate effort "to make a fool of him" and so he mistakenly hates the Negro "with a fierce raw fresh hate" to mirror his grandfather's racist dislikes.

When Nelson and Mr. Head walk unawares into the kitchen, much to the amusement of everyone who knows better, the grandfather counters with a quick wit about the peril of cockroaches in

the kitchen making it off limits for passengers. Nelson's awareness changes:

> ...Nelson felt a sudden keen pride in [his grandfather]. He
> realized the old man would be his only support in the strange
> place they were approaching. He would be entirely alone in
> the world if he were ever lost from his grandfather. A terrible
> excitement shook him and he wanted to take hold of Mr.
> Head's coat and hold on like a child. (218)

A few paragraphs later this attitude is repeated: "For the first time
in his life, he understood that his grandfather was indispensable
to him." O'Connor artfully constructs the story toward the climactic moments of betrayal and alienation. After their arrival Mr.
Head ushers the boy around the maze of streets and crowds. He
is intent upon keeping the terminal's dome in sight lest they get
lost. He remembers the insults of people when he had ventured
into one of the stores on an earlier trip and could not find his way
back out. Mr. Head's pride will not allow the boy to know about
that humiliating incident; most of all he is too proud to repeat the
humiliation in front of his grandson. A stop at the weighing
machine (affirming that Nelson has "a great destiny ahead" but
incorrectly stating his weight) and an encounter with the yawning
sewers that frighten the boy lead Mr. Head to advise him that he
will get "your fill" of the city.

When the boy perceives that they have traveled in a circle, he
charges, "I don't believe you know where you're at!" They wan-
der into a black neighborhood and Mr. Head again insults his
grandson, "...this is where you were born—right here with all
these niggers" (221). The old man insists that he has not gotten
them lost. They discover that they have lost their lunch of "bis-
cuits and a can of sardines" (213)—diminutive symbols of the
Eucharist and the gospel's loaves and fishes, a meal that these two
will not share in the story. O'Connor's deft handling of this symbolism is a powerful reminder of reconciliation as the prerequisite
for Eucharist: "If you bring your gift to the altar and then recall

that your brother has anything against you, leave your gift at the altar, go first to be reconciled with your brother, and then come and offer your gift" (Matt 5:23–24).

Nelson Betrayed

Nelson's vulnerability is evident in his fear of the unfamiliar black men and children; he is a victim of generations of racism. The compound alienation symbolizes the effects of original sin as inherited sin. But it is from the maternal presence of the "large colored woman" that the boy discovers a generous response to his frightened questions. O'Connor vividly shows the boy's terror when he asks the Negro lady the question, "How do you get back home?" but the narrator adds, "in a voice that did not sound like his own" (222). On one level the question is about directions and geography; but at the deepest level it is a question about spiritual orientation and the return to a "strange country" of grace where alienation from God is overcome by reconciliation. "The Artificial Nigger" thrusts Nelson into the visible world of racism as concrete evidence of original sin, the South's particular symbol of the inherited evil of a flawed human condition.

The absence of feminine presence in Nelson's life (he was orphaned at the age of one) becomes obvious when he wants the huge lady "to reach down and pick him up and draw him against her and then he wanted to feel her breath on his face." Images of darkness have accumulated throughout the story, beginning with the first mention of Nelson in the third paragraph: "The only dark spot in the room was Nelson's pallet, underneath the shadow of the window" (210). Nelson's intuitive awakening to this feminine presence suggests many levels of meaning. There is splendid irony in the fact that this affective element in the story comes through the person of the black woman. And there is even a Jungian psychological dimension to Nelson's coming into contact with the anima side of his personality as well as the animus that Mr. Head has cultivated. It is at this juncture of the story that

Nelson grows beyond his literal "head" identity (symbolic of the rational) and discovers unexplored sides of his identity. O'Connor writes to Ben Griffith in May 1955 about this symbolism: "I meant for [the Negro woman] in an almost physical way to suggest the mystery of existence to [Nelson]—he not only has never seen a nigger but he didn't know any women and I felt that such a black mountain of maternity would give him the required shock to start those black forms moving up from his unconscious" (931).

Mr. Head intervenes and insults his grandson once again, saying, "You act like you don't have any sense!" The boy's ensuing "shame" at having turned to one of the "niggers" and then being ridiculed by his grandfather leads him to take hold of the old man's hand in "a sign of dependence that he seldom showed" (223). O'Connor compounds the irony of the story with this brash reclaiming of the boy by his grandfather (and the boy's submission), thereby anticipating Nelson's moment of greater vulnerability.

They follow the railroad tracks because Mr. Head has the idea that they will lead back to the railroad station. But Nelson reminds him that they might be following the tracks in the wrong direction. Disoriented, Nelson succumbs to sleep. His dreams are vividly described as Nelson is "half conscious...of black forms moving up from some dark part of him into the light" (225) and Jungian interpretations of the story gain momentum. The old man, himself tired, is so distraught about being lost that he cannot sleep. Then he hits upon an idea of how "to teach a child a lesson he won't forget"—and in the process recover his position of authority.

He quietly walks to the corner and sits "hunched like an old monkey" on a trash can in the alley where he can watch Nelson awaken alone. The image of the monkey sitting on the garbage can lid in the alley of the city makes for a sardonic figure. The symbolism of garbage in the alley compounds the grandfather's spiritual demise. Mr. Head reminds O'Connor's readers of the dehumanization of Enoch Emery in *Wise Blood*. Enoch revered the "shrunken mummy" in the museum—his "new Jesus"—and he also became so jealous of the ape-man Gonga that he violently attacked the man wearing the costume and wore it himself. The impatient grandfather kicks his foot against the can and the sudden booming noise rouses the startled Nelson. He flees in panic and collides with an elderly lady; a crowd of bystanders condemns him and calls for justice to be done as she complains that her ankle is broken. At the very height of this turmoil, Mr. Head steps forward. With the boy clinging to him, the women turn their wrath toward the old man's responsibility for the child. But he denies knowing his vulnerable grandson with the words "This is not my boy. I never seen him before" (226). The echo of Peter's denial of Jesus (Matt 26:72) is unmistakable.

In the aftermath Nelson follows Mr. Head at a distance. When the old man glances over his shoulder for a glimpse of the boy, the narrator describes his "two small eyes piercing" the back of the grandfather "like pitchfork prongs." The narrator tells us that this is "the first time [Nelson] had ever had anything to forgive. And Mr. Head had never disgraced himself before." The choice of the word "dis-graced" is not casual because O'Connor's point is to identify Mr. Head's alienation not only from Nelson but from God and from his own true self. Nelson rejects the light-hearted overture to have a Coca-Cola and turns his back upon his grandfather "with a dignity he had never shown before." The choice of the word "dignity" is crucial to O'Connor's story. Without this gesture and the sinned-against Nelson's self-knowledge of his worth, Mr. Head would not feel or recognize "the depth of his denial." Nelson's is not an evil pride but a sense of self-worth experienced by a maturing boy. The effect upon the grandfather is devastating:

> He knew that if dark overtook them in the city, they would be beaten and robbed. The speed of God's justice was only what he expected for himself, but he could not stand to think

that his sins would be visited upon Nelson and that even now, he was leading the boy to his doom. (267)

Original sin echoes in this line, with Adam's fault being passed on to subsequent generations. When the thirsty boy arrives at the water spigot, "disdaining to drink where his grandfather had," the depths of betrayal become clear. Nelson reacts as if his grandfather had poisoned the very sources of life. Mr. Head looks "ravaged and abandoned" and loses hope. The alienation initiated by the grandfather has ushered him through purgatory to the threshold of Dante's *Inferno*.

Mr. Head's Redemption

The scene presents anew an adultery of the heart that is reminiscent of biblical stories. Mr. Head is described as "wandering into a black strange place where nothing was like it had ever been before." Everything in the elegant suburban section where they pass is "entirely deserted." Mr. Head waves his arms "like someone shipwrecked on a deserted island." He has come to the desert places of the human heart like an Israelite on exodus or a desert father, his faith tested on the anvil of suffering. Out of the depths he cries in abandonment, "Oh Gawd I'm lost! Oh hep me Gawd I'm lost!" It is not only a literal statement about his need for directions to the railroad station but a plea for reconciliation with his grandson and with God.

When a fat man volunteers information about a suburban stop where they can still board the train, Mr. Head becomes euphoric, "We're going to get home." But the boy is indifferent and distant. The narrator describes him still stinging from the betrayal: "...his eyes were triumphantly cold....Home was nothing to him." At this very moment, Mr. Head recognizes the abyss that threatens to engulf his soul. "He felt he knew now what time would be like without the seasons and what heat would be like without light and what man would be like without salvation." He stands on the brink of despair as he realizes the enormity of his sin.

O'Connor writes to "A" that "Mr. Head's redemption is all laid out inside the story" (1108). For the story transfigures the protagonists who embark upon the journey of salvation. An attentive reading bears out this careful crafting of "The Artificial Nigger." When the pair happen upon the lawn statuary, "the plaster figure of a Negro sitting bent over," O'Connor offers her trademark gesture that is both "in character" but "beyond character"—and yet entirely believable. The damaged figure with its chipped eye and "a wild look of misery" stands at an unsteady angle. Here is the perfect mirror for both characters to recognize their own misery in sin and their capacity for reconciliation: "It was not possible to tell if the artificial Negro were meant to be young or old; he looked too miserable to be either." O'Connor reinforces this perception by describing both Mr. Head and Nelson standing before the statue "with their necks forward at almost the same angle and their shoulders curved in almost the same way and their hands trembling identically in their pockets."

Three characters—Mr. Head, Nelson, and the lawn statue—share a sudden solidarity in misery and suffering. The next lines perhaps interpret too directly the meaning of the symbolism and stray into a moralizing tone, not "showing" but "telling" the reader. The "great mystery, some monument to another's victory that brought them together in their moment of common defeat" (230) and that resolves "their differences like an action of mercy" is Christ's death and resurrection. The paschal victory brings forgiveness and God's unconditional love to all Adam's offspring. The penultimate paragraph of the story identifies Mr. Head with the mystery of both the first man and Christ, the second Adam: "He realized that he was forgiven for sins from the beginning of time, when he had conceived in his own heart the sin of Adam, until the present, when he had denied poor Nelson" (231).

When Nelson's eyes implore some "explanation" from his grandfather to reassure him of his guide's wisdom, O'Connor ironically has him fail to deliver a "lofty statement." His name, "Mr. Head," symbolizes his propensity to respond with clear and direct "explanations" or answers, to be the ideal guide and esteemed mentor. Yet the only words that come from his mouth are a racist exclamation: "An artificial nigger!" A few paragraphs later he elaborates, "They ain't got enough real ones here. They got to have an artificial one" (229). Commentators shy from interpreting these jarring lines embedded between two passages of tender affection and religious mystery. I find in them one of O'Connor's supreme ironies. This Negro statue personifies the ultimate humiliation of America's enslaved people. The lawn-figure version of the black jockey first reminds us that thoroughbred horse racing was originally considered too dangerous for white riders, so slaves were pressed into this risky entertainment for white patrons. The figure is bent over the stereotypical slice of watermelon, a figure of ridicule. He is not even the version of the statue that holds the reins of horses or a lantern—familiar variations on the theme of servitude.

The key to interpreting Mr. Head's comment lies in the reference for the pronoun, "They." Mr. Head and Nelson are now lost among the mansions in the "elegant suburban section" of the white neighborhood, symbolized by "deserted" environs and "submerged icebergs" (228). It is not blacks who display these statues, but the prosperous whites who benefit most from racism's persistent economic, political, and social domination. "They" are the affluent, the powerful establishment class. There are, no doubt, many black domestics, gardeners, and other workers on their estates. Whatever rights and dignity they enjoy in the wake of the Civil War and the Emancipation Proclamation, at this point in American history O'Connor chooses to cauterize the wound of racism with this "artificial" representation. And here she ventures much more than a liberal political statement.

The striking contraries (in Lynch's sense of the term) in "The Artificial Nigger" are the poised, "coffee-colored man" on the train who presents a haughty figure of majestic elegance "gazing over the heads of the passengers" and wearing "a light suit and a yellow satin tie with a ruby pin on it" (215); and the humiliation of the watermelon-bearing lawn statue's "chipped eye" and "wild look of misery" (229). The former provokes Mr. Head to reflex condemnations and epithets to assure his own superiority and social domination. Sinful pride seeps out of every pore of Mr. Head in his unrelenting efforts to teach Nelson that "niggers" are the deserving scapegoats for the world's evil, contemporary crucified figures of Christ. When he and his grandson encounter the figure of agony during their own lacerating quarrel, they both recognize how the redemptive power of suffering reorients them. Ralph C. Wood succinctly captures the effect of their confronting this contemporary crucifixion symbol:

> I believe that "The Artificial Nigger" was Flannery O'Connor's favorite story because it is the work that gives the fullest fictional embodiment to her firmest convictions about both race and religion. Here she instructs herself no less than her readers in the meaning of the Gospel. Perhaps O'Connor knew that her own racial sinfulness had been dissolved in an unbidden gift of artistic liberty. It enabled her to turn a broken lawn jockey into an ironic testament to the mystery of Charity—a mystery that, though always hidden, is deeper by far than the mystery of iniquity. This "artificial nigger" thus becomes the ultimate anti-racist emblem. It reveals much more than the evident evils of slavery and discrimination; it discloses the subtle grace inherent in suffering that can be redemptively borne because God in Christ has borne it Himself. It is the sign of a divine courtesy that, by reconciling us to both God and each other, offers the one true and radical remedy for our unmannered, unjust, and deeply discourteous society.[7]

When the train delivers them home again, the moon's "full splendor" floods the clearing with light. Mr. Head has come to experience "the action of mercy" which no words (except the artist's, in this case O'Connor's) could name. He comes to understand that the action of mercy grows out of the "agony" of both men and ("in strange ways") children. No one is denied either agony or mercy—what William F. Lynch would call the "contraries" of the human condition. While Mr. Head can be "appalled" as he judges himself as thoroughly as God would, he also experiences how "the action of mercy covered his pride like a flame and consumed it."

O'Connor remarks succinctly that Mr. Head's "depravity"[8] (231) was hidden from him so as not to lead him to despair. It is another way to name the reality of original sin that O'Connor so effectively dramatizes in "The Artificial Nigger." Once this grandfather is awakened to his need for mercy and his radical dependence upon God (mirrored in Nelson's dependence upon him), then the unconditional love and extravagant forgiveness of God become evident to him. At the end of the story the metaphor of the train disappearing "like a frightened serpent into the woods" recalls Christ's victory over Satan through echoes of Adam and Eve with the serpent in the Garden of Eden (Gen 3:15).

Nelson's fatigue and suspicion in the final sentences are a measure of his own loss of innocence and his coming to the knowledge of good and evil. His serious demeanor relaxes in the final words when "his face lightened." As he mutters, "I'm glad I've went once, but I'll never go back again!" we encounter O'Connor's Christic imagination. The Christian tradition calls original sin the "necessary fault" and "The Artificial Nigger" reiterates this truth. Nelson had moments earlier wanted to maintain a grudging alienation from his grandfather—"his mind had frozen around his grandfather's treachery as if he were trying to preserve it intact to present at the final judgment" (228). But in the meantime, he and Mr. Head have happened upon the mystery made visible in the "miserable" figure of the statue depicting the much abused and ridiculed slave figure. Face to face with the mystery of such agony and the redemptive power of such suffering, Nelson and Mr. Head neither rebel nor escape their world. They are reinserted back into their home place, but transformed and redeemed by their encounter with the power of sin and reconciliation. It is the pattern of Christ's death and resurrection written in their lives. As she writes to Ben Griffith in mid-1955, "[I]n those last two paragraphs I have practically gone from the Garden of Eden to the Gates of Paradise" (931).

The "True Country" of Grace

The story's early reference to Mr. Head being like the angel Raphael to the Tobias-like Nelson earns particular meaning in this final scene. The "true country" becomes the symbol of grace and redemption in her fictional universe. O'Connor elaborates in her essay "The Fiction Writer and His Country":

> [The writer's "country" suggests] his true country, which the writer with Christian convictions will consider to be what is eternal and absolute. This covers considerable territory, and if one were talking of any other kind of writing than the writing of fiction, one would perhaps have to say "countries," but it is the peculiar burden of the fiction writer that he has to make one country do for all and that he has to evoke that one country through the concrete particulars of a life that he can make believable.[9]

O'Connor's arresting image of the "true country" has earlier origins in the prayer to St. Raphael. In early 1956 she writes to "A" about receiving "a couple of years ago" from *The Catholic Worker* a card with the prayer to St. Raphael printed on it. She acknowledges that she "took over" some of the imagery and put it into "The Displaced Person"—"the business about Mrs. Shortley looking on the frontiers of her own true country." But O'Connor adds that this "true country" involves the archangel "guid[ing] us to the province of joy so that we may not be ignorant of the concerns of our true country" (983–84). A month before her death, Flannery corresponds with another person and remarks that the prayer of St. Raphael is "a prayer I've said every day for many years." She emphasizes how the words "Light and Joy" (1214) are found in the prayer. In fact, early in the prayer we find: "May all our movements be guided by your [Raphael's] Light and transfigured with your joy." This is followed by, "Lonely and tired, crushed by the separations and sorrows of life, we feel the need of calling you and pleading for the protection of your wings, so that we may not be strangers in the province of joy, all ignorant of the concerns of our country." O'Connor's art in "The Artificial Nigger" transforms the prayer into symbols of faith.

Applying Merton's Interpretation of Original Sin

Thomas Merton, an O'Connor contemporary, appreciated "all the truth and all the craft with which she shows man's fall and his dishonor."[10] His sense of the meaning of original sin affords a keen insight into the dynamic of her stories. This can be seen in concert with Merton's suggestion that the "key word" in O'Connor's stories is "respect." He insisted, "She never gave up examining [respect's] ambiguities and its decay." Merton points out how O'Connor "wrote in and out of the anatomy of a word that became genteel, then self-conscious, then obsessive, finally dying of contempt but kept calling itself 'respect.'"[11] In this collection of stories, *A Good Man Is Hard to Find*, Merton's observation that "Her beings are always raising the question of worth," becomes transparent when she succeeds in what he called "peel[ing] away the whole onion of respect layer by layer."[12] The monk's description of the spiritual predicament of original sin helps to clarify both the pervasive racism and the concluding scene of "The Artificial Nigger":

> Each one slaved in the service of his own idol—his consciously fabricated self. Each one then pushed all the others away from himself, and down, beneath himself: or tried to.

> This is Original Sin. In this sense, Original Sin and paradise
> are directly opposed....[O]nce we break free from the false
> image, we find ourselves what we are: and we are "in
> Christ."[13]

The "consciously fabricated self" speaks to the real "artificial"-
ity in the story, a false self that Mr. Head idolatrously cultivates.
(The "artificial Mr. Head" becomes a compelling irony in
O'Connor's story about original sin.) All through his writings,
Merton elaborates on the seductions of a security found in various kinds of delusion. In his posthumously published collection of
essays entitled "The Inner Experience," he relates it to the story
of Adam's fall in Genesis 3. In Merton's theological anthropology,
the result of the fall is human alienation—from God, from self,
and from others. Redemption becomes a return to the paradise
state, a recovery of lost unity. In Merton's language, the soul then
awakens and becomes conscious of its alienation. The soul can
then begin on the illuminative way.

Merton interprets our original sin as an "ontological lapse"
and not a moral lapse: sin violates a person's very *being*. Sin, like
grace, engages the person's deepest levels of freedom and identity.
Merton's is a contemplative understanding of original sin. So he
insists that the mission of the contemplative today is "to keep
alive a sense of sin" as ontological lapse, not merely the violation
of any explicit moral code of conduct.[14] It is this discovery that
Mr. Head and his grandson, Nelson, both make. But first they
had to taste the experience of alienation through betrayal and the
need for forgiveness. Once awakened to their ontological restoration as persons redeemed by Christ—conversion—Nelson's final
words in the story ring true to this transformation: "but I'll never
go back" (231).

In the scene of Mr. Head and Nelson's return home, the
reader's attention is drawn to "the sky which was hung with
gigantic white clouds *illuminated* like lanterns" because "the
moon [is] restored to its full splendor...and flooded the clearing

with light" (230, emphasis mine). Grandfather and grandson have begun their illuminative way, a life's journey foreshadowed by the literal awakening of Mr. Head under "half of the moon" (210) at the beginning of the story. O'Connor's famous statement, "It seems to me that all good stories are about conversion, about a character's changing" (1067), comes in the context of an April 1958 letter to "A" and her pointed reflections about "The Artificial Nigger."

> The action of grace changes a character. Grace can't be experienced in itself. An example: when you go to Communion, you receive grace but you experience nothing; or if you do experience something, what you experience is not the grace but an emotion caused by it. Therefore in a story all you can do with grace is to show that it is changing the character. Mr. Head is changed by his experience even though he remains Mr. Head. He is stable but the same man at the end of the story. Stable in the sense that he bears his same physical contours and peculiarities but they are all ordered to a new vision. (1067)

Equally important is O'Connor's reminder that part of the difficulty for the fiction writer is the audience "who doesn't know what grace is and doesn't recognize it when they see it." She emphasizes that her stories are "about the action of grace on a character who is not very willing to support it (1067)—and Mr. Head is one of the stellar examples of such an O'Connor character.

Trusting the Blind Imagination

There is another correspondent with whom O'Connor shares her most intimate thoughts about the racial question and the emerging civil rights movement. Maryat Lee was the sister of the president at Milledgeville's Georgia College and a lifelong friend of Flannery. Their correspondence is often satiric, playing off roles: Flannery as the stereotypical southerner and Maryat as the

southerner-transplanted-in-the-North and become a "white liberal." In a six-month period during the first half of 1957,
O'Connor writes nine letters to Lee. Twice she mentions her
story, "The Artificial Nigger." The first time, already noted, she
claims the short story as "my favorite and probably the best thing
I'll ever write" (1027). But the second time O'Connor nuances
her meaning. It appears that there has been some misunderstanding about Flannery's response to news of Maryat's engagement to
David Faulkes-Taylor (*HB*, 225). She engages in their usual banter and satire: "The following is good Georgia advice: don't
marry no foreigner. Even if his face is white, his heart is black"
(1027). She admits that her subsequent letter of 9 June 1957 was
"inadequate and cliche-ridden." Perhaps it was her reference to
"grace" and "the blood of Christ" that provoked Maryat. Or her
quoting from *Mourning Becomes Electra* to address Maryat's
upcoming nuptials—"Pity the man who loves what death can
touch" (224–25)—that occasions their apparent falling out.
Flannery describes the language she used as "the coin of the realm
which has the face worn off it" and laments her own hatred of
"pious language...because I believe the realities it hides." Then
O'Connor makes an emphatic point:

> Nevertheless, you do misinterpret me if you think I mean that
> it all ends in tatattatum and a tragic little pie. I believe in the
> resurrection of the body. I also believe in it before it gets that
> way, dear girl, so don't put me down in yr Associate
> Reformed Presbyterian black books. It's my own & your
> own but also the Essential.
>
> Anyway, what I said in the letter, I also said in The
> Artificial Nigger, and that is the way I should keep on saying
> it, it being my vocation to say it that way. (1035–36)[15]

O'Connor's reflections about her own work include the clue that
she always has her eye on "the act, the acceptance of grace particularly...as the thing which makes the story work."[16] She identifies
it in "The Artificial Nigger" as "what the artificial nigger does to

reunite Mr. Head and Nelson. None of these things can be predicted. They represent the working of grace for the characters." Her insight clarifies her understanding of the writer's "discovery" of the moment of grace through "an action that is totally unexpected, yet totally believable,...an action that indicates that grace has been offered." O'Connor insists that it is not an action she "consciously put into my stories; it is a discovery that I get out of them."[17] In this context we begin to understand her appeal to the "blind imagination" in fiction. Faith, for O'Connor, is "a walking in darkness and not a theological solution to mystery."[18] No wonder her short stories are peopled with variations of the archangel Raphael who heals the blind Tobias, the paradigm of pilgrims being welcomed into their "true country."

"A CIRCLE IN THE FIRE"

Few characters in O'Connor's fiction are as succinctly introduced as Mrs. Cope in this story. After describing Mrs. Pritchard (a helper on the farm) with "her arms folded on a shelf of stomach,....a large woman with a small pointed face and steady ferreting eyes," we are forewarned: "Mrs. Cope was the opposite," meaning she is "very small and trim with a large round face and black eyes that seemed to be enlarging all the time behind her glasses as if she were continually being astonished." The feature of those constantly dilating eyes, unsteadily reacting to whatever astonishing new catastrophe presents itself, tells us that Mrs. Cope is equal to her name. She "copes" in the sense of coming to blows with, engaging, and contending in a never-ending battle, a contest on whatever field of encounter she finds herself[19]—be it symbolically working "fiercely" against the weeds and nut grass "as if they were an evil sent directly by the devil to destroy the place" (232), in a duel of wits with the constant threat of "fire in her woods" (232), or dealing with the mischievous intrusion of the three adolescents, Powell, Garfield, and W. T. Mrs. Cope does not fare well with the less than perfect human condition she finds around her, all evidence of original sin. She is stubbornly oblivious to her own share in Adam's fall.

What proves ironic throughout the story, however, is that the seemingly invincible Mrs. Cope (symbolized by her sunhat that remains "still stiff and bright green" while Mrs. Pritchard's is "faded and out of shape") proves unsuccessful in this latest test. She proudly tells Mrs. Pritchard, "I can always find something to be thankful for," and we learn from the narrator that "she has everything" (234). But her companion, whose husband, Mr. Pritchard, works on the farm, knows better and responds with a revealing contempt, "I reckon *you* can" (234). The contempt/ respect dialectic lies at the heart of the story. Mrs. Pritchard's fatalism opens the story by recounting the death of a distant kinswoman in an iron lung and her infant child, an O'Connor trademark grotesquerie. It serves to contrast this woman's life as fertile—both by having sex with her husband and giving birth to a child, the iron lung notwithstanding—with Mrs. Cope's life as ironically more confined and sterile than this recently deceased victim's.

Another symbolic cameo event happens when Mrs. Cope grows impatient with Culver, the Negro helper who drives the tractor past the gate and chooses the long way around to the field "at her expense." In a single sentence we learn a great deal about Mrs. Cope's attitudes: "Her Negroes were as destructive and impersonal as the nut grass" (233). Once again her eyes looked like they would enlarge "until they turned inside out" over this new astonishment at inefficiency. There is a mock humor and foreshadowing of events when she responds, "I thank the Lord all these things don't come at once. They'll destroy me" (234). But the key to Mrs. Cope's blessing of "rich pastures and hills heavy with timber" is her work ethic: "I have the best place in the country and do you know why? Because I work." It cues us to a self-righteousness that makes her insistence on prayers of thanksgiving superfluous. She reinforces her self-sufficient pride with the declaration "I don't let anything get ahead of me and I'm not always looking for trouble. I take it as it comes" (235). Flannery O'Connor has re-created in her the personification of Adam's pride. Mrs. Cope's prayers of thanksgiving are a matter of self-congratulation and not directed with gratitude toward God.

When the three boys led by Powell arrive, a subtle description of the bespectacled leader interprets Mrs. Cope's worst fears: "One of his eyes had a slight cast to it so that his gaze seemed to be coming from two directions at once as if it had them surrounded" (235). Already Mrs. Cope is beyond her depth in warding off a single adversary at a time; her defenses are compromised because she is not accustomed to being "surrounded." The return of Powell from the Atlanta housing development to the farm where his father once worked suggests the return to a happier place and time of childhood innocence and play. There is an unmistakable nostalgia for the symbolic Eden, before original sin's eruption. Gene, his small companion, volunteers this remembrance: "Said he had the best time of his entire life right here on this place. Talks about it all the time." The mention of riding the horses triggers Mrs. Cope's possessiveness and fear of an injury with the result that someone would "sue her for everything she had" (237). Both loss and the gratuity of grace are a threat to Mrs. Cope. There are mixed motives in the trio's visit but Mrs. Cope does nothing to defuse their bravado and air of delinquency. When the narrator tells us that "Powell's stare seemed to pinch her like a pair of tongs" (236), we ascertain vital information about Mrs. Cope, who does not recognize Powell.

The sullen demeanor of the boys persists even as Mrs. Cope blushes and experiences "a peculiar look of pain" when she realizes they must be hungry. But it is not compassion that motivates her. The "muted conference" with Mrs. Pritchard in the kitchen is followed by Mrs. Cope's saccharine but empty statement: "'Those poor children are hungry,' Mrs. Cope said *in a dead voice*" (238, emphasis added). For a moment there is the specter of evil on the lawn with Ashfield's cigarette stub and the potential for fire in the woods. Her reaction—"She stopped instantly as if a snake had been slung in her path"—reminds readers of the serpent in the Garden of Eden and the same metaphor used to show The Misfit's resistance to grace in "A Good Man Is Hard to Find"; Mrs. Cope is neurotic about the threat of some potential evil. Her offering of crackers and Coca-Colas is meager fare for hungry boys. Gene protests, "I don't like them kind of crackers," and returns his to the plate. Powell had already declined them. The stakes for hospitality increase when Powell asks if they can stay overnight in the barn and promises they won't smoke. She refuses twice, the second time repeating it "as if she were talking politely to a gangster" (239). It is not difficult to see the parallel between "A Circle in the Fire" and "A Good Man Is Hard to Find" in terms of the central character coming to a moment of self-recognition vis-à-vis a criminal—either real or potential. Again O'Connor connects the story to "A Good Man Is Hard to Find" through the gangster metaphor.

When Mrs. Cope encounters the boys again at the end of their afternoon in the woods, they ask for water. Once again she exclaims, "They certainly *looked* hungry," in the wake of Mrs. Pritchard's keener observation that "They only played with what we gave them to eat." But the hunger of these boys is different from a need for food, and Mrs. Cope's failure to engage it betrays her own selfish and patronizing ways. Earlier in the story she observed, "They looked as if they were used to being hungry and it was no business of hers" (237). She offers some cold guinea, which the boys first decline as dogs' food, but then devour once the plate is placed on the step (a symbolic detail to suggest that she considers them no more than pets to be domesticated by her superior gifts).

No sooner do the boys pick up the sandwiches than Mrs. Cope interrupts with her question, "Do you boys thank God every night for all He's done for you?" Nothing can alienate the adolescents more than this intrusion of a moralizing note. O'Connor signals the reaction by the narrator's note of "an instant hush" as

"They bit into their sandwiches as if they had lost all taste for food." When she persists, the narrator deftly describes the boys: "They were as silent as thieves hiding. They chewed without a sound." When Mrs. Cope breaks the silence, "Well, I know I do," and retreats to the house with an air of victory, her self-righteousness appears invincible. But the great revelation in this scene centers on a parody of Eucharist, the meal shared by a community in celebration of the presence of Christ among the circle of Christian disciples. For all her claims of perpetual "thanksgiving" there is no real Eucharist (in Greek, "thanksgiving") in Mrs. Cope's life; her claim that "we have everything" (234) is the epitome of a greedy heart that resists any sharing—she extends only a begrudging handout to ward off intruders and thereby connives to tame their presumably evil inclinations. The boys acknowledge the dynamic when they decline her bacon breakfast the next morning and respond, "We don't want nothing of yours." Her feigned hospitality carries a controlling proviso: "'You boys know that I'm glad to have you,' she said, 'but I expect you to behave. I expect you to act like gentlemen" (242).

Mrs. Cope exposes her own lie the day before when the boys grabbed her expression "my woods" (240) and proceed to challenge her greed by defiantly sleeping in the barn, riding the horses, letting the bull loose, crossing the tree line, and inhabiting the woods. Gene, the smallest of the boys, responds to Hollis Pritchard, "Man, Gawd owns them woods and her too"—a remark that he reports to Mrs. Cope. The boy tells her things she does not want to hear. It all adds to her "shocked look" the day before when she encountered the boys and is shaken to a dawning realization, "as if she had had a searchlight thrown on her in the middle of the night" (243). Mrs. Cope's grace is about to arrive in the dark and disruptive violence soon to erupt on her farm.

At this juncture in the story Mrs. Cope's daughter, Sally, breaks her silence and eavesdropping by sticking her head out the window and shouting, "Ugggghhrhh." O'Connor renders her entrance in grotesque fashion, "crossing her eyes and hanging her tongue out as far as possible as if she were going to vomit" (242). It is a remark aimed unconsciously as much at her mother, Mrs. Cope, as at W. T., the "big boy" who is the object of her blind rage. This twelve-year-old girl is another of O'Connor's adult-child pairs who serve as foils for one another in her fiction, much like Mr. Head and Nelson in "The Artificial Nigger." They also make visible the socialization process (one dimension of the doctrine of original sin and our "learned" propensity toward evil) and the child's innocent recognition of sin in this adult character.

When Sally is first mentioned in the story, she stares at "the blank sky" and thinks that it "looked as if it were pushing against the fortress wall, trying to break through" (232). O'Connor reinforces the imagery of battle by describing them later in the same paragraph as "the gray-blue sentinel line of trees." The metaphor of the tree line of woods—"The fortress line of trees was a hard granite blue"—recurs at the precise moment that the child appears to engage the boys in combat. She is armed with two pistols and a "very tight" hat that is pulled down to her glasses and "seemed to be squeezing the redness into her face." Her once again "astonished" mother confronts her with the questions "Why do you have to look like an idiot?" (247); "When are you going to grow up?"; "What's going to become of you?" (248). The questions recoil upon Mrs. Cope when her daughter replies, "Leave me be...I ain't you." Her preteenage identity struggles with the individuation process, but O'Connor suggests something spiritually deeper in terms of identity. Sally comically appears as a mirror image of her mother, an image that Mrs. Cope identifies as "an idiot." Early in the story we learn of the girl's passive-aggressive relationship with her mother. When Mrs. Cope invites her to watch the beautiful sunset against the horizon of the woods, she only mutters "meanness" and taunts her mother with the ironic suggestion that "It looks like a fire" (233).

As Sally crashes through the woods in pursuit of Mrs. Cope's pursuers, we begin to see how different she is from her mother. Her earlier threat to "handle" the boys by strangling them is impulsive, a genuine response to her feelings. Mrs. Cope, on the other hand, speaks in controlled, military, and strategic circumlocutions: "I do not fold my hands" (243). When W. T. first encounters Sally in the window, he "looked up and stared at her, 'Jesus,' he growled, 'another woman'" (242). It is a teenager's habitual abuse of the Redeemer's name. But it serves well O'Connor's irony. Readers of the title story in *A Good Man Is Hard to Find* recall The Misfit's complaint that "Jesus thown everything off balance" (151). It is no coincidence that Powell first appears as he leads the procession of boys from the gate. He is described as "bent to the side carrying a black, pig-shaped valise" (235). From the opening of the story Powell and his companions, like Jesus, throw Mrs. Cope's world off balance as they initiate her into the mystery of grace. There is a connected irony early in the story when she mistakes Powell for his brother, "J. C.," when she finds out that he is Mr. Boyd's son (J. C. being the same initials as Jesus Christ).

Sally's foray into the woods is interrupted when she sits on a tree stump and places her feet "carefully and firmly on the ground." There is a christological overtone in imagery reminiscent of Mary's role in salvation, the victory over the serpent's temptation at Eden: "She lifted [her feet] and put them down several times, grinding them fiercely into the dirt as if she were crushing something under her heels" (248). She comes upon the naked boys cavorting in the cow trough and racing around the field. They are described as lying down to rest "with their ribs moving up and down"; thus O'Connor has playfully inserted an allusion to the creation story and the myth of Adam's rib. Sally overhears when W. T. announces that he would build a big parking lot there. But she fails to fathom Powell's gesture as he shows the matches "[f]or more than a minute."

When the "narrow line of fire" begins to blaze in the woods, the girl watches almost like her mother, "with a dazed stare." The boys "disappeared shrieking" into the woods. The most obvious biblical allusion of the story (and an explanation of the title) is from the Book of Daniel in the Hebrew scriptures. The text is a distinctive type of writing known as apocalyptic, or a sudden, violent destruction that is revelatory. Apocalyptic literature has its roots in the prophets of Israel. It speaks of God ultimately vindicating his people. It proves most apt for "A Circle in the Fire" because O'Connor's story coincides with two elements in the story of King Nebuchadnezzar's three Jewish administrators of the province of Babylon—Shadrach, Meshach, and Abednego. The first concerns their refusal to serve the king's god or worship the god statue he has set up. Neither will Powell and his companions worship Mrs. Cope's mammon or engage in her idolatry of possessions, symbolized by the woods and her puritan work ethic. But the second concerns Mrs. Cope's persecution of the boys. The boys' "wild high shrieks of joy as if the prophets were dancing in the fiery furnace" (251) are reminiscent of Nebuchadnezzar's test and persecution of the Jews and of the trio being spared. The king's recognition of the God of the Jews echoes in O'Connor's story: "I decree for nations and peoples of every language that whoever blasphemes the God of Shadrach, Meshach, and Abednego shall be cut to pieces and his house destroyed. For there is no other God who can rescue like this" (Dan 3:96).

Sally registers "some new unplaced misery that she had never felt before" as she witnesses the conflagration. After she runs to her mother's side, she stares "at her face as if she had never seen it before." It is a moment of recognition for the child, not unlike Nelson observing Mr. Head in "The Artificial Nigger." "It was the face of a new misery she felt, but on her mother it looked old and it looked as if it might have belonged to anybody, a Negro or a European or to Powell himself." The universality of this "old" misery and the identification with the lowly, the displaced persons of World War II, and even the "gangster" Powell reflected in Mrs. Cope's face are O'Connor's signature of original sin in the story— the "old" origins of alienation and pride. The invincible Mrs. Cope has come to recognize her own vulnerability. She is now displaced from her coveted woods and all the autonomy and self-righteousness they symbolize. O'Connor has poised Mrs. Cope to recognize that the original sin of selfishness and pride belongs to anybody and everybody, even to her righteous self. Whether she accepts the grace offered in this violent moment remains an unfinished, or a new story.

"A LATE ENCOUNTER WITH THE ENEMY"

If ever an O'Connor character were nominated for the award for unadulterated vanity, the protagonist from "A Late Encounter with the Enemy," General Tennessee Flintrock Sash of the Confederacy, would be without peers. The reader reels from the first line of the story where we learn that he was "one hundred and four years old" and that "[l]iving had got to be a habit with him" (252). Twelve years earlier he was "the hit of the show" when he first appeared in the general's uniform at the Atlanta movie premiere of a Civil War movie—O'Connor's obvious comic lampooning of *Gone with the Wind* as a cinema extravaganza. The fact that he and his granddaughter, Sally Poker Sash, were introduced sixteenth on the premiere's program could not diminish that he inflated his role on stage at the "nashnul event" (254). No matter that he was probably only a Confederate foot soldier (or that his granddaughter told the organizer that his name was "George Poker Sash" and that he had "only been a major"), he boasted of having his picture made with his arms around the waists of beautiful Hollywood girls in the stage spotlight.

Sally Poker Sash serves O'Connor's comic intent with her own possessiveness and derivative celebrity. The story begins with her anticipating her college graduation (at the age of sixty-two!) and having her famous grandfather sitting on the stage for the occasion. Sally is another of O'Connor's neurotic antiheroines. Her worry focuses upon "the sense that she might be cheated out of her triumph" if he did not survive long enough. She shares with "General Sash" a romanticized nostalgia that distorts reality and claims undeserved status over others.

> She wanted the General at her graduation because she
> wanted to show what he stood for, or, as she said, "what all
> was behind her," and was not behind them. This *them* was
> not anybody in particular. It was just all the upstarts who had
> turned the world on its head and unsettled the ways of decent
> living....
> She meant to hold her head very high as if she were say-
> ing, "See him! See him! My kin, all you upstarts! Glorious
> upright old man standing for the old traditions. Dignity!
> Honor! Courage! See him!" (252–53)

The spotlight that centers on General Sash catches only "a weird
moon-shaped slice of Sally Poker"—a crescent that literally and
symbolically eclipses her from celebrity. When she suddenly discovers that she appears on stage in formal attire (with corsage, rhine-
stone buckle, and white gloves and handkerchief) but wearing her
two brown Girl Scout shoes "protruding from the bottom of her
dress," the humiliated Sally races off, pushing his wheelchair.

We learn that "since then life had not been very interesting" for
the General. His spirit's ennui is mirrored in a broken body: dead
feet, knees that worked like hinges, poor kidneys, but a persistent
heartbeat. Lethargic, "he had no more notion of dying than a cat"
with nine lives. General Sash is reduced to providing "atmosphere"
by wearing his uniform, carrying his sword, and saluting at the
museum on Confederate Memorial Day or during the spring open-
ings of the old homes (257). He is reduced to being a moveable
piece of furniture. The abyss of his discontent and malaise registers
in his cantankerous and ornery disposition when he is readied for
the academic procession for Sally's graduation. Oblivious to the
nature of the occasion, the General knows he will be on display
with uniform and sword. He is a portrait of vanity: "Put the soward
acrost my lap, damn you...where it'll shine....God damn it....God
damn every goddam thing to hell" (258).

The ensuing stroke that proves fatal to the General while he is
on the graduation stage is first imaged as "a little hole beginning
to widen in the top of his head." Disoriented, he knows that a

procession coming to meet him "must be something connected with history, like they were always having. He had no use for any of it. What happened then wasn't anything to a man living now and he was living now." With that ironic circumlocution, O'Connor completes her sketch of his dementia and death-in-life. The graduation speaker's address confronts the General with his shallow life and the deceit upon which he has staked his identity: "'If we forget our past,' the speaker was saying, 'we won't remember our future and it will be as well for we won't have one.'"

Considering this story in the context of the collection *A Good Man Is Hard to Find,* the crux of the problem is the failure to recognize sin as sin. The Civil War itself stands as a metaphor of Cain and Abel, brother embattled against brother. The mention of places and names inspired by his military history (or his claim to celebrity at the battles of Chickamauga and Shiloh, and in concert with Johnston and Lee) assault "the dark places of his brain...as if they were trying to wrench themselves out of place and come to life" (260).

General Sash finally cannot "protect himself from the words" that now come in "a regular volley" that he meets with "quick curses." The stroke seizes him with a hundred stabs of pain and he literally falls. It is a symbolic gesture pointing to his fall after a career of pride. But key events in his life flash before him in these moments before death:

> As the music swelled toward him, *the entire past opened up on him out of nowhere* and he felt his body riddled in a hundred places with sharp stabs of pain and he fell down, returning a curse for every hit. He saw his wife *looking at him critically* through her round gold-rimmed glasses; he saw one of his *squinting* bald-headed sons; and his mother ran toward him with an *anxious look;* then a succession of places—Chickamauga, Shiloh, Marthasville—rushed on him *as if the past were the only future now* and he had to endure it. Then suddenly he saw the black procession was almost on him. He recognized it, for it had been dogging all his days. He made

such a desperate effort to see over it and find out what comes after the past that his hand clenched the sword until the blade touched the bone. (261, emphasis mine)

All the family relationships where his identity as husband, father, and son has been dishonored by sin or some alienation mediated through these microseconds of painful flashback are reclaimed in a moment of recognition. Vanity and deceit have given the General a veneer of honor. The "black procession" dogging all his days is this unresolved admission of deep inner guilt he has been carrying around. This is the "enemy" of the title that he encounters only in his final breaths—a literal "deathbed" conversion scene. In the same moment, the General searches for something to follow this past. It is a dazzling openness to grace. The stroke's final surge sends a reflex gripping motion to his hand and the honorific blade creases the flesh. It is a conclusion bristling with irony.

Sally Poker has unwittingly been cheated out of her triumph as she sees him "sitting fixed and fierce, his eyes wide open" but nonetheless already a corpse as she receives her diploma and holds her head higher. "What all was behind her" has expired but not before a final revelatory moment. The discovery of that reality will confront Sally Poker at the peril of her own vanity and deceit. Her grandfather has confronted the counterfeit of the "spotlight" and spiritual enlightenment that has quaked the heart of his being, and so now must she. General Sash and his granddaughter commence a spiritual journey at the end of this story that is far beyond anything they ever expected.

"GOOD COUNTRY PEOPLE"

The introduction of Mrs. Hopewell in "Good Country People" signals how O'Connor once again explores the precincts of original sin: "Mrs. Hopewell had no bad qualities of her own but she was able to use other people's in such a constructive way that she never felt the lack....Nothing is perfect. This was one of Mrs. Hopewell's favorite sayings" (264). What greater flaw than to believe oneself to be flawless? In addition to her pride, Mrs. Hopewell perpetrates a deceitful optimism in the face of reality's uglier aspects—her daughter, Joy, a.k.a. "Hulga," in particular: "Mrs. Hopewell said that people who looked on the bright side of things would be beautiful even if they were not" (267).

Paired with Mrs. Hopewell is Mrs. Freeman. She and her husband were hired to work the farm in spite of a previous employer's alarming caution about her nosiness. They are hired because there are no other applicants for the job—and because Mrs. Hopewell knows them to be "good country people," "not trash" (264). This woman of "great patience," the narrator tells us, "realized that nothing is perfect and that in the Freemans she had good country people and that if, in this day and age, you get good country people, you had better hang onto them" (265). Already in the first paragraph of the story, however, we are alert to a flaw in Mrs. Freeman that mirrors Mrs. Hopewell's flaw: "Mrs. Freeman could never be brought to admit herself wrong on any point" (263). O'Connor's use of eye imagery to describe Mrs. Freeman's three expressions (neutral, forward, and reverse) is masterful. In "forward," her unswerving eyes "turned as the story [she was telling] turned as if they were following a yellow line down the center of it." But on the rare occasions she needed to "retract a statement" she halted in "reverse" as her "black eyes" receded; and any observer "would see that...[she] was no longer there in spirit" (263). This same spiritual torpor foreshadows the action surrounding Joy-Hulga in the story.

The thirty-two-year-old daughter of Mrs. Hopewell is introduced as "highly educated" (263). The next mention of her comes on the heels of her mother's observation that "nothing is perfect." Joy-Hulga's response to her mother's stream of clichés is one of "constant outrage" that leaves her expressionless; it is a fitting index of her own lack of feelings and her insensitivity to others' feelings. O'Connor describes her attitude as "the look of someone who has achieved blindness by an act of will and means to keep it" (265). O'Connor once again employs the artistry of imaginative eye imagery to serve as a metaphor for Joy-Hulga's spiritual state. Perhaps more successfully than anywhere in her fiction, O'Connor here dramatizes the lesson she learned from Romano Guardini: "...the roots of the eye are in the heart." Although she borrows his insight in her essay "The Church and the Fiction Writer" to describe the fiction writer's eye as the "testing point" that "involves the whole personality and as much as can be got into it" (807), the same metaphor ironically applies to Hulga.

It is no surprise, therefore, that Hulga has heart trouble—both physically and spiritually. In fact, O'Connor's next sentence in this same essay describes the impasse of Hulga: "In fact, for the Catholic [the roots of the eye] stretch far and away into those depths of mystery which the modern world is divided about—part of it trying to eliminate mystery while another part tries to rediscover it in disciplines less personally demanding than religion" (807–8). Hulga the Ph.D.-philosopher who every day "sat on her neck in a deep chair, reading" (268) personifies the modernist elimination of religious mystery that we encounter in so many O'Connor characters. She has retreated so far into her own ideal world that even on her occasional walks she dislikes everything: dogs, cats, birds, flowers, nature—and young men. There are echoes of Nietzsche's "God is dead" theology in Hulga's blue-underlined text that Mrs. Hopewell picks up and reads: "Nothing—how can it be for science anything but a horror and a phantasm?...[S]cience wishes to know nothing of nothing. Such is after all the strictly scientific approach to Nothing" (269).

Mrs. Hopewell describes her daughter—"She was brilliant but she didn't have a grain of sense"—and considers her emotionally "still a child" (268) because she wears her yellow sweatshirt with the embossed faded cowboy on a horse. Joy declares her independence of her mother by legally changing her name when she reaches the age of twenty-one. Mrs. Hopewell finds her choice of

"Hulga" to be "the ugliest name in any language" (266). Ironically, Joy-Hulga prizes her name both for its ugliness but also as a metaphor for the mythic character Vulcan's working in the furnace (266). By a willful act of inversion, Hulga reverses her symbolic naming by her mother ("Joy") and turns herself into Hulga. This alienation from her given identity serves as a powerful symbol. Hulga's claim that her new name was "her highest creative act" (267) will prove to be a devastating irony. Mrs. Hopewell herself is befuddled by her daughter's exchanges. At one of their volatile meals, Hulga stands up with "her face purple and her mouth half full" and confronts her mother: "Woman! do you ever look inside? Do you ever look inside and see what you are *not*? God!" Her negative question brims with the scientific materialism and Nothingness of her reading. But it nonetheless serves as an ironic question that Hulga herself will confront as the story unfolds. O'Connor's comic sense plays with the ambiguity of the exclamation "God!" in Hulga's outburst. On the literal level it is a blasphemous curse. But seen from another perspective, it is an ironic declaration that the flawless Mrs. Hopewell—in spite of her pride—cannot usurp God's place.

No sooner does Mrs. Hopewell shut Hulga's book and retreat with a "chill" than she recalls the Bible salesman who had come by yesterday. O'Connor's insertion of this detail catches the reader by surprise. But the juxtaposition of the focus on Hulga's philosophy books about Nothingness with the reference to the Bible serves as a creative pairing of contraries in the story. The Bible salesman is described at the door, "carrying a large black suitcase that weighted him so heavily on one side that he had to brace himself against the door facing" (269). The suitcase and the posture are reminiscent of Powell's first appearance in "A Circle in the Fire." Again, O'Connor connects this story with the title story of the collection where The Misfit reveals that "Jesus thown everything off balance"—a fitting description, both literally and symbolically, of Hulga's fate at the end of this story. After a moment of banter about her name ("I hope you are well"), the young man gives her "an earnest look" and says, "Lady, I've come to speak of serious things." The false intimacy of his conversation manipulates Mrs. Hopewell: "I know you believe in Christian service....I know...that you're a good woman." But she is quick to see beyond his flattery and replies, "What are you selling?" The alert salesman observes that no Bible is evident in the parlor. Mrs. Hopewell knows that she cannot admit that her daughter is an atheist and prohibits the Bible, so she lies about it being at her bedside (it is actually in the attic). When he pleads ("I'll tell you the truth") that not many people buy Bibles "nowadays," he adds a self-deprecating line about his identity, "I'm just a country boy" (270). Mrs. Hopewell takes the bait and registers her praise of good country people as "the salt of the earth."

Manley Pointer, Ironic Seducer

We get the first hint of the salesman's identity when he pursues Mrs. Hopewell's mellowing to him. The name Manley Pointer foreshadows his seductive intentions for Hulga. But even more telling is his remark that he is from "out in the country around Willohobie," and "not even from a place, just from near a place." It is not unfair to derive his "hobo" identity from this combination of the town's name and his constant displacement. He patronizes her again by calling her "real honest people" when she directs him to pack up his Bibles. As he explains that he has no desire to go to college but to devote himself to Christian service because of a heart condition, Mrs. Hopewell connects him with Joy-Hulga and spontaneously invites him for dinner. There lurks here the same dark motive of the self-serving maternal matchmaker that we found in Lucynell Crater (and, in a paternal parallel, that Asa Hawks intends for Sabbath Lily in *Wise Blood*). Mrs. Hopewell's immediate remorse has less to do with her own motives than her realization that Hulga will respond with "deliberate rudeness" (272)—which she does.

It comes as no surprise that Manley Pointer is so full of himself that he dominates the dinner conversation. When he quotes Jesus' saying (Matt 16:25) from the New Testament, "He who losest his life shall find it," O'Connor compounds the irony of the story. Mrs. Hopewell finds him "so sincere, so genuine, and earnest." She is not oblivious to his repeated efforts to catch Hulga's eye with "a keen appraising glance" (272). When Hulga encounters the departing Manley at the gate, she detects his "excited gesture with his free hand." They have surreptitiously planned the next day's meeting. She is so cerebral that she has no clue as to the sexual desire when "his look was different from what it had been at the dinner table" and he was "breathing as if he had run a great distance to see her." Hulga lies about her age, claiming to be seventeen, and her spiral downward begins. She mistakes his every flirtation. When he asks, "You're shy, aren't you?" she merely nods unknowingly. When Manley offers, "I like girls that wear glasses," his flattery strains credibility. But it does make even more apparent O'Connor's satiric mirroring of a dimension of herself in the intellectual, bookish Hulga, complete with the eyeglasses. She writes to "A" in September 1955: "Hulga in this case would be a projection of myself into this kind of tragic-comic action—presumably only a projection, because if I could not stop short of it myself, I could not write it. Stop short, or go beyond it, I should say. You have to be able to dominate the existence that you characterize" (958–59).[20]

In a supreme moment of irony we move from a description of Manley giving Hulga "a dying look as if he felt his insides about to drop out of him," indicative of his lust, to the revelation of Hulga's imagining that night that she "seduced" him the next morning at their picnic. When she considers that she will have to deal with Manley's "remorse" after the seduction, the reader finds the familiar environs of Adam and Eve in the Garden of Eden, hiding in their shame (Gen 3:10).[21] "[Hulga] imagined that she took his remorse in hand and changed it into a deeper understanding of life. She took all his shame away and turned it into something useful" (276). Here is the ultimate misunderstanding of original sin by Hulga, the Nihilist philosopher. It adds to the complexity of her pride that precedes her fall at the story's end.

When Manley is bold enough to ask Hulga, "Where does your wooden leg join on?" and then offers a patronizing remark about her courage, she reveals her atheist stance, "I don't even believe in God" (277). Again we glimpse the true Manley when he responds, "'No!' ...as if he were too astonished to say anything else." The interlude of a kiss from Manley, with "more pressure than feeling behind it," triggers a charge of adrenaline to Hulga's brain and she triumphs as "a matter of the mind's control." When Manley asks, "Then you ain't saved?" she proudly boasts, "In my economy...I'm saved and you are damned but I told you I didn't believe in God." The mutual seduction scene continues. Hulga signals the barn as a resting place. She gives him a "contemptuous look" when he raises the question of her wooden leg interfering with the climb to the loft. The lack of respect is mutual. The clumsy foreplay continues. Just as the narrator reminds us that Hulga's mind, "throughout all of this, never stopped or lost itself for a second to her feelings" (279), Manley adds another protocol to the seduction: she must reciprocate and say that she loves him. Because Hulga the philosopher "was always careful how she committed herself," she advises him,

> "I don't have illusions. I'm one of those people who see
> *through* things to nothing....You poor baby....It's just as well
> you don't understand....We are all damned...but some of us
> have taken off our blindfolds and see there's nothing to see.
> It's a kind of salvation." (280)

In fact, it is Hulga's illusions that keep her from touching reality. Her idealistic philosophy sets her up to become the victim of Manley's demonic violation by taking her wooden leg at the very moment that she is convinced that "She had seduced him without even making up her mind to try" (280). O'Connor's supreme irony comes when Hulga realizes that seduction involves more than the mind—and that the mind can, in fact, completely mistake the reality of seduction.

When Manley insists that the wooden leg makes her different—"You ain't like anybody else"—she feels "as if her heart had stopped and left her mind to pump her blood." It is a devastating image of Hulga's predicament. O'Connor's irony keeps reminding us of Hulga's disproportionately large intellectual life that comes at the expense of her truncated spiritual and emotional life. She totally mistakes Manley's intentions, thinking that for the first time in her life she is "face to face with real innocence." Just as she prepares to surrender completely to him, O'Connor revisits the line from the gospel (Matt 16:25) and twists ironically: "It was like losing her own life and finding it again, miraculously in his" (281). Manley wants to know about the mechanics of the wooden leg. After he removes it and declines to replace it, the narrator tells us, "Without the leg she felt entirely dependent upon him. Her brain seemed to have stopped thinking altogether and to be about some other function that it was not very good at." The revelation comes in her vulnerability and feeling of dependency. She no longer has her artificial leg—her misguided intellect that eclipses the spiritual and emotional realities—to stand on.

Manley simultaneously opens the hollowed-out (not "hallowed") Bible and removes the whiskey bottle, the obscene playing cards, and the packaged condoms. Her question comes from under a murmur: "Aren't you just good country people?" And his response, "I'm as good as you any day of the week," rounds out O'Connor's irony. The religion that Manley Pointer sells (just as Asa "hawks" his religion in *Wise Blood*) is nothing but a phony facade. Hulga's angry and sarcastic reaction, "You're a fine Christian! You're just like them all—say one thing and do another...," mirrors Hazel Motes's philosophical quest for the truth in *Wise Blood*. She shares with Haze the virtue of recognizing what is untrue. Manley's rejoinder, a chain of clichés (much like Mrs. Hopewell's habit of speech) ironically exposes his plight:

"I know which end is up and I wasn't born yesterday and I know where I'm going." His departing glance as he descends through the loft lid and down the ladder mirrors her contempt for him: "he turned and regarded her with a look that no longer had any admiration." Manley Pointer admits that he has been using an alias and not his real identity. As he spits out his departing words, Joy-Hulga recognizes for the first time her own emptiness and alienation: "You ain't so smart. I been believing in nothing ever since I was born!" (282). It is the beginning of her awakening and her acknowledgement of the "swollen pride"[22] that identifies her share in original sin.

We gain further insight into O'Connor's imagination through an August 1956 letter to "A" that emphasizes Hulga's contempt, the root of her sin. Eight months earlier she had written to "A" about her story "A Temple of the Holy Ghost" and defined sin as "the contradiction, the interference, of a greater good for a lesser good" (976). Hulga's preoccupation with the intellect is just such interference.

> About GCP let me say that you are not reading the story itself. Where do you get the idea that Hulga's need to worship "comes to flower" in GCP? or that she had never had any faith at any time? or never loved anybody before? None of these things are said in the story. She is full of contempt for the Bible salesman until she finds he is full of contempt for her. Nothing "comes to flower" here except her realization in the end that she ain't so smart. It's not said that she has never had any faith but it is implied that her fine education has got rid of it for her....Now that Hulga is repugnant to you only makes her more believable... (999–1000)

O'Connor renders Hulga eminently believable as a character who recognizes how she has impersonated herself. At the striking conclusion of this story she penetrates her own illusion and is ruthlessly put in touch with reality, a reality that once again comes through a dark and disruptive grace.

"THE DISPLACED PERSON"

The longest O'Connor short story in *A Good Man Is Hard to Find* is the concluding story, "The Displaced Person." Once again she initiates a story with formidable female characters. Mrs. Shortley, the wife of the dairy worker, personifies resistance and pride as she mounts the hill in order to gaze upon the scene of the arriving Polish immigrants: "She stood on two tremendous legs, with the grand self-confidence of a mountain, and rose, up narrowing bulges of granite, to two icy blue points of light that pierced forward, surveying everything." No sooner do we read this detailed description than we are told that she "ignored the white afternoon sun" that crept behind "a ragged wall of cloud as if it pretended to be an intruder" and instead cast her gaze toward the red clay road leading from the highway." Both her haughty stance and the fact that she is oblivious to sun and sky signal a neglect of the transcendent in O'Connor's shorthand symbolism. The peacock that follows her in what O'Connor describes as a "procession" symbolizes pride as it protects its tail from touching the ground. At this juncture we meet the thrice-widowed Mrs. McIntyre, owner of the farm and employer of the Shortleys, and the arriving immigrant, Mr. Guizac. There is an air of deceit when we learn that Mrs. McIntyre wears "her largest smile,"[23] and Mrs. Shortley detects the false pretense when she notes that the smile has "a narrow slide in it" (285).

As Mrs. Shortley's vision both "narrowed" and "widened" to take in Mr. Guizac and his family (the unnamed wife and son, Rudolph, and daughter, Sledgewig), O'Connor already plays with the theme of appearances and reality. "The first thing that struck [Mrs. Shortley] as peculiar was that they looked like other people." Xenophobia threads throughout the story and grows more complex. Mr. Guizac's gallant gesture—suddenly "he bobbed down from the waist and kissed" Mrs. McIntyre's hand—is a foreign act of grace and respect, as alien to the two Georgia women as the Polish name that they ridicule by pronouncing it "Gobblehook" (286).

There is a subtle but telling note early in the story as O'Connor describes Mrs. McIntyre and Mrs. Shortley preparing the living quarters for the immigrants. It is a makeshift collection of discarded furnishings and curtains made from chicken feed sacks. The women insist that the immigrants "should be grateful for anything they could get" because they are "lucky" to "escape." Mrs. Shortley recalls a graphic description of a newsreel of Holocaust victims that she had once seen: "a small room piled high with bodies of dead naked people in a heap, their arms and legs tangled together, a head thrust in here, a head there, a foot, a knee, a part that should have been covered up sticking out, a hand raised clutching nothing." But the word *Holocaust* and the Nazi genocide of Jews and other victims of their xenophobia do not enter her consciousness. In fact, before any viewer "could realize that it was real and take it into your head," O'Connor interjects, the picture changes and a "hollow-sounding voice" on the newsreel says, "Time marches on!" No wonder Mrs. Shortley continues to be oblivious to the deeper currents of original sin manifest in the Third Reich. She persists in her caricature that such things "were happening every day in Europe where they had not advanced as in this country." Her only "intuition" comes with the suspicion that, "like rats with typhoid fleas," the Guizacs might now perpetrate the same atrocities on others—"do it to others," an inversion of the Golden Rule. She descends from her proud perch to be introduced and find out "what they were capable of" (287). It is not a concern with their capacity for goodness but a presumption of malice that tells us far more about Mrs. Shortley's flaws than about the immigrants. A few paragraphs later we encounter her predatory personality in an apt metaphor: "Her look first grazed the tops of the displaced people's heads and then revolved downwards slowly, the way a buzzard glides and drops in the air until it alights on the carcass." It is an ominous foreshadowing of the story's lethal conclusion.

Mrs. McIntyre meets the Guizacs and we simultaneously learn some important details of her background. She is described as a three-times widowed "small woman of sixty with a round crinkled face and red bangs" over penciled eyebrows (287–88). O'Connor's trademark eye imagery reveals essential details about her character. Mrs. McIntyre's eyes are "soft blue" when she opens them wide; but they become "more like steel or granite when she narrowed them to inspect a milk can." This is a woman who reminds readers of Mrs. Cope from "A Circle in the Fire," a frugal and exacting taskmaster. We are told that Mrs. Shortley respects Mrs. McIntyre "as a person nobody had put anything over on yet— except, ha, ha perhaps the Shortleys" (288), and once again we glimpse flaws. In this scene the priest who shepherds the Guizacs to their new-world life appears, and immediately Mrs. Shortley contrasts him with her son, "H. C.," who is going to start a church after going to Bible school because he "could sell anything." Her son also has a "sweet voice for hymns"; by contrast, she describes the priest's "foreign"-sounding English as someone speaking with a "throatful of hay" (289). The most important judgment she makes about the priest is that Catholics "did not have an advanced religion" (288). His "pleasure" in admiring the peacock's beautiful "tail full of suns" will figure prominently in this story—and contrast starkly with Mrs. McIntyre's loss of pleasure after the death of her last husband, the late Judge McIntyre. Once again it is eye imagery that reveals her condescending attitude toward the priest: "Mrs. McIntyre raised her orange eyebrows and exchanged a look with [Mrs. Shortley] to indicate that the old man was in his second childhood" (289). It is an ironic and playful metaphor for the life of grace (the "born again" life of the "new creation," and the gospel advice [Matt 18:3–4] to become like a little child and be humble) that contrasts sharply with the alienation of original sin. In this sense, of all the O'Connor characters in *A Good Man Is Hard to Find*, Mrs. Shortley most resembles The Misfit in the collection's title story because she also plumbs the abyss of alienation and echoes his hollowness, "It's no real pleasure in life" (153). As nowhere else in her fiction, O'Connor in this story consciously confronts the anti-Catholic bias in American culture and offers readers an imaginative and compelling invitation into the Catholic sacramental ethos that takes pleasure in God's creation.

The group drives the displaced people to the "shack" where they will live and leaves Mrs. Shortley alone to summon the hiding Negro farmhands from behind the mulberry tree. She invites their reaction to the immigrant arrivals and a familiar repartee ensues. The old man, Astor, and the younger Negro, Sulk, engage in clever "signifying" in the story, a familiar Negro verbal device that O'Connor uses often in her fiction. By a series of exchanges, the blacks taunt oppressive whites with false praise. Ralph C. Wood describes it well: "What often appears as 'Tomming'—an abject acquiescence to the white man—can be used to get revenge by indirection, to save oneself from returning evil for evil, and thus to preserve one's own sense of dignity and worth when the white world has denied it."[24] When Astor asks what "displaced person" means, Mrs. Shortley defines their predicament: "...they ain't where they were born at and there's nowhere for them to go." When Astor replies, "If they here, they somewhere," and Sulk chimes in, "Sho is," Mrs. Shortley shrugs it off as "[t]he illogic of Negro-thinking." She menaces them by attributing a statement to Mrs. McIntyre: "This is going to put the Fear of the Lord into those shiftless niggers!" (290). However, we soon learn that the Shortleys dismiss the Guizacs as no threat to their job security or status. He sums up the situation, "She ain't any better off than if she had more niggers."

But in three weeks time Mrs. McIntyre discovers that Mr. Guizac is "an expert mechanic, a carpenter, and a mason" as well as "thrifty and energetic" (292). She declares that after thirty years of hiring "sorry people" (293), "That man is my salvation!" (294). The context reveals her self-serving attitude when she acknowledges exploiting him, saying: "One fellow's misery is the other fellow's gain." O'Connor describes how Mrs. McIntyre "sighed with pleasure" (293), but we will discover the word "pleasure" to be shallow and mistaken. A few paragraphs later in the story she will qualify her salvation claim by reducing it to a preoccupation with material possessions: "He saves me money" (295). Mr. Guizac has caught Sulk in the act of stealing one of her turkeys and dragged him to Mrs. McIntyre's back door for justice. When she discounts the incident by saying that "all Negroes would steal," Mr. Guizac is described as going off "with a startled disappointed face" (293). Once again, we glimpse deeply into the soul of both the immigrant and the farm owner by contrasting his vigilance with her compromised kowtowing to the status quo and a double standard.

Mrs. Shortley counters her boss's satisfaction with Mr. Guizac by responding, "I would suspicion salvation got from the devil." An insight into her character comes through the omniscient narrator's telling us that "she felt religion was essentially for those people who didn't have the brains to avoid evil without it." Her unmistakable pride reduces religion for people like herself to "a social occasion providing the opportunity to sing." We are told, however, that "if she had ever given it much thought, she would have considered the devil the head of it [religion] and God the hanger-on"—another ironic inversion in the story. We also learn that with the coming of the displaced Guizacs, Mrs. Shortley "was obliged to give new thought to a good many things" (294). But Mrs. McIntyre is undaunted and volunteers that Mr. Guizac is "worth raising" in salary. Mrs. Shortley detects that her husband's job is in jeopardy. She says that the doctor tells him that he suffers from "over-exhaustion" but Mrs. McIntyre's eyes, "almost closed as if she were examining the bottom of a milk can," ferrets out the truth. She claims that he must be working a second job. Mrs. Shortley's realization of her husband's vulnerability comes through a metaphor: "...her dark suspicion grew like a thunder cloud."

A Confederacy of Xenophobes

The fact that both Mr. Shortley and the Negroes worked afternoons at whiskey stills in the woods meant that they refrained from reporting one another to Mrs. McIntyre. What dawns on Mrs. Shortley is that the Guizacs were "all eyes and no understanding" (295) and therefore liable to expose her husband's greater transgression just as Mr. Guizac had reported Sulk's theft. She adds another remark relayed from her daughter (obviously fabricated in the desperation of the moment) claiming that Sledgewig has said that her father is saving to buy a used car. "Once they get them a used car, they'll leave you." The counterpunching continues with Mrs. McIntyre pointing out that Mr. Guizac doesn't smoke, and Mrs. Shortley insisting that "No man...is more of a Christian" than her husband. (This superiority claim dovetails with her disparaging remark about Polish Catholics embracing an "unreformed" religion.)

The tractor, cutter, and wagon pass in front of Mrs. McIntyre and again she applauds Mr. Guizac's efficiency in getting the harvest completed in two days. She imagines how long it would have taken with "men and mules to do it," and Mrs. Shortley inserts an ominous note, "'Maybe,' [she] muttered, 'if don't no terrible accident occur.'" O'Connor's irony bristles at this point because she has just reported on Mrs. Shortley's appraisal of Mr. Guizac's smile as a metonym for Europe, "mysterious and evil, the devil's experiment station." In her every act of desperation, Mrs. Shortley plays the role of the tempting devil, luring Mrs. McIntyre into the spiral of evil that will end with the story's calculated murder.

The poison of displacement proves the perfect motive for Mrs. Shortley to coerce Astor and Sulk into her conspiracy against Mr. Guizac. She preys upon *their* vulnerability in being displaced: "'All you colored people better look out....The time is going to come,' she prophesied, 'when it won't be no more occasion to speak of a nigger.'" She employs the metaphor of the mule being displaced by the tractor to emphasize her point. Sulk proves arrogant after she departs. He protests, "Big Belly act like she know everything." But Astor reminds him, "Never mind...your place too low for anybody to dispute with you for it." The truth of the matter comes from Mr. Shortley, who admits, "I'm a dead man" (297) because Mr. Guizac is about to *displace* him from his dairy job. Mrs. Shortley remains in denial and refuses to comprehend her husband's admission. "'I suspect,' she said, 'that before long there won't be no more niggers on this place. And I tell you what. I rather have niggers than them Poles. And what's furthermore, I aim to take up for the niggers when the time comes.'" She adds a line that resonates with an irony that escapes her: "A nigger don't know when he has a friend." The dairy worker's wife is unrelenting. She protests that she hates "to see niggers mistreated" and insists, "I have a heap of pity for niggers and poor folks." Her ultimatum comes when she righteously announces, "When the time comes...I'll stand up for the niggers and that's that. I ain't going to see that priest drive out all the niggers" (298).

Part 1 of "The Displaced Person" draws to a close with the narrator reporting that Mrs. McIntyre "had changed" since Mr. Guizac had been working for her. We are told of the transformation from Mrs. Shortley's careful vantage: "...she had begun to act like somebody who was getting rich secretly." The fact that she also no longer confides in Mrs. Shortley contributes to this perception. Again when Mrs. McIntyre alludes to plans to dismiss some of the other help in order to raise the Displaced Person's salary, the wife of the dairyman misinterprets and offers a defense of the wrong victims: "You can always tell a nigger what to do and stand by until he does it." She learns from Astor the secret about young Sulk's transaction with Mr. Guizac. Without yet knowing the details, the reader anticipates a dramatic reversal when O'Connor describes her telling the compromising secret about Mr. Guizac to her husband: "Mr. Shortley had risen straight up in bed like Lazarus risen from the tomb" (299). Finally, Mrs. Shortley eavesdrops on the priest and Mrs. McIntyre during one of his now frequent visits. She is paranoid that he will bring more and more immigrants, "uproot niggers," and transplant the Roman Catholic Church ("the Whore of Babylon," to use the worst of Reformation-era slurs against Catholicism) "in the midst of the righteous" like herself.

The intermittent vision of Mrs. Shortley one Sunday afternoon after she has climbed an incline presages the revelation that is about to come to her. The image of the clouds as "rows and rows of white fish washed up on a great blue beach" (301) serves well as a subconscious metaphor for the waves of new European immigrants arriving on American shores. However, another "vision" early in the story has cautioned us about Mrs. Shortley's dim perception. She earlier failed to attend to the peacock's tail, "a map of the universe [that] she didn't notice...any more than she did the spots of sky that cracked the dull green of the tree." She is totally oblivious to the transcendent, whether symbolized by the peacock or the sky itself.[25] O'Connor tells us with deadpan irony, "She was having an inner vision instead." And in that vision she ironically emerges as the "giant angel" telling the Negroes that they were being displaced by the "ten million billion" immigrants. Described with an expression "lofty and satisfied" (291), the proud Mrs. Shortley gravitates toward her and her husband's downfall.

A clenching and unclenching in Mrs. Shortley's heart accompanies the second "vision." It is a fitting image because her heart shows no signs of compassion; she remains in the clenches of the devil, who tempts her to exploit others to the advantage of her slothful husband. The call in this vision to "prophesy" inverts a genuinely religious vocation by her pretending to defend the vulnerable Negroes. When Mrs. McIntyre tells the priest that she will tomorrow give Mr. Shortley "a month's notice," Mrs. Shortley is literally floored. There is comic irony in her glance at the calendar in the feed house, advertising a laxative. She does not see the man in the picture who holds up "his marvelous discovery." She is so traumatized by her own frightening discovery that her husband is

being fired that, "She looked ahead as if she saw nothing what-
soever....her face an almost volcanic red" (303). She mobilizes
her husband and two daughters to flee at four in the morning to
avoid the indignity of being fired. There is irony in the description of their automobile, stealthily moving "slowly, like some
overfreighted leaking ark" past the Guizacs' shack and Mrs.
McIntyre's house. Her stroke in the departing car echoes the
reaction of familiar protagonists from earlier stories in *A Good
Man Is Hard to Find*—the grandmother's death in the title story;
Ruby in "A Stroke of Good Fortune"; Mr. Head's shame and
vulnerability in "The Artificial Nigger"; Hulga's predicament in
"Good Country People"; and the General's stroke in "A Late
Encounter with the Enemy." Thrashing and clutching, she finally
submits: "...then all at once her fierce expression faded into a
look of astonishment and her grip on what she had loosened."
Her collapse and stillness suggest that Mrs. Shortley has recognized her own vulnerability and dependence upon some reality
outside her own pride. The narrator describes her two daughters,
seated in the car beside their father, who stared ahead, "imitat-
ing a dead man":

> They didn't know that she had had a great experience or ever
> been displaced in the world from all that belonged to her.
> They were frightened by the gray slick road before them and
> they kept on repeating in higher and higher voices, "Where
> we goin, Ma? Where we goin?" while their mother, her huge
> body rolled back still against the seat and her eyes like blue-
> painted glass, seemed to contemplate for the first time the
> tremendous frontiers of her true country. (305)

If the contemplative is indeed one who penetrates illusions and
touches reality, then Flannery O'Connor's description of Mrs.
Shortley's death suggests that in a final moment of grace she has
at least begun to admit her flawed human ways and to see from a
distance ("frontiers") the "true country" of love and reconciliation, not xenophobia and exploitation. What remains open is the

fate of both her husband and her daughters. There could be no better symbol of original sin than the perplexed, directionless Annie Maude and Sarah Mae, who have inherited this existential exile and alienation.

By the conclusion of part 2, Mrs. McIntyre resembles Mrs. Shortley. She climbs to the top of a slope, stands with folded arms, looking "grimly out over the field," and watches Mr. Guizac maneuver the new machinery through the cornfield. Her pride has swollen to boast that she "handled" all the previous farm help and is now capable of handling Mr. Guizac. In a classic O'Connor use of eye imagery, the narrator describes Mrs. McIntyre: "...she narrowed her gaze until it closed entirely around the diminishing figure on the tractor as if she were watching him through a gunsight." She condemns him along with the others: "You're just like all the rest of them...only smart and thrifty and energetic but so am I. And this is my place." It is a moment of pride that foreshadows her demise (and literal *displacement*) in the final part of the story. O'Connor includes an ominous note, as Mrs. McIntyre stands "equal to anything. But her heart was beating as if some interior violence had already been done to her" (315). Indeed, this very heart imagery recalls Mrs. Shortley's stroke and the gracious moment of conversion— once again a dark and disruptive grace in O'Connor's fiction.

Mrs. McIntyre's Greed and Pride

This second part of the story opens with Mrs. McIntyre speaking to Astor, the old Negro. She frames the departure of the Shortleys in one of Judge McIntyre's clichés, "We've seen them come and seen them go." She describes the Shortleys as "not quite trash" and adds that the wife of the dairyman "was a good woman" whom she would miss. The dialogue turns to the "signifying" that O'Connor employs so deftly in her fiction. When the old man reminds her that "me and you...is still here," the narrator tells us, "She caught exactly what he meant her to catch in his tone" (305). The old man follows her observation that she has spent her life fooling with "worthless people": "'Black and white,' he said, 'is the same.'" Astor is the only one of the Negroes who knew the Judge, her third husband, and he claims "title" (308) because of this distinction. He quotes the Judge's wisdom to Mrs. McIntyre, "Judge say he long for the day when he be too poor to pay a nigger to work....Say when that day come, the world be back on its feet." She misunderstands his mixture of signifying and "Tomming" and claims that she has "somebody now who *has* to work!" Astor repeats the cliché, "We seen them come and we seen them go," and adds observantly: "'But we ain't never had one before,' he said, bending himself up until he faced her, 'like what we got now.'"

O'Connor's description of the old "cinnamon-colored" man "with eyes that were so blurred with age that they seemed to be hung behind cobwebs" (306) echoes the eye imagery associated with her characters all the way back to the blinded Hazel Motes. This old black man who pushes the wheelbarrow and forgets "which direction he wanted to move in" (308) personifies the wisdom of the lowly and the outcast. O'Connor symbolizes this eccentric status by describing his occasional conversations with the peacock that follows Astor around the farm. We learn that Mrs. McIntyre keeps the peacock "only out of superstitious fear of annoying the Judge in his grave. He had liked to see them walking around the place for he said they made him feel rich" (309). A further hint comes when she reminisces about meeting the Judge when she worked as his secretary. "[T]he old man with his sharp eye had seen at once that here was a woman who admired him for himself. The three years that he lived after they married were the happiest and most prosperous of Mrs. McIntyre's life, but when he died his estate proved to be bankrupt" (309). O'Connor's description of the Judge's death and bankruptcy coincides with Astor's quote from the Judge: the day when he was "too poor to pay a nigger to work" would be the day "the world be back on its feet." It is an image of redemption from slavery, the very aboriginal sin that O'Connor described in referring to "The Artificial Nigger" as "the tragedy of the South" (954).

Astor has referred to the fact that the Poles "got different ways of doing" (307). Mrs. McIntyre presses him to report if Mr. Guizac is doing anything he shouldn't. "'It warn't like it was what he should ought or oughtn't,' he muttered, 'It was like what nobody else don't do'" (307). Mrs. McIntyre, the survivor of the Judge's bankruptcy, continues to discredit Mr. Guizac for not struggling (i.e., suffering) enough. In a telling admission, she volunteers: "The truth was that he was not very real to her yet. He was a kind of miracle that she had seen happen and that she talked about but that she still didn't believe" (310). This passage is crucial to discern Mrs. McIntyre's eventual transformation. Congruent with William Lynch's insight that the fiction writer's task is "to imagine the real," O'Connor will not only *tell* us to expect it, she will employ the third part of the story to *show* it. Mrs. McIntyre will come to appreciate Mr. Guizac as her "salvation" in a far different light after his death than before.

The vague reference by Astor to the Displaced Person's doing "what nobody else don't do" becomes clear when Mrs. McIntyre finds Sulk meeting with Mr. Guizac. An unthinkable violation of the South's racial code is about to be discovered. Sulk surrenders the photograph of the twelve-year-old Polish girl who is Mr. Guizac's cousin and tells Mrs. McIntyre, "She going to mah [marry] me." Before he can explain that the girl, now sixteen, seeks to be freed from the Polish camp and that Sulk is paying three dollars a week for her redemption, Mrs. McIntyre looks down the road toward the tractor. She collapses on her bed "and pressed her hand over her heart as if she were trying to keep it in place." Her pessimism about human nature erupts with the judgment, "They're all the same. It's always been like this" (311), and then she falls back flat on the bed. She retreats to the "closet-like space" where the empty, but locked safe is "set like a tabernacle" because it was a memorial to the Judge's business transactions there. When the narrator tells us, "...with her intense constricted face turned toward the empty safe, she knew there was nobody poorer than she was" (312), her self-pity only magnifies her pride. Her despair at this moment is a form of pride; she is too proud to acknowledge her dependence upon a benevolent reality like the God of compassion. She drives to the cornfield and confronts Mr. Guizac. She asks him, "What kind of a monster are you?" (313). She accuses him of arranging the ultimate moral offense, an inter-racial marriage in the American South.

Mrs. McIntyre is impervious to the Polish immigrant's attempt to explain that his cousin has been a prisoner of the camps for three years. His desperate effort to impress upon her that the girl's mother died in the camp after two years meets deaf ears. In an ironic moment Mrs. McIntyre resembles Mrs. Shortley's self-righteous defense of the blacks and the status quo: "I will not have my niggers upset. I cannot run this place without my nig-gers. I can run it without you but not without them...." Mr. Guizac's final appeal, "She no care black....She in camp three year," meets only her arbitrary claim that this is "my place" and she says who comes and who goes. The narrator as "an after-thought" describes her disclaimer, "I am not responsible for the world's misery." And she climbs the slope, arms folded in a stance of defiant pride, and heart beating under the damage of some previous "interior violence."

Part 2 of the story ends with the scene of the cornfield, reduced to stubble by Mr. Guizac's daylong cutting that extended into the night. It concludes with the presence of the Judge in the graveyard located in the center of this field. He is described by the narrator as "grinning under his desecrated monument" (315). We learned earlier that one of the farm workers, Mr. Herrin, had stolen the cherub atop the Judge's tombstone when he and his wife left because his wife admired it. The Judge had purchased it one day "partly because its face reminded him of his wife and partly because he wanted a genuine work of art over his grave" (312). But it is not Mr. Herrin's theft of the cherub from the grave that desecrates the monument. It is Mrs. McIntyre's stubborn refusal to assist the world to be "back on its feet" and refrain from exploiting others that desecrates both the monument and the dignity of human persons (herself included). Her pride will spiral recklessly out of control in part 3 of the story. But after her fall, she will be offered the yet unimagined but believable grace of redemptive suffering.

Pietà and Transfiguration

Part 3 of the story opens with the priest steadfastly visiting Mrs. McIntyre and instructing her in the Catholic faith—rambling on this time about purgatory—while her mind nervously recites the argument that she has no "moral obligation" to keep Mr. Guizac. She interrupts. "'Listen!' she said. 'I'm not theological. I'm practical!'" In spite of the Polish man's efficient work, she argues that he is "not satisfactory" because he "doesn't understand how to get on with my niggers." She complains about his attitude, "He's not in the least grateful for being here" (316). When the priest intercedes that the Guizacs have "no where to go," she defends herself, "I didn't create this situation, of course." For a second time in their conversation, the old priest turns his attention to "that beautiful birrrrd" of hers, the peacock.

The double entendres in their conversation are an index of the radically different worldviews of the priest and the farm owner. Suddenly the mystery of original sin and Christ's redemptive action overlap. Mrs. McIntyre, in fact, did not "create this situation" of original sin. When the peacock dances and displays its tail in a "timbrous noise"—"Tiers of small pregnant suns floated in a green-gold haze over his head"—the transfixed old priest's reaction addresses her complaint: "'Christ will come like that!' he said in a loud gay voice and wiped his hand over his mouth and stood there, gaping." The Christian mystery is the coming of Christ into a situation he did not create, original sin. But the priest's next murmur, "The Transfiguration," names the redemptive effect of Christ's transforming grace. O'Connor describes

Mrs. McIntyre's face posed in "a set puritanical expression" that reacts by blushing. "Christ in the conversation embarrassed her the way sex had her mother." Faith and religion are at best ephemeral for her. When Mrs. McIntyre says, "He didn't have to come in the first place," the ambiguity of "he" in their exchange adds further irony. The priest's reply, "He came to redeem us" (317), connects original sin and redemption in an evangelizing response.

O'Connor's purpose becomes all the more evident when the next paragraph shifts attention to the return of Mr. Shortley to solve her dilemma of where to find a white man to replace Mr. Guizac. We recall the earlier description of the dying Mrs. Shortley contemplating "for the first time the tremendous frontiers of her true country." Mrs. McIntyre "had the feeling that she was the one returning, after a long miserable trip, to her own place." She is on the brink of her most definitive breakthrough. She will soon discover and begin to reclaim her own identity as a graced person. But first she must be displaced from her "own place" of original sin. She must yield to the misery of her own making in order for grace to be believable. Mrs. McIntyre's realization that she has been missing Mrs. Shortley's company proves to be one of her final mistaken perceptions. There is a three-day interlude after which she gets over the death, symbolic of her own potential for resurrection life.

Mr. Shortley's physical appearance suggests his identity as the devil of this O'Connor story. The cliché that runs like a refrain throughout the story proves literally true when Mrs. McIntyre rehires him: "The devil you know is better than the devil you don't" (299). He wears a shirt "with red and blue palm trees" and looks like "a man who had gone for a long time without water." The desert environs of his recent sojourn are unmistakable. But this is no desert father according to the Christian design. He is no doubt the devil who is familiar with the desert as the tempter of souls. One imagines him having fled from some harrowing exorcism by an authentic modern desert father and returning now to Mrs. McIntyre's farm. "The change in his face seemed to have come from the inside" and he has deeper "hollows in his long bitten blistered face." This description contrasts him with the Guizacs, who are described as "getting fat" because finally the "hollows had come out of their cheeks." Mr. Shortley's xenophobia vis-à-vis "foreigners" fuels Mrs. McIntyre's resolve to hire him and fire Mr. Guizac. But in the midst of his World War I recollection of a man throwing a hand grenade (a man who resembles Mr. Guizac), she momentarily glimpses an important truth that she nonetheless ignores: "But Mr. Guizac is a Pole, he's not a German." O'Connor contrasts Mr. Shortley's recognition of the Negroes' "limitations" with Mr. Guizac's expectation that they "work as hard as he worked himself." It is a stark, symbolic representation of original sin versus grace. O'Connor adds a subtle element to this symbolism by having the priest next admit that Mrs. McIntyre has "no legal obligation" to keep the Displaced Person if he is unsatisfactory; instead he introduces "the moral" obligation. Law and grace are classic metaphors for the contrast between Mrs. McIntyre's puritanism and the old priest's Catholic ethos.

O'Connor cannot resist the ironic metaphor of Mr. Shortley's nativism ("a man that's fought and bled and died in the service of his native [sic] and don't get the consideration of one of them like them he was fighting"); it serves to remind the reader of Mr. Shortley's exile from the "true country" of grace that his wife has begun, through death, to contemplate. The priest's persistent and patient visits to convert Mrs. McIntyre by instructions on the sacraments and Catholic dogma have the opposite effect upon her. The most telling exchange during their visits occurs as he ventures to explain, "...when God sent his Only Begotten Son, Jesus Christ our Lord...as a Redeemer to mankind...," only to meet her interruption, "Father Flynn!...I want to talk to you about something serious." She discredits his evangelization with her proclamation: "'As far as I'm concerned,' she said and glared at him fiercely, 'Christ was just another D.P.'" The truth of this statement escapes her. It will only be when Mrs. McIntyre witnesses the death of the long-suffering Mr. Guizac that O'Connor succeeds in showing this mystery of faith reaching her consciousness. And then, she will find that it was "as if he spoke of something that had happened yesterday in town" (320). She ends their visit with a striking inversion of the same gospel call (Matt 18:3–4) that Manley Pointer quoted and then promptly ignored, "He who losest his life shall find it" (272): "She told him how the poor who looked rich were the poorest of all because they had the most to keep."

The subsequent description of Mrs. McIntyre's beginning to look "thin" and "fidgety," "as if something were wearing her down from the inside" (321), alerts the reader to her self-destructive behavior. The final five pages of the story unfold some of O'Connor's most compelling images of the Christian mystery. The priest again confronts her to think about the Holocaust's "ovens and boxcars and the camps and the sick children and Christ our Lord." Her rebuttal is to retreat to her practical, one-dimensional stance: "He's [the Displaced Person, Mr. Guizac] extra and he's upset the balance around here...and there are no ovens here and no camps and no Christ our Lord..." (322). The echo of The Misfit from the title story of this collection galvanizes the complex of symbols in the story. The escaped convict said, "Jesus thown everything off balance," and now Mrs. McIntyre admits her refusal to accept the same mystery. It comes with an outright denial of the knowledge of both evil and good.

Her claims on paradise are short-lived. No sooner has she spoken than the tempter steps out of the final coil in this story's lethal spiral. While Mrs. McIntyre is warning Mr. Guizac of her financial obligations, Mr. Shortley stealthily moves under the guise of the serpent in the Garden of Eden: "At the other end of the barn, she saw a long beak-nosed shadow glide like a snake halfway up the sunlit open door and stop." He personifies the tempter's ability to distort, to seduce people into choosing an apparent good. Sulk, the young Negro, falls victim to Mr. Shortley's demonic conspiracy. He conjures up "the power of making other people see his logic" (323) by asking Sulk why he doesn't return to Africa. He makes the distinction that Sulk's grandfather was "brought." "It's the people that run away from where they come from that I ain't got any use for," says Mr. Shortley. He adds one final appeal by pointing to the barrier of language. According to Mr. Shortley, "our mistake" is "letting all them people onto English"; he predicts that there would be less trouble "if everybody only knew his own language." O'Connor strikes the perfect symbol to identify Mr. Shortley with pride. It is the myth of the Tower of Babel (Gen 11:1–9) that narrates the confusion of languages as the consequence of the ambition to be immortalized by building a tower to the heavens. This pride is symbolically reversed in the Pentecost phenomenon when everyone hears and understands Peter's preaching of the paschal mystery of Christ (Acts 2:5–13), despite their different languages. Mr. Shortley usurps the place of God, ignoring the very biblical saying that he repeats: "Revenge is mine, saith the Lord" (324).

In the final scene, Mr. Guizac is repairing the small tractor. Mrs. McIntyre postpones her "unpleasant duty" of firing him because she first wants Sulk and Mr. Shortley to leave them alone. O'Connor describes her "stamping her feet" on this cold morning to ward off the "paralysis." She has "cold feet" in every sense of the phrase. Her heart and arteries constrict, explaining her poor circulation and symbolizing her lack of compassion. Mr. Shortley starts up the large tractor, "warmed by it as if its heat and strength sent impulses up through him that he obeyed instantly." His obedience to these impulses is a perfect metaphor for concupiscence, the inclination to sin that results because our freedom is damaged by original sin. But he compounds the sin by premeditation and the knowledge of the murderous consequences about to happen. On cue, Sulk moves out of the way ("as if a spring in the earth had released him") of the tractor whose brake Mr. Shortley has disengaged. The tractor heads for Mr. Guizac's mud-splattered boots and body lying totally vulnerable in the path of the rolling tractor. Few lines in O'Connor's fiction implicate her characters in evil as distinctly as the next one. Mrs. McIntyre remembers both Mr. Shortley's calculated inertia and the fact "that she had started to shout to the Displaced Person but that she had not" (325). In an instant, her eyes, Mr. Shortley's eyes, and Sulk's eyes meet "in collusion" and conspiracy against the victim and his backbone cracks under the weight of the tractor.

The earlier allusion to the priest's speaking of Christ's redemptive sacrifice "as if it had happened yesterday in town" (320) is made manifest as Mr. Guizac's family gathers at the foot of his cross. This mid-twentieth-century crucifixion is as heinous as the Holocaust from which the Displaced Person and his family have fled. The priest bends over to offer communion *(viaticum)* to the dying man. The symbolism of the Eucharist as the church's thanksgiving and both the sacrifice of Christ and the ongoing sacrifice of the faithful members of the Church anchors the story in redemptive grace. Once again, the human mind fails when there is the epiphany of mystery in O'Connor's fiction. "[Mrs. McIntyre's] mind was not taking hold of all that was happening. She felt that she was in some foreign country where the people bent over the body were natives, and she watched like a stranger...." It is a perfectly ironic reversal as she is ushered from the precincts of original sin into the "true country" of grace and redemption.

The final paragraph of the story reads almost like a coda to this narrative and perhaps even to this entire collection, *A Good Man Is Hard to Find*. Mr. Shortley, Sulk, and Astor abandon Mrs. McIntyre. She is left helpless and becomes a victim ("she came down with a nervous affliction"). The farm that she had made into an idol is auctioned off "at a loss" (326) and her health declines as paralysis and Parkinson's symptoms combine with weakening vision and the total loss of speech. She is ironically rendered absolutely dependent upon the "colored woman" who attends her needs. O'Connor achieves in Mrs. McIntyre the kind of human suffering self-imposed by sin that makes this story more credible than her earlier effort with Hazel Motes at the conclusion of *Wise Blood*. In helping her readers to recognize sin, she succeeds in making grace believable.

"The Displaced Person" ends with the report that "Not many people remembered to come out to the country to see her except the old priest." His weekly visits ostensibly offer her an explanation of the doctrines of the Church. However, at a deeper level, O'Connor shows us that this eighty-year-old priest teaches her the corporal works of mercy. As her body shrivels and atrophies, his fidelity and love feed her spirit. It is a telling portrait of the old priest's life as Eucharist. Perhaps this is O'Connor's way of signaling that Mrs. McIntyre's "country" has become the "true country" of grace, the environs of her displacement where redemptive suffering has brought her. The final sentence of the story is not really a contrast between the dying Mrs. McIntyre and the proud peacock who is fed from the priest's "bag of breadcrumbs" (327). He also feeds her. But his faithful visits and pastoral love are a "showing" of the mysteries of faith, true nurture, and in that way more than in his parroting of formulas as he "explain[s] the doctrines of the Church." Already he recognizes in Mrs. McIntyre the beginnings of the transfiguration which he identified with the peacock's display of the "green-gold haze over his head" (317). Flannery O'Connor's genius radiates through this climactic, concluding story in *A Good Man Is Hard to Find*, showing us how redemption and glory, crucifixion and transfiguration, are a single paschal action.

Chapter Five

Violent Grace:
The Violent Bear It Away

I have got to the point now where I keep thinking more and more about the presentation of love and charity, or better call it grace, as love suggests tenderness, whereas grace can be violent or would have to be to compete with the kind of evil I can make concrete.
　　　　—Letter to Andrew Lytle, 4 February 1960

In a letter to "A" three years after the publication of *Wise Blood,* Flannery O'Connor honestly admitted that Hazel Motes's self-blinding was problematic because he did not seem "very human" (963). She consciously strove to remedy this dimension of her writing in her second novel, *The Violent Bear It Away.* Its protagonists, Mason Tarwater, Francis Marion Tarwater, and George Rayber especially, emerge as fully human and complex characters. The first novel had been five years in the making and this second would occupy her imaginative powers for seven years.

This span in United States history—from late 1952 through 1960—encompassed dramatic events: U.S. troops' involvement in the Korean War; the supreme court's ruling on public school integration, *Brown v. Board of Education of Topeka* in 1954; Senator Joseph McCarthy's Communist witch-hunts menacing literary artists, movie producers, and theater personalities; the Soviet Union's 1958 launch of Sputnik and the reaction that gave birth to America's space program and new emphasis upon students' science studies. O'Connor voiced her lament over the continuing drift of the culture in one late 1958 letter: "...the religious sense seems to be bred out of [modern people] in the kind of society we've lived in since the 18th century. And it's bred out of them double quick now by the religious substitutes for religion" (1077). America beckoned for prophets to awaken it from spiritual complacency. Flannery O'Connor fixed upon this very metaphor, the prophet, as the fulcrum for her new novel.

She describes *The Violent Bear It Away* as "a novel built around a baptism" (*HB*, 341)—and an initiation story it is. However, the art of this O'Connor novel becomes fully apparent only when the reader appreciates the symbolism of "the prophet" and her imaginative presentation of the violence of grace in conflict with concrete evil. She was well aware of a blind spot in the audience's field of vision: "[T]he modern reader is so far de-Christianized that he doesn't recognize the Devil when he see him..." (*HB*, 361). Her new novel offers all the density and intensity of fully human characters engaged in spiritual struggle. My analysis of the novel addresses four elements: (1) a theological understanding of prophet vis-à-vis Mason Tarwater and Francis Marion Tarwater; (2) O'Connor's meticulous development of Rayber; (3) the necessary presence of Bishop, the idiot child; and (4) Francis Marion Tarwater's experience of grace and O'Connor's ecumenical pioneering.

A THEOLOGY OF PROPHET

Walter Brueggemann is one of the foremost contemporary theologians studying the prophets and their biblical literature. He identifies the task of prophetic ministry: "...to nurture, nourish, and evoke a consciousness and perception alternative to the consciousness and perception of the dominant culture around us." He contrasts this definition with both conservative and liberal misconceptions and reductionisms: the prophet as future-teller, predictor of ominous things to come; or the prophet as voice of righteous indignation or social action. Brueggemann insists that contemporary preoccupation with exclusively future or present realities inadequately comprehends what is at issue in the Israelite understanding of prophecy. A twofold alternative consciousness emerges in the prophet: (1) to criticize; and (2) to energize. In the first instance, the prophetic consciousness dismantles the institutions, power structures, and prevailing consciousness of the dominant culture. In the second instance, it energizes persons and communities by God's promise of a "new time" and a "new situation" toward which the community of faith may move.[1] Brueggemann points to the contemporary American ethos of consumerism to illustrate. Persons and even Church institutions in the United States are so inculturated into this dominant culture of consumerism, with its idols and illusions, that we are not conscious of any liberating alternative or even the need for one.

> The internal cause of such enculturation is our loss of identity through the abandonment of the faith tradition. Our consumer culture is organized against history. There is a depreciation of memory and a ridicule of hope, which means that everything must be held in the now, either an urgent now or an eternal now. Either way, a community rooted in energizing memories and summoned by radical hopes is a curiosity and a threat in such a culture. When we suffer from amnesia every form of serious authority for faith is in question, and we live unauthorized lives of faith....[2]

Because O'Connor describes herself as a "God conscious writer" (942), she promotes the viability of this prophetic alternative. Rayber repeatedly insists that his uncle, Mason Tarwater, personifies the prophet who is "almost extinct" (339, 348, 378), reminding us how easily the prophet's radically countercultural alternative can be domesticated. Brueggemann alertly points out that while none of us relishes criticism, neither do we relish energizing because it demands something costly from us. He returns to the dominating figure of Moses as the source of our primary understandings of Israel to evoke a principle that informs a theological interpretation of O'Connor's imaginative efforts:

> [T]he shaping of Israel took place from inside its own experience and confession of faith and not through external appropriation from somewhere else....I am urging in parallel fashion that if the church is to be faithful it must be formed and ordered from the inside of its experience and confession and not by borrowing from sources external to its own life.[3]

Understanding Moses' Exodus ministry as socially revolutionary in terms of "newness and radical innovativeness" (by breaking with the social reality of Pharaoh's Egypt: slavery, oppression, and exile), Brueggemann's insight bears special scrutiny. He places the event in the category of "revelation" because it is unprecedented. "Prophecy is born," he reminds us, "precisely in that moment when the emergence of social political reality is so radical and inexplicable that it has nothing less than a theological cause." The break of the Israelites from Egypt's imperial reality is two-dimensional: (1) Moses dismantles Egypt's "religion of static triumphalism" by exposing the impotence of their gods and disclosing an alternative religion of the freedom of God; and (2) Moses dismantles Egypt's politics of oppression and exploitation by countering these with a politics of justice and compassion.[4] In other words:

> [I]f a God is disclosed who is free to come and go, free from and even against the regime, free to hear and even answer

slave cries, free from all proper godness as defined by the
empire, then it will bear decisively upon sociology because
the freedom of God will surface in the brickyards and manifest itself as justice and compassion.

...The point that prophetic imagination must ponder is
that there is no freedom of God without the politics of justice and compassion, and there is no politics of justice and
compassion without a religion of the freedom of God.[5]

Although Walter Brueggemann is professor of Old Testament
at Columbia Theological Seminary in Decatur, Georgia, he shares
much more than geography with O'Connor. His presentation of
the theology of prophecy helps us to understand that a changed
social reality comes about only when the false pretenses of the
oppressive culture's myths and gods are made apparent and then
dismantled. The unfolding of plagues against the Egyptians ultimately proves that the gods of the oppressors "could not" do
what the God of the Israelites could do (Exod 8:18). False claims
to authority, power, and promises are unmasked. Brueggemann
connects the beginnings of prophetic criticism with another
dimension, the *grieving* complaint of Israel in Exodus 2:23–25:
"Israel groaned under their bondage...and cried out for
help....And God heard their groaning, and God remembered his
covenant." He calls that cry "the primal criticism." When
Yahweh acknowledges the grievance, it signifies that this first step
permits the new reality to emerge: "I have seen the affliction of
my people who are in Egypt, and have heard their cry....I know
their sufferings, and I have come down to deliver them out of the
land of the Egyptians" (Exod 3:7–8). Brueggemann borrows
Dorothee Soelle's suggestion that prophetic criticism mobilizes
people to "their real restless grief" and nurtures them away from
the numbed and dull empire, "the cry-hearers who are inept at listening and indifferent in response."[6]

Brueggemann's analysis of Israel's prophets contrasts them
with the dominant culture's "royal consciousness." When God
becomes so captive that the king is completely relaxed in God's

presence, the prophetic consciousness fails and the royal consciousness dominates. Brueggemann uses the example of Solomon
to confirm that the prophet's purpose is much more radical and
profound than social change. Solomon's kingdom offered the possibility of affluence and access to God in the Temple, dissipating
the prophet's appeal for an alternative. He describes the myth
embraced by the Jerusalem establishment during Solomon's reign:
"...the king-temple-royal-city complex guarantees social and cosmic order, protecting persons and communities from anarchy.
Such a faith "tended to give questions of order priority over questions of justice."[7]

In the wake of the Solomonic establishment comes the loss of
passion, the inability to care or to suffer. (As I will analyze
momentarily, this vacuum becomes the storm center of
O'Connor's *The Violent Bear It Away;* it both names and interprets the matrix of Rayber's struggle.) Brueggemann names this
numbness and apathy as the absence of *pathos.* As a result, the
royal regime "manages" external behavior. In other words, people become preoccupied with proper behavior "because they are
no longer able to experience their own *experience.*" There is an
absence of adequate symbols to counter the official denial of
death's reality and potential. We discover the theologian's antidote: "The task of prophetic imagination is to cut through the
numbness, to penetrate the self-deception so that the God of endings is confessed as Lord." Brueggemann's outline of the prophet's
task unfolds three distinct parts that parallel in an uncanny way
the dramatic action of *The Violent Bear It Away:*

> (a) To *offer symbols* that are adequate to the horror and mas-
> siveness of the experience which evokes numbness and
> requires denial....[T]he prophet is to reactivate out of our
> historical past symbols that always have been vehicles for
> redemptive honesty....
> (b) To *bring to public expression those very fears and terrors*
> that have been denied so long and suppressed so deeply that
> we do not know they are there....

(c) To *speak metaphorically but concretely about the real deathliness that hovers over us and gnaws within us,* and to speak neither in rage nor in cheap grace, but with the candor born of anguish and passion.[8]

With this threefold task, the prophet becomes much more than a scolding, reprimanding figure. By voicing the dread of endings and the collapse of our security and self-sufficiency, the prophet invites the king to experience what he most fears and denies: that the royal consciousness and perception of reality is ending. For that reason, Brueggemann argues that the capacity of the prophet to use lamentation language and a symbolic death scene makes real what the royal consciousness must see, but resists seeing. Such grief and crying in pathos becomes the ultimate form by which the prophet criticizes the status quo. It announces a definitive end—and makes way for a new beginning.[9] Seen against this theological understanding of Israel's prophets, O'Connor's "novel built around a baptism" (*HB,* 341) explodes with meaning. Christian initiation is the story of conversion, but also of the dawning of prophetic consciousness.

Definitive endings and new beginnings punctuate *The Violent Bear It Away.* Two of the novel's major characters, Mason Tarwater and his great-nephew, Francis Marion Tarwater, are ultimately defined in terms of prophetic consciousness. The opening paragraphs introduce the dead man by way of flashback: "The old man, who said he was a prophet, had raised the boy to expect the Lord's call himself and to be prepared for the day he would hear it." Mason had educated Tarwater about the world's rejection of prophets. But more important than such "trifling" evils, he prepared him to expect evils "that come from the Lord and burn the prophet clean" (332). In the second paragraph, the narrator introduces the theme of rescue. Mason's nephew, George Rayber, was raising Francis Marion Tarwater after his sister died giving birth. A prelude to the story (again by way of flashback) informs us that Mason himself had earlier lived for three months in Rayber's house, thinking it was "Charity," only to discover that his atheistic nephew's "ideas" were diametrically opposed to his own prophet's worldview. When Rayber's surveillance of Mason's behavior results in a psychology journal article demeaning him, the old man rages, rescues the infant Tarwater, and flees to the margins of society into the woods called Powderhead. He later declares that he was "Betrayed" and shamed (344) by Rayber's secular humanist analysis of his life. His metaphor convinces the reader that he, Mason, is the true prophet who criticizes Rayber and energizes Tarwater to resist the dominant culture personified by Rayber: "I been leavened by the yeast he don't believe in." He adds, "and I won't be burned" (344), precipitating one of the novel's major symbolic actions. The prophet gives the boy the charge to bury him—not burn his body—upon his death and to baptize the idiot child named Bishop, subsequently born to Rayber and the wife who abandoned them.

The opening sentence of *The Violent Bear It Away* reveals that Tarwater refused to carry out his great-uncle's request that his body receive a proper Christian burial—"with the sign of its Saviour at the head of the grave"—and that the devoted Negro named Buford Munson finished the task. Tarwater defies his great-uncle and in his drunken stupor blasphemously burns the house where he thought his uncle's body still lay. He discovers the truth of Mason's burial by Buford only in the final pages of the novel. Tarwater's romanticized notions of the prophet veer away from Mason's talk of "the sweat and stink of the cross, of being born again to die, and spending eternity eating the bread of life." He prefers fiery visionaries and the classical prophet's symbolic actions—Moses striking water from the rock, Joshua making the sun stand still, or Daniel staring down the lions in the pit. Tarwater cannot countenance Mason's conviction that his calling comes in terms of the mundane charge to baptize Bishop, the retarded child of Rayber.

The boy mistakes for genuine prophetic visions his uncle's disappearance in the woods for days at a time, after which Mason returned looking "bedraggled and hungry," looking as if he had "wrestled with a wildcat" (334–35). Those interludes were brought about after the old prophet recognized his failure to rescue Rayber, whom he had also baptized and instructed "in the facts of his Redemption" at the age of seven. Mason's depression is evident as he halts in midstory and stares in front of him, "as if he were looking into a pit which had opened up before his feet" (333–34). The abyss that yawns before the prophet is nothing less than despair over failing in his vocation. His thrashing out his "peace with the Lord" for days in the woods is O'Connor's euphemism alluding to the great-uncle's avocation, producing and selling moonshine liquor. Drunkenness has been an occasional escape for the old prophet—"A prophet with a still" (358), as Tarwater's new stranger-friend (alias the devil) mocks Mason—as liquor is for Tarwater at the novel's opening. Nonetheless, the crucial encounter between Mason's prophetic consciousness and the twentieth century's "royal consciousness" personified by Rayber and his embrace of secular humanism and scientific techniques is starkly drawn.

O'Connor presents the immediate fact of Mason's death as a transitional moment foreshadowing definitive endings and new beginnings: "The boy knew he would have to bury the old man before anything would begin" (336). The imagery reflects Paul's baptismal metaphors of the *death* of the "old man" and the *birth* of the new man, "Christ is living in me" (Gal 2:20; cf. 1 Cor 15:49) and the grain of wheat dying in order to produce much fruit (John 12:25). This pattern of death and resurrection-life, the pattern at the center of prophetic consciousness, reverberates throughout the novel. Rehearsing his funeral by lying in the coffin, the old man says with satisfaction, "This is the end of us all" (337). Tarwater's glee about his freedom from school ironically dissolves when his great-uncle picks up the story of the boy's life with Rayber and the old man's liberation from the asylum where Rayber's mother had him confined for four years: "Well that wasn't the end of it!...You were born in bondage and baptized into freedom, into the death of the Lord, into the death of the Lord Jesus Christ" (342).

Whenever Mason begins talking to Tarwater, the boy intuitively interjects, "get on with the rest of it," because he knows that a story "always had to be taken to completion" or ending (372). The old man's appeal to Tarwater is reduced to essential Christian symbols that bear prophetic echoes—"All I'm asking you to do is to get me in the ground and set up a cross" (338). When Tarwater objects that he might lack the strength to bother with "trifles" of setting up a cross, Mason insists that the burden will rest on Tarwater because the prophet knows that his school-teacher nephew would blasphemously have him cremated. After allusions to plague, sword, and fire—from the prophet's lexicon of apocalyptic death imagery—Mason shouts the prophet's fundamental preoccupation with liberation: "I saved you to be free, your own self...and not a piece of information inside [Rayber's] head!" (339).

The truth of Mason's insight collides with Rayber's surmise that the challenge of his raising Tarwater involves "a monumental job of reconstruction" (391) according to his post-Christian consciousness. When they finally meet in chapter 3, O'Connor laces Rayber's first words with irony. He tells the boy that Mason did him "a great injustice" and "It's a blessing he's dead at last." Without resurrection faith rooted in the prophetic consciousness, death does not liberate for authentic new life or justice or compassion. Rayber can boast that he will make a man out of Tarwater. His pride swells to the point that he is oblivious to Tarwater's body language described in O'Connor's deftly drawn imagery:

> The boy's face darkened. His expression hardened until it was a fortress wall to keep his thoughts from being exposed; but the schoolteacher did not notice any change. He gazed through the actual insignificant boy before him to an image of him that he held fully developed in his mind. (388)

Rayber's announcement that he will get Tarwater "started now in the right direction" adds a final ironic note. His efforts to "turn" around, or convert, the boy to his own mindset and consciousness becomes a challenge to everything that Mason had initiated. Tarwater's "fortress wall" expression is a harbinger of the struggle to come. What is even more devastating is Rayber's ambition to re-create Tarwater in his own image and likeness—at least the sanitized image and likeness that he holds in his rationalistic head. The most damning description of Rayber comes in the detail: the schoolteacher gazes past the boy who stands directly before him, a boy dubbed "insignificant." He can no more accept the given reality of Tarwater, disciple of Mason, than he can accept the flawed creation, his retarded son.

O'Connor's imagination gives evidence here of a response (both conscious and unconscious) to William F. Lynch's plea for the literary artist to exercise the analogical imagination. Rayber holds the Manichean theology that distorts and dissociates the body from the mind; he yields to the temptation to win immediate freedom by seeking quick infinities through the rapid and clever manipulation of the finite; he refuses to acknowledge let alone penetrate and pass through the rigors, densities, limitations, and decisions of any created reality that he dismisses as "insignificant." The prophet's analogical ("Christic") imagination embraces a flawed creation because the prophet knows that only through what Lynch calls the positive and athletic penetration of the finite do we arrive at the infinite. And so, O'Connor offers the drama of Tarwater's ambivalence and struggle over his calling as a prophet. He knows a "terrible disappointment" over inheriting Mason's hunger for the bread of life and Jesus. He fears the truth of his calling and tries to keep his vision fixed on the surface of things—a spade, a hoe, a mule's hindquarters, or the ploughed red furrow—and "avoid this threatened intimacy of creation" (343). Tarwater fears that, like Adam, he will be expected to "name" each thing, revealing his awe at the primordial human contemplative who penetrates illusion and touches reality.

O'Connor's humor erupts in the scene of the first encounter between the uncle and nephew. The traveling copper flue salesman, Mr. Meeks (a surrogate for the devil) drives Tarwater to the city and his uncle's house after he leaves Powderhead. His axiom, "love was the only policy that worked 95% of the time," dissolves into a banality because it is only a lubricant to manipulate customers. A client's wife who dies of cancer evokes from Meeks a grateful, uncaring sigh; death only means "that's one less to remember" (362). Tarwater suddenly thinks they are headed in the wrong direction when he sees the distant glow of lights from the city that he mistakes for the fire at Powderhead. It is a symbolic response. Tarwater resists the seduction of Meeks's Calvinism that preaches hard work as the path to success: the Hard Lesson from Life degree. True to the military tactics of his Revolutionary War namesake, Francis Marion, he evades Meeks's questions. He resists the salesman's exploitative offer to employ him if he were jobless and hungry next week. Even more revealing is Meeks's condescending attitude toward the girlfriend he telephones—and toward Tarwater's awe at the telephone Meeks dials to connect him to his uncle. The irony is that the mentally challenged child, Bishop, answers the phone and breathes heavily like "someone struggling to breathe in water." This stunning "revelation" that the boy cannot yet decipher (383) foreshadows his wrestling with Mason's claim that baptizing the child is the beginning of Tarwater's prophetic life and the tragedy of the child's drowning.

When Rayber finally opens the door that Tarwater is kicking with his work shoe, the uncle stands symbolically with the face of a sleepwalker "who wakes and sees some horror of his dreams take shape before him." The irony is prescient because Rayber will progress to precisely such a horror in his battle of wills with the boy. Rayber mutters that he is "deaf" and retrieves the ear plug and metal box of his hearing aid—symbolic of his inability to hear or respond to God's Word preached by the prophet. His weak eyes require eyeglasses that O'Connor describes as "twin glass caverns" to remedy nearsightedness—another symbolic clue to alert the reader that Rayber is a man who lacks depth of vision in every sense. When Tarwater thinks that Rayber's head runs by electricity (386), O'Connor's comic sensibility indicates that this man is completely artificial and mechanical. There is an echo of Meeks's advice about the city's ethos with its gadgetry as surrogate deities: "Meeks told him to learn to work every machine he saw" (383).

Once again flashbacks allow O'Connor to dramatize the interaction between Mason and Tarwater and fill in pivotal elements of plot. The boy strains to remember Mason's description of Rayber's face in anticipation of their imminent encounter. When the old prophet admits that he has forgotten the color of Rayber's eyes, he emphasizes that he knows "the look" and "what's behind them": "Nothing. He's full of nothing." Even worse, Mason nails his nephew with an apt description: "He don't know it's anything he can't know." Rayber's satisfied Enlightenment pride, magnified in mid-twentieth-century science and secular humanism, admits no place for sacred mystery. Mason reminds the boy how he became the victim of Rayber's testing his head and attempting to control his thoughts. He warns against contacting the uncle: "And before long you wouldn't belong to your self no more, you would belong to him" (366).

The old prophet's stories unfold and reveal Rayber's personality. When Mason went to live with him for three months, he baptized Tarwater. But Rayber turned it into a blasphemous joke, pouring the water of his baby bottle a second time—over his bottom—and repeating the baptismal formula. The baptism occurred within ten minutes of Mason's arrival. O'Connor's irony uncoils in Rayber's initial refusal to let Mason live with him and interfere with the upbringing of his nephew, Tarwater. His atheistic stance contradicts the old man's faith: "He's going to be brought up to expect exactly what he can do for himself. He's going to be his own savior. He's going to be free." That absolute autonomy abhors any admission of dependence on another. As we will see in analyzing O'Connor's development of Rayber in the middle section of the novel, it is a stance that ends in spiritual inertia.

The final principal character appears in the wake of Tarwater's encounter with Rayber. The diminutive figure of Bishop is described earlier by Mason. This "dim-witted" child is the offspring of Rayber and the welfare woman, Bernice Bishop, who had accompanied him to Powderhead in an attempt to reclaim Tarwater. Rayber's later recollection of his violent abuse of Bernice—a source of enduring satisfaction for him (442)—corrects the distorted impression of his victimization in the marriage she abandoned. Mason's shooting of Rayber's ear is reminiscent of the impetuous act of Peter in cutting off the ear of the soldier when Jesus is betrayed and arrested in the Garden of Gethsemane. It is ironic that Matthew's gospel (from which the title of the book is taken) presents Jesus responding: "Those who live by the sword will perish by the sword" (Matt 26:53). As a symbol, Rayber's defective eardrum tells us that he is not only physically but spiritually deaf, unable to hear or respond to the prophet's proclamation of God's Word as an energizing word of mercy and unconditional love.

DEVELOPING THE CHARACTER OF RAYBER

On New Year's Day 1956, Flannery O'Connor writes to "A": "My novel is at an impasse." She had written to her publisher Robert Giroux in mid-1953 that she expected writing *The Violent Bear It Away* to take a long time. "It's a theme that requires prayer and fasting to make it get anywhere," she indicates, and adds a characteristically comic note, "I manage to pray but am a very sloppy faster" (*HB, 59*). In July 1957 O'Connor again writes to "A," ruminating on the title of the book and remarking that it "seems" that now more than ever before the kingdom of God "has to be taken by violence, or not at all." Her own prophetic task as a fiction writer becomes self-evident in the same letter:

"You have to push as hard as the age that pushes against you" (*HB*, 229). Finally, in April 1959 the long awaited breakthrough arrives. She writes first to Catherine Carter, her editor, advising her to interrupt her reading of the manuscript and "wait until I send you the new middle" (*HB*, 327). Two days later she explains the creative process more succinctly in a letter to Sally and Robert Fitzgerald.

> Rayber has been the trouble all along. I think one thing that is needed is to make his reactions to the boy more dramatic and have some of the stuff happen other than in flashbacks. Anyway I aim to do a good deal more work on the middle section.
> ...Just tear the ms. up....I am going to renovate the whole thing (HB, 329).

Less than three weeks later she explains to Caroline Gordon Tate, her most loyal and trusted critic, that she had wrongly telescoped the middle of the novel in order to get on with the end. "[B]ut now that I've got to the end, I see there isn't enough middle" (*HB*, 332). A week later she writes to "A" that she will persevere through the summer on the novel and adds, "It is too good a book not to be a better one" (1096). By October of 1959 the manuscript is complete and she remarks to John Hawkes that Rayber "was always the stumbling block" and that "I spent most of the seven years on Rayber" (1108).

To appreciate fully *The Violent Bear It Away* is to recognize O'Connor's meticulous development of Rayber as a very human and complex character. The structure of the novel assigns six of the twelve chapters to this process,[10] indicating how she invests half of her creative effort in Rayber's struggle. Four months after the publication of the novel she writes to "A" that she has sent her a copy of William F. Lynch's *Christ and Apollo*. She recommends it for good answers to "A's" quandary about responding to people who ask a writer "what-are-you-saying." "There is no answer for them," she insists, "except to say you are saying what can't be said otherwise than with your whole book, that you can't substitute an abstraction and have the same thing" (*HB*, 400). It is no coincidence that *Christ and Apollo* is on her mind as O'Connor meticulously renovates the "caricature" of Rayber that she confesses she had made of him in 1954 (*HB*, 352). Lynch's concrete examples of the anagogical imagination reinforce her conviction that the fiction writer does *not tell* but *shows* her audience the truth through the actions of very human characters.

Rayber's habit of abstraction pointed out earlier is captured in one of Mason's graphic metaphors. In chapter 2, young Tarwater ironically puzzles over why Rayber did not "use his head" and make a greater effort to rescue him from Mason. He suggests that he might have brought "the law" to Powderhead on his behalf. (Here is a subtle but unmistakable sign that Tarwater has not yet fully understood the prophet's alternative to Rayber's deathly status quo; he appeals for the law to restore order and mistakes the grace of a deeper freedom offered to him as Mason's apprentice.) The old prophet unmasks Rayber's trafficking in abstractions and fleeing from the dense, finite world: "It was because he found you a heap of trouble. He wanted it all in his head. You can't change a child's pants in your head" (378). The prophet's intuitive grasp of Rayber's narrow-mindedness unfolds in scene after scene in the middle of O'Connor's novel. Perhaps as nowhere else in her fiction she succeeds with Rayber in making "corruption believable before [she] can make the grace meaningful" (1182). The texture and complexity of the novel genre allows O'Connor to accomplish her most compelling drama of violent grace. She overcomes the temptation to reduce Rayber, who lives abstractly, to an abstraction. By discovering and developing his character, O'Connor takes her readers through the dense turmoil and finite pathos that Lynch identifies as the task of the anagogical imagination.

Before analyzing steps in Rayber's demise, it is crucial to realize that O'Connor carefully qualified her insight on the sequence of corruption-grace. In a 1963 letter to a new correspondent, she reminds Sister Mariella Gable that people who ask fiction writers "to make Christianity look desirable" distract a writer from "what you see" and seek a description of Christianity's "essence." But such an "Ideal Christianity," she reminds, doesn't exist because everything a human being touches ("even Christian truth") "he deforms slightly in his own image." Flannery considers this to be one of the effects of original sin. She finds Catholics acting as if this doctrine itself is "perverted" and an indicator of Calvinism. Her conclusion deserves to be pondered: "[Calvinists and Catholics who act like Calvinists] read a little corruption as total corruption" (1182). The vortex of pathos and despair that engulfs Rayber by the end of chapter 9 can easily sweep away readers in its wake. They risk missing how O'Connor makes grace even more meaningful as the father of the drowned-and-baptized boy anticipates "the raging pain, the intolerable hurt that was his due." When Rayber, however, "continued to feel nothing" (456), the irony brilliantly compounds.

On Halloween 1959, shortly after completing the writing of this novel, O'Connor writes to "A" to tell her that she "would have liked for [Rayber] to be saved, and it is ambiguous whether he may be or not" (*HB*, 357). Three weeks later she writes to John Hawkes and unequivocally reiterates an openness as far as her character's ultimate fate: "With trial and error I found that making Rayber pure evil made him a caricature and took away from the role of the old prophet since it left him nothing worth trying to save" (HB, 359). In the six chapters comprising the middle section of the novel, readers witness O'Connor's imagination creating Rayber (himself prone to abstraction) as her very human, concrete, and finite living person. At the core of his personality she equips him with a free will that galvanizes the action of the novel.

In chapter 2, just after the infant Tarwater's double baptism is recounted, Rayber's "rage" erupts in his confrontation with the prophet Mason, whom he claims "ruined my life." In a revealing exchange the schoolteacher compares his baptism by the old man when he was seven years old with the baptism of the infant Tarwater.

> "You're too blind to see what you did to me. A child can't defend himself. Children are cursed with believing. You pushed me out of the real world and I stayed out of it until I didn't know which was which. You infected me with your idiot hopes, your foolish violence. I'm not always myself, I'm not al..." but he stopped. He wouldn't admit what the old man knew. "There's nothing wrong with me," he said. "I've straightened the tangle you made. Straightened it by pure will power. I've made myself straight." (376–77)

Every line of Rayber's outburst brims with irony as the rest of the novel will evidence. Earlier in the same chapter we learn how Mason's sister, the mother of Rayber, had "worked a perfidy on him" (368) by having him confined to an insane asylum for four years. The fact is that she was a whore and Mason knew this about Rayber's mother and her moral lapses; that her daughter, Tarwater's mother, conceived him out of wedlock with the divinity student whom Rayber arranged to be her "lover"; and that Rayber's father, the divinity student, shot himself before Tarwater was born. This is the knowledge of evil that Mason remembers and Rayber denies. His protest that "There's nothing wrong with me," proves ironic in light of guilt over his father's desperate suicide and his own abandonment. The "perfidy" of Mason's sister is a betrayal of trust repeated when Rayber betrays trust and writes the journal article demeaning the old man's identity as prophet. The prophet Hosea's marriage to a wife who is a whore (the adultery metaphor of Israel the harlot breaking the covenant with Yahweh) echoes through O'Connor's novel. But true to his prophet's calling, Mason does not give up on Rayber. The cruelest irony comes later as Rayber relives the "viper's tangle" reminiscent of the François Mauriac novel by that title.

O'Connor ends chapter 3 with a cluster of events to set the stage for the middle and ending of the novel. Tarwater's first sight of Rayber's son, Bishop, comes with "the revelation" that his call to be a prophet and baptize the child is irrevocable and unavoidable, though he will resist and wrestle with this vocation and its meaning. It is Rayber who interrupts this vision and describes Tarwater's freedom after Mason's death as "just like coming out of the darkness into the light." It is especially ironic that the baptismal symbols of moving from darkness (sin) to light (Christ) are misstated by Rayber. For the first time the schoolteacher admits he is vulnerable. His mouth is "stretched painfully" as he explains Bishop to the boy. "All the things I would do for him—if it were any use—I'll do for you," he tells him. Then the innocent retarded child reaches his hand to "touch" Tarwater—an example of O'Connor's signature "gesture" that reveals grace—and he immediately knocks it away. In the wake of a primal violence, Tarwater's "vision" of the pair, father and son, prophetically intuits a truth: "The child might have been a deformed part of himself [Rayber] that had been accidentally revealed." Tarwater denies that he'll get used to the child in "clear and positive and defiant" words "like a challenge hurled in the face of his silent adversary" (388–90). Characters stake out polarized positions and part 1 of the novel ends. Both Rayber and Tarwater spend the rest of the novel struggling with illusions and discovering that their real adversary resides within.

O'Connor's fourth chapter opens part 2 of the novel with Rayber's euphoria over the return of his sister's son. He gazes on the sleeping Tarwater and admires him "like a man who sits before a treasure he is not yet convinced is real" (391). His emotions are described "like an intense stab of joy" because of a striking father-son physical resemblance. His purchase of new clothes (that Tarwater refuses to wear) is an attempt to symbolize "a new life" (392) for the boy. The baptismal symbolism of being "clothed in Christ" (Gal 3:27) is, however, ironically inverted. Rayber's defensive explanation for not risking Mason's gunshots and rescuing the boy proves equally ironic on two counts. First, he claims that "a dead man is not going to do you any good" and contradicts the first prophetic element—criticism of the status quo—climaxing in Christ's death and resurrection. Second, he claims that "This is our problem together" and projects onto Tarwater-the-fourteen-year-old his own resentment upon returning to Powderhead at the age of fourteen to curse Mason (395–96). It is the same rationalist psychologizing that he has used to discredit Mason in the journal article. Rayber confirms his resistance to the prophetic impulse as he explains how the city is run and "the duties of a good citizen" (398).

The boy suddenly recognizes the exact place in the city where he had leaned too far forward in the window of the lawyer's office and lost his hat. On that occasion the law could not assist Mason in wrestling the inheritance of Powderhead from Rayber as his successor. Now a symbolic grace comes as Tarwater is again "precariously balanced" in front of the garagelike pentecostal tabernacle. O'Connor knits the two incidents together through Rayber's observation that these two experiences in the city are unique times when the boy showed "a particular interest" (398). A poster advertises, "Hear the Carmodys for Christ"—an event unfolded in chapter 5. Tarwater finds an interrogative voice when his uncle ridicules the evangelist's resurrection belief. When the boy asks, "They won't rise again?" Rayber thrills over the fact that for the first time the boy seeks his opinion. It provides Rayber the occasion to observe Tarwater and reconsider a battery of psychological tests to "ferret out the center of the [boy's] emotional infection" (399).

But what the interlude triggers is a revelation of Rayber's own spiritual paralysis. We discover that the "outrageous" love he feels for Bishop leaves him "shocked and depressed" for days at a time. In keeping with his habit of abstraction, "love in general" evokes no fear in him. Nor is Rayber overcome by the utilitarian quality of what he considers to be "love" when it improves people.

> It was love without reason, love for something futureless, love that appeared to exist only to be itself, imperious and all

demanding, the kind that would cause him to make a fool of himself in an instant. And it only began with Bishop. It began with Bishop and then like an avalanche covered everything his reason hated. He always felt with it a rush of longing to have the old man's eyes—insane, fish-coloured, violent with their impossible vision of a world transfigured—turned on him once again. (401)

Unconditional love, the mystery of mercy that transfigures, both attracts and awes the secular humanist hiding behind his rational calculus. Once again, Mason epitomizes Brueggemann's prophetic consciousness as an alternative consciousness—heralding a vision impossible for those mired in the "royal consciousness" that is now manifest in post-Enlightenment, post-Christian scientific certitude. The prophet is not concerned to implement the vision because it must first be imagined before it can be implemented[11]— an aggravating element of the prophet's task.

Rayber calls this unconditional love a family "affliction...flowing from some ancient source, some desert prophet or pole-sitter," avalanching over everything his reason hated. Unlike Mason who submitted to it, Rayber staves it off. "What the boy would do hung in the balance," he concedes. The schoolteacher's claim to "a rigid ascetic discipline" (402) by his own admission collapses into "bare will." Rayber's rigidity compromises any asceticism; he lives so totally in the head that he violates the fundamental Christian principle of the incarnation, wrought memorably by William Butler Yeats: "The body is not bruised to pleasure soul."[12] Flannery explains her intent in a June 1959 letter: "The violent are not natural. St. Thomas's [Aquinas] gloss on this verse ["the violent bear it away"] is that the violent [whom] Christ is here talking about represent those ascetics who strain against mere nature. St. Augustine concurs" (1101). Authentic Christian ascetics such as the desert fathers practice and promote disciplines that ultimately reverence the body. Through renunciation, purity of heart, and freedom from the illusory cares of the world they reclaim the lost simplicity of Adam's freedom in paradise. They reclaim a contemplative intimacy with all creation[13]—the very discovery that Tarwater will make!

Once again, O'Connor employs the metaphor of the character "off balance" to dramatize the moment of grace offered; she places Tarwater's ongoing struggle—"his fate hung in the balance"—in striking contrast. Rayber's willful refusal resides for now in an abstraction: "He kept himself upright on a very narrow line between madness and emptiness, and when the time came for him to lose his balance, he intended to lurch toward emptiness and fall on the side of his choice" (403).

Chapter 5 revives the parade of evangelists in O'Connor's fiction. Seeing the child-evangelist Lucette eclipses the comic moments that open the chapter with Rayber's barefoot and pajama-clad chase as Tarwater wanders and then flees to the pentecostal tabernacle. Rayber's "transparent nightmare" erupts into consciousness. The schoolteacher reexperiences the event when his father reclaimed him from Mason. The adult Rayber resents the "childhood pain" that he associates with leading helpless children to baptism and faith. But he cringes when he recognizes that Lucette "was not a fraud,...only exploited" (411). Her evangelical patter recounts the major faith claims about Christ. Rayber ironically mistakes the "miraculous communication" (414) between him and the child. Instead of the possibility of him rescuing her, she bolts him by recognizing and pointing to him as a "damned soul" and asks if he is "deaf to the Lord's word." Rayber's only recourse is to snap the button on his hearing aid in a symbolic act of "irreversible defiance" (415). O'Connor allows Rayber his freedom to defy redemption in a way that makes his corruption believable. She also allows her imagination the freedom to discover his complex character.

The plot turns in chapter 6 as Rayber resolves to be infinitely patient with Tarwater and thereby win him over. He plans an excursion for the museum but they never arrive because en route there Bishop gallops into the shallow pool fed by the fountain at the center of the park. Moments earlier, the grip of Rayber's "hated love" has returned as Bishop sits in his lap. The habit of abstraction repeats: "He knew that if he could once conquer this pain, face it and with a supreme effort of his will refuse to feel it, he would be a free man." A revelation comes as the narrative confides to the reader Rayber's earlier failed attempt to drown Bishop. With perfect irony a newspaper caption accompanies the photograph of a rescuer administering artificial respiration beside the victim's kneeling father: "OVERJOYED FATHER SEES SON REVIVED" (419). Once again O'Connor ironically plays with Christian death and resurrection metaphors.

The Cherokee Lodge anchors the action in chapter 7. Rayber secretly plans a side trip from this ostensible fishing trip; he will take Tarwater to Powderhead to reveal and begin to heal the boy's psychological trauma. Tarwater's long face and bulb-shaped hat conjure up for Rayber the image of "a root jerked suddenly out of the ground and exposed to the light"—a metaphor for the schoolteacher's analytic designs on the boy's "compulsion." The woman at the lodge reception desk brings a new perspective on each character. When she questions whether the unkempt, taciturn Tarwater belongs with them, Rayber condescendingly claims him—"to impress on him that he was wanted, whether he cared to be wanted or not" (425). She observes Rayber's disheveled appearance and concludes that the schoolteacher is having a nervous breakdown.

Two simultaneous events in this chapter add significant momentum to the novel. First, Tarwater responds to the woman's reprimand, to "Mind how you talk" to the afflicted child, with an awakening realization. O'Connor describes her fierce look, "as if he had profaned the holy." Tarwater's total attention rivets on Bishop, "as if his gaze had slipped and fallen into the center of the child's eyes and was still falling down and down and down" (427). From this point onwards he makes eye contact with Bishop, symbolizing a new quality of relationship. The child's untied shoes, already noted by the woman, are thrust upward to

Tarwater as Bishop suddenly interrupts his stair climbing. "He leaned over and began to tie them." Only pages before, in chapter 6, Rayber had tied the same shoelaces, feeling the "hated love" grip him, only to refuse it with "a supreme effort of his will." Tarwater's tying the shoes surprises the woman because she had judged him as abusing the retarded child. Her confusion at "this act of kindness" calibrates with O'Connor's habit of offering a gesture of grace totally right but also surprisingly unexpected. If ever there was a contemporary reenactment of Jesus' footwashing at the last supper, here it is. In John's gospel (13:1–20), Jesus *not only tells* the disciples to "Love one another," he *shows* them how by humbling himself and washing their feet.

Romano Guardini, O'Connor's adopted theological mentor, had used the example of Francis of Assisi in the chapter of *The Lord* entitled "God's Humility." Francis was humble when he bowed before the poor, "as one whose heart has been instructed by God flings himself to the ground before the mystery of paltriness as before that of majesty." Guardini concluded that the God revealed in Jesus "must be one who loves," and so when Tarwater humbly bends down and ties Bishop's shoes, we discover through this subtle gesture how "love does such things."[14] When the woman sees and then discounts that she sees "something fleeing across the surface of [Tarwater's eyes], a lost light that came from nowhere and vanished into nothing," the tension of intent between drowning and baptizing Bishop reaches a crescendo. The resolution of this ambiguity has already been presaged in Tarwater's eye contact and symbolic act of humility on behalf of Bishop. We enter chapter 8 oriented by his truth: "You got to show you're not going to do one thing by doing another. You got to make an end of it. One way or another" (427–28).

Rayber escalates his confrontation with Tarwater in chapter 8. We learn that he watches "for something that he planned to make happen" on the trip and thereby trap the boy. Meanwhile, Tarwater intuits that he is on the verge of decision as the silence of the lake meets the prophetic call that confronts him with silence.

O'Connor teases out the anticipation by calling it a "waiting silence." "It seemed to lie all around him like an invisible country whose borders he was always on the edge of, always in danger of crossing." It is the same "silent country" that he finds reflected in the center of Bishop's "limitless and clear" eyes (431). O'Connor's essay, "The Fiction Writer and His Country," confirms the symbolism: "...the writer with Christian convictions will consider [his true country] to be what is eternal and absolute" (801).

Rayber takes the trio to a park and they come to another fountain and shallow pool. Predictably, Bishop gallops for the water. The sun shines with "blinding brightness" on a stone lion's-head fountain and "like a hand on the child's white head." Bishop's face "might have been a mirror where the sun had stopped to watch its reflection." The symbols suggest the transfiguration of Jesus (Mark 9:2–8; Matt 17:1–8; Luke 9:28–36), an event before his passion and crucifixion that for the first time reveals to the disciples Jesus' resurrection. In O'Connor's story it serves the same purpose vis-à-vis Bishop's drowning and baptism in the next chapter. Tarwater's reaction captures his ambiguity: he starts forward and "at each step the boy exerted a force backward but he continued nevertheless to move toward the pool" (432). Rayber intercepts him as his foot reaches the ledge of the pool and snatches Bishop from baptism. The "friend," alias the devil, tempts the boy in this chapter at an unprecedented pace, a sure sign that a climactic scene is near. He has ridiculed him for not having a clear, unmistakable sign of calling like real prophets. As Tarwater peers into the water, he glimpses his own reflection and denies he was intent on baptizing Bishop; the "silent face" appears to say that he should drown the child—and Tarwater recognizes that his true adversary is his own pride. Rayber confides that he once attempted to drown Bishop, but before he does, the memory of his failed attempt evokes a "convulsive motion" that he willfully clears out of his head.

Rayber warns Tarwater that he has an unconscious mind and that he and all children "are cursed with believing" (436). He ridicules baptism as "futile rites" and claims that the greater dignity is simply to be a self-sufficient, neighborly man. His verbal assault peaks when he criticizes with a psychological projection: "You're eaten up with false guilt." Tarwater's response is nausea—another bodily function that ironically counters the schoolteacher's preference for abstraction. Moments later, when the boy leaves his clothes in the boat and swims ashore, Rayber has second thoughts about the confrontation. When he sees Tarwater back at the lodge, the boy wears his new clothes, "a changeling, half his old self and half his new." O'Connor's image captures the ambiguity. The boy looks "triumphantly, boldly" into the center of Bishop's eyes and puzzles Rayber, who suggests a ride that Tarwater declines. The final line of the chapter comes full circle with the chapter's opening paragraph: "He wanted to escape before the boy changed his mind" (440). Besides the clinical psychological testing that Rayber plans in order to "fix" Tarwater, it is more than plausible that he has unconsciously "tested" and manipulated the boy into drowning Bishop—a demonstration of Tarwater's ability to undertake decisive "action" that he continually boasts about and that Rayber seems to masterfully exploit.

The rationale for Rayber's trip to Powderhead in chapter 9—to rehearse confronting Tarwater with the fact of his compulsion to baptize Bishop and become a prophet—takes on a new dimension as he drives "without destination" (441) only to unconsciously take the dirt road and walk to the lookout point above Powderhead. It dawns upon him that he has now inherited the place, but his mind quickly abstracts the dollar value of the timber to finance a college education for Tarwater. Bishop gazes from the ravaged scene of the fire and then to Rayber, and "a dreaded sense of loss" (445) comes over the schoolteacher. It is as if he unconsciously knows that the boy's drowning is imminent—just as he drove to Powderhead in unconscious defiance of reason. Rayber's belief ("What we understand, we can control" [450]), Tarwater's "fresh contempt" for his uncle, and the schoolteacher's invincible conviction that "certain laws determine every man's conduct" symbolize the apex of his indifference. The coming cataclysm of Bishop's drowning coincides with his achievement of a nihilism that he sees as the summit of human dignity: "To feel nothing was peace" (454).

When the "unmistakable bellow" of Bishop's drowning reveals the struggle on the lake, Rayber has just awakened to switch on his hearing aid. His facial expression betrays spiritual anguish. He willfully silences every impulse to cry out. "[T]he dull mechanical beat of his heart" is less than human, and Rayber is an unrepentant accomplice to Bishop's death. The anesthesia of alienation that Rayber desired and chose completely numbs him. Flannery O'Connor has masterfully made sin believable through the paralysis of his stony heart. The truth of his damnation is earned through his human, sinful character. In the manner that garnered multiple O'Henry Short Story Awards, O'Connor presents Tarwater not only drowning the "idiot child" but also baptizing Bishop, and himself going on to discover that Buford has properly buried his uncle. When Rayber intuits the fact that Bishop's baptism comes simultaneous with his drowning, the irony of the story brims.

THE NECESSARY PRESENCE OF BISHOP

Bishop's presence in *The Violent Bear It Away* concretely connects Rayber to Tarwater. The distinct way that each ultimately relates to the child shows how Tarwater's consciousness arrives at a striking alternative to that of his schoolteacher uncle's. O'Connor's first description of Bishop, "gnawing on a brown apple core" (349), conjures up symbols of the myth of original sin and the consequences of Adam and Eve's eating from the tree of the knowledge of good and evil. Rayber mockingly admits Bishop's resemblance to Mason, "grown backwards to the lowest form of innocence." But Rayber reduces the relationship with his son to the only "problem" he had not conquered: "He had only learned to live with it and had not learned to live without it"

(400). When he tells Tarwater to forget that Bishop exists because "He's just a mistake of nature," Mason's apprentice already perceives a "secret affliction" (403). Arriving at the Cherokee Lodge, Rayber "absently" touches Bishop's ear before pushing the child aside. The touch leaves his fingers "tingling as if they touched the sensitive scar of some old wound"—another echo of original sin but also O'Connor's playing on his physical and spiritual deafness and Mason's role in both. Rayber even refers later to his own baptism at age seven as a lasting scar (437). The original sin motif recurs in the description of Tarwater's birth "at the scene of a wreck" from which his mother dies and in which his grandparents are killed.

Tarwater's sudden entry into Rayber's life serves as a foil to expose the lack of a meaningful human relationship between the schoolteacher and his retarded son. The gospel injunction, "Where your treasure is, there will your heart be also" (Matt 6:19), gets inverted in Rayber's case. Tarwater is a "treasure"— imagined as a new, healthy, potential son—while Bishop, his real, though mentally defective son, is readily ignored. Perhaps Rayber intimates more than he realizes when we learn that he has no doubt that Bishop was "formed in the image and likeness of God"—but did not believe this truth applied to himself (401). He experiences a range of feelings from compassion to fury toward Tarwater (424), but he symbolically drowns all affective responses when it comes to the child. Even in the final chapter in which Rayber appears, he "automatically" (read, "numbly") sits Bishop on the seat of the car while his mind returns to "Tarwater's future" (441). For all intents and purposes, Bishop de facto drowned at the ocean the day his father attempted to take his life, even though Rayber's actual "failure of nerve" was ironically reported in the newspaper as a rescue.

O'Connor's disappointment that so many readers get a hold of "the wrong horror" (942) when reading her stories applies especially to the interpretation of *The Violent Bear It Away*. The "horror" of this story is not the death by drowning of Bishop (no more so than the death of Solace Layfield in *Wise Blood* is the right horror). Brueggemann's three elements of prophecy offer a lens through which to interpret the novel's genuine horror. (1) The true fears and terrors that O'Connor has brought to expression in this prophetic story are Rayber's indifference, lack of pathos, and the rigor mortis of a cold, mechanical heart. (2) She demonstrates through concrete and detailed events the horror of the secular, rationalist preoccupation with the surfaces of reality at the price of excluding mystery; in Rayber's world, both Mason and Bishop are "freaks," the one a freak of nature, the other a freak of religious superstition. (3) Finally, the real deathliness (about which O'Connor speaks metaphorically) hovers over us and gnaws within us as we witness Rayber willfully strangling his capacity to experience anguish or passion. It is a portrait of Dante's *Inferno,* complete with the icy pit of inertia.

In an essay that O'Connor presented in October 1960 at Wesleyan College for Women in Macon, Georgia, "The Grotesque in Southern Fiction," she defends the necessary presence of characters like Bishop in her fiction. She first argues the larger issue of the modern romance tradition of the novel distinct from the given orthodoxy of the past two hundred years. "Since the 18th century," she observes, "the popular spirit of each succeeding age has tended more and more to the view that the ills and mysteries of life will eventually fall before the scientific advances of man"—an attitude personified by Rayber. That literary orthodoxy, she insists, limits rather than broadens the novel's scope because it confines the novelist to mirroring the social status quo of the dominant culture. A startlingly prophetic element lives in the romance tradition that O'Connor finds leaning "away from typical social patterns" (815). She points to Thomas Mann's claim "that the grotesque is the true anti-bourgeois style." The romance novelist in the tradition of Nathaniel Hawthorne finds interest "in what we don't understand rather than in what we do." O'Connor's concrete distortions embodied in her contemporary grotesques become "a [cultural] reproach, not merely an eccentricity."

> I believe that [the grotesques] come about from the prophetic
> vision peculiar to any novelist, but particularly and, in these
> times, deliberately peculiar to the novelist whose concerns I
> have been describing. In the novelist's case, prophecy is a
> matter of seeing near things with their extensions of meaning
> and thus of seeing far things close up. The prophet is a real-
> ist of distances, and it is this kind of realism that you find in
> the best modern instances of the grotesque. (817)

No wonder she writes to Cecil Dawkins on 25 October 1958 that
she supposes people will call the new novel "another Southern
Gothic" because "I have an idiot in it. I wish I could do it without the idiot but the idiot is necessary" (*HB,* 301).

O'Connor's memorable comeback, when asked why southern
writers populate their works with freaks, bristles in this essay: "I
say it is because we are still able to recognize one." She goes on
to explain that grotesques, properly understood, measure how far
we are displaced from our own spiritual depths, especially from
the South's healthy theological conception of the "whole man."
Along these same lines she endorses Hawthorne's purpose in writing romances as an attempt "to keep for fiction some of its freedom from social determinisms and to steer it in the direction of
poetry" (818). This essay, written on the heels of the publication
of *The Violent Bear It Away,* identifies O'Connor's task as a novelist interested less in conventional probability and open to
prophetic possibility. For that reason she chides the novelist
whose sense of evil is so diluted that he forgets "the price of
restoration" (820). In contrast, the writer who is a "realist of distances" and accepts the theological mystery of life "will be interested in characters who are forced out to meet evil and grace and
who act on a trust beyond themselves—whether they know very
clearly what it is they act upon or not" (816).

It is especially important to read O'Connor's essay on the
grotesque with an eye toward Brueggemann's theology of the
prophet. She resists her audience's demands for "a literature
which is balanced" and that domesticates the prophetic process.

With scorn and ridicule O'Connor rejects the notion of the novelist who "in the name of social order, liberal thought, and sometimes even Christianity" abdicates the prophetic vision and compromises to become "the handmaid of his age" (817). She concedes that Dante's thirteenth century afforded a balanced picture of the world, but contends that our world no longer reflects for the novelist "a balance from the world around him." O'Connor's prophetic imagination begins with the newly given recognition that our world is indeed off balance, and "the novelist now has to achieve [a balance] from a felt balance inside himself." Her grotesques are necessarily "more drastic" in order to get across this vision (820–21).

During the last week of 1956, O'Connor writes to "A" and remarks on Guardini's recent essay on Dostoevsky's *The Idiot* "as a Christ symbol." She notes the coincidence of her character, Bishop, from the novel-in-progress as "a kind of Christ image," then goes on to qualify him "probably just as a kind of redemptive figure." Prince Myshkin in *The Idiot* suffered from a combination of epilepsy and childish innocence. Three comments in Guardini's interpretation of Dostoevsky's novel bear an uncanny resemblance to O'Connor's novel. First, he sees the beauty of Nastasya touch the prince at the point of his most intimate strength—the capacity to empathize and "experience himself in another's misery" in the religious love of compassion. Second, the German theologian points to the "scandal" of Christ's incarnation "under the form of a slave" (Phil 2:5–11). His exegesis of the very text that is the source of O'Connor's title for the novel (Matt 11:2–15) places emphasis upon the verse "And blessed is he who is not scandalized in me." Guardini's interpretation of Myshkin points to a parallel with Bishop: "It seems that at [Myshkin's] touch, the evil that is hidden everywhere is obliged to reveal itself, and that through him 'men's hearts are displayed.'" Only the poor and children respond to Jesus in the gospel; it is "the clever, conformists and right-thinking people" who discount the prophetic alternative of living in such liberating love. Third and finally,

Guardini ends with the scene of the madman-murderer Rogozhin lying beside Myshkin. Rather than be repulsed, Myshkin-the-Idiot touches the hair and cheeks of the "evil genius."

> [W]hat emanates from [Myshkin] is the image of the Redeemer himself. It is the image of that love which is so perfectly forgetful of itself that no consciousness can grasp it any more, nor any will penetrate it; it is the image of our Lord dying with the words, "Father, forgive them, for they know not what they do."
>
> Thus these pages, which seem to describe an ultimate catastrophe, resound with the notes of victory....[A] song of triumph...arises from total collapse. Divine strength and a victory of love spring up here out of the most frightful distress.[15]

O'Connor's character, Bishop, proves to be a *scandal*—literally a "stumbling block"—to both Rayber and Tarwater. Her imagination's debt to Dostoevsky, prodded by Guardini's insights, shows an unmistakable bearing upon the Christian horizon of *The Violent Bear It Away*. Tarwater's capacity for compassion withstands the whirlpool of Rayber's apathy. The boy's recalcitrant temperament equips him to discover how the devil's temptations only constrict his desire for spiritual freedom, confirming O'Connor's axiom: "...the Devil teaches most of the lessons that lead to self-knowledge" (1150). Out of the novel's distressing horror emerges the victory of love through violent grace. Like his predecessor Hazel Motes, Tarwater leaves the world of inherited faith, passes through complex stages of the journey away from faith, and at the end returns to faith on a higher plane.

TARWATER'S EXPERIENCE OF GRACE AND O'CONNOR'S ECUMENICAL PIONEERING

To speak of Flannery O'Connor as an ecumenist catches most people off guard. Pockets of Georgia in her lifetime were labeled "no-priest land," and the minority Catholic enclaves in the Protestant Bible Belt scrupulously avoided conversations about religion with those they condescendingly dubbed "non-Catholics." However, the address O'Connor delivered for the one hundred and seventy-fifth anniversary of Georgetown University in 1963, "The Catholic Novelist in the Protestant South," gives ample evidence of her informal and implicit dialogue with Protestantism. She fiercely respected Protestant Christians for their *experience* of faith, so much so that in searching for a self-definition she spoke metaphorically about her own total commitment to a Catholic identity: "I am a Catholic not like someone else would be a Baptist or a Methodist but like someone else would be an atheist" (930). Her second novel becomes the epiphany of a profoundly ecumenical spirit, not in the sense of seeking the visible unity of churches at the institutional levels, but more in the sense of "spiritual ecumenism,"[16] the striving to integrate all Christians at the deepest levels of a common experience of Christ's paschal mystery. She offers a compelling argument that the South's best traditions, rooted in the Protestant habit of seeing religion biblically, are the same as the Catholic novelist's. The Catholic's "kinship with backwoods prophets and shouting fundamentalists," she insists, comes far more naturally than any affinity for "those politer elements for whom the supernatural is an embarrassment and for whom religion has become a department of sociology or culture or personality development" (859). O'Connor's imagination deftly renders a theological appreciation of grace and sacrament with striking ecumenical insights.

Six months after the publication of *The Violent Bear It Away*, Flannery writes to her protégé, William Sessions, to correct his apparently mistaking Mason Tarwater for a Southern Baptist. She describes him as "an independent, a prophet in the true sense," who is inspired by the Holy Spirit. Traditional Protestant churches in the South "are evaporating into secularism and respectability," she observes, and being replaced by a wide new spectrum of sects that do not resemble Protestantism. She appeals to Hawthorne to justify the prophetic tenor of her romance novel, not the kind of realistic novel that traffics in social determinisms. "[Mason] was a prophet, not a church-member. As a prophet, he has to be a natural Catholic" (1131). Two weeks later she exchanges a second letter with Sessions and develops her appreciation of Protestant salvation theology. She responds with alarm that he has reduced Protestantism to "Baptist Orthodoxy" and specifically mentions infant baptism among Methodists. O'Connor points to Mason Tarwater's "one very dominant Protestant trait," which is to follow the voice of the Lord "regardless of whether it runs counter to his church's teaching." Precisely because of their Protestantism, she argues, both Mason and Francis Marion Tarwater can respond to "a truth held by Catholics."[17]

Almost three years later O'Connor writes to Janet McKane and compliments her for understanding the novel's ending in terms of redemption in the lives of the characters. In contrast, she points to the many who find the novel depressing because they see Tarwater warped by Mason and en route to being a fool or a martyr. These readers, she reports, would prefer Tarwater to be civilized by Rayber, who would then send him to college for an engineering degree. "A good many Catholics are put off because they think the old man, being a Protestant prophet, so to speak, has no hold on the truth. They look at everything in a confessional way" (*HB*, 536). She has little time for nominal Catholics or the clergy who pander to their tepid understandings of the faith.

Contemporary Catholic theology offers radical new insights on the theology of sin and grace. The key to these reinterpretations lies in the mystery and paradox of human freedom. O'Connor's *The Violent Bear It Away* succeeds in dramatizing this very reality in the characters of both Rayber and Francis Marion Tarwater. She comments to "A" in an early 1960 letter about the fierce nature of human freedom: "...there is very much the business of the characters not wishing to be swallowed up in another's will" (1124). Roger Haight, one of North America's foremost Catholic theologians, points to a crucial insight from revisionist Catholic theology that identifies the ecumenical genius of O'Connor: "The Protestant theology of grace tends to be understood against the background of the horizon of sin; Catholic theology of grace tends to define grace in response to the finitude of human nature and death, although it does not neglect the problem of sin." He argues that there is "no compelling reason to consider these two frameworks in exclusion of each other; they can be combined."[18] And combine them O'Connor does in this novel, as we will see momentarily.

Haight identifies the symbolic sources of original sin.[19] He proceeds to analyze the structure and dynamics of the story, uncovering the experience of sin and guilt not merely in psychological terms, "but precisely in the terms of the symbols themselves." I summarize and paraphrase his theological reflection in what I reframe as four theological principles of Christian anthropology:

1. The Adam and Eve story indicates our fallen existence, not from a past state, but from our essential potentiality and from God's design for human persons: we are alienated from God's creative and salvific intentions;

2. We share a condition of the universal propensity to both personal and social sin;

3. Temptation in the story is an external symbol reflecting the universal human tendency to find excuses; the serpent's deceit in the story thematizes the illusion of unlimited human freedom;

4. Sin emerges out of human freedom, that is, it is not from God (who creates "good") or from creation, but discovered as a power with its source in human existence itself.

In this schema, the doctrine of sin accurately portrays human persons as both sinful and free. Haight emphasizes that sin emerges out of human freedom. In Romans 5:12–21 Paul places the power of sin within the divided self, within each person. This contrasts sharply with Romans 7:19–20, which was misread as everyone participating in original sin by inheritance; the real meaning of that entire passage is based on Christ as Savior. The paradox lies in the fact that this deep structure out of which human freedom operates is: (1) prior to any concrete exercise of human freedom; and (2) actualized only in the exercise of human freedom itself. As a result, sin is seen as both a structure and a dynamic process. The Christian tradition speaks of many instances of such "prior sin": pride, unfaith, idolatry, disobedience, rebellion, self-centeredness. These are well represented through the characters of O'Connor's stories and especially in her second novel. They demonstrate the tension between spirit and nature in human freedom. Haight stresses "egocentric autonomy" as the most central sin. It is manifest actively as aggressivity and domineering acts, passively as the escape from freedom and responsibility. Rayber personifies this sin emerging from passive freedom that negates itself, refuses to act, and escapes the responsibility and potential of his freedom to respond in unconditional love to Bishop.

The Catholic theology of grace, central to O'Connor's imagination, offers a positive purpose for human freedom: the struggle to resist sin. Haight presents grace as "a more positive indication" that resisting sin's power and effects within the self and history is "the intrinsic God-given purpose of human freedom."

> Speaking generally the notion of God's grace refers to God's goodness, graciousness, and benevolence toward human beings. Grace is God's love for human existence. But this grace is always understood against the background of a human dilemma. In relation to human sinfulness God's grace appears as mercy and forgiveness. Against the background of human finitude and death, God's love appears as a power unto ultimate salvation in eternal life.[20]

Karl Rahner is credited with restoring grace to its position close to the center of Christian thought.[21] One of his "Copernican" revolutions was to reorient grace as first and foremost

God's self-communication and presence to human persons, opening grace to the possibility of interpersonal categories to analyze it. Grace ceased to be identified with the static understandings of Neoscholastic theology as "a "habit" or "quality" of the human soul infused by God. Rahner's second contribution was to insist that grace is not extrinsic to human existence; God's presence is an offer of salvation that is already part of the condition for human existence, a salvation that God wills from the beginning. Third, rather than present a God who is frugal with grace, Rahner's theology presents the universality of grace in terms of God's universal will for salvation. Fourth, and finally, Rahner insists that human persons experience supernatural grace as experiences of genuine self-transcendence. Haight places particular emphasis upon this last theological contribution because it "opens the theology of grace to phenomenological and narrative methods of analyzing grace in and through experience."[22] In the case of Flannery O'Connor, she presages this shift from a Catholic Neoscholastic position (that grace is extrinsic to human experience) and offers her compelling stories of human freedom emerging through the drama of sin and grace in real human lives. This revisionist theology of grace is perfectly congruent with her conviction that for the Catholic novelist "the natural world contains the supernatural," and for that very reason her "obligation to portray the natural" is not diminished but increased. It becomes a matter of the artist's concern "with the mystery as it is incarnated in human life."[23]

In *The Violent Bear It Away,* O'Connor guards human freedom when she corrects Dr. T. R. Spivey, with whom she dialogues, about his impression that Mason is a Calvinist "and sees people dammed [sic] by God. He sees them as dammed [sic] by themselves" (HB, 507).[24] She insists in her essay on the Catholic novelist that the task is not to write abstractly about general beliefs "but about men with free will."[25] No wonder her second novel explores the struggle between Mason and Rayber for Francis Marion Tarwater's free will. Her recurrent dialogue with John

Hawkes concerning the novel leads her to speak of it as "a more ambitious undertaking" than *Wise Blood*. She insists that she accepts again in her second novel "the same fundamental doctrines of sin and redemption and judgment that they do" with the "do-it-yourself" religion of the South. She sees there an "unconscious pride" worked out dramatically. "Wise blood [the wisdom ultimately not to deny Christ] has to be these people's means of grace—they have no sacraments," she recognizes (1107). She credits young Tarwater as "one who will have the struggle, one who knows what the choice is" (1108).

Chapters 10, 11, and 12 lead us to the climactic resolution of Tarwater's struggle. His simultaneous baptism and drowning of Bishop in the previous chapter dramatizes the ambiguity about sin and grace. The "queer ups and downs in his voice" and his contradictory statements about being hungry in chapter 10 give evidence of the same disturbance. Tarwater protests to the truck driver that the baptism was an "accident" and claims that you cannot be born again. But his nightmare reenacting the events with Bishop only hours earlier reasserts the tension: "an inner eye…piercing out the truth in the distortion of his dream" (461). The metaphor of Jonah "clinging wildly to the whale's tongue" (462) aptly describes the boy's tenacity; but the raw voice of the "defeated boy" crying out the words of baptism in the dream confronts him with the act of baptism. In the chapter's final sentence, anticipating his return to Powderhead, he defiantly reasserts his free will to "begin to live his life as he elected" and thereby make good "his refusal" (463).

Although Tarwater persists in thinking himself "tried in the fire of his refusal" that burned off Mason's influence, his spiritual hunger and thirst persist in chapter 11. Early in chapter 12, his first sight of the clearing at Powderhead describes the place as "burned free of all that had ever oppressed him" (475). He confronts the large woman at the crossroads filling station early in the penultimate chapter. She appears like an archangel, "all knowledge in her stony face and the fold of her arms indicated judgment" (467). With penetrating, fixed eyes she indicts his behavior: "It shames the dead." O'Connor's description of Tarwater gauges his fundamental option for sin:

> The boy pulled himself together to speak. He was conscious that no sass would do, that he was called upon by some force outside them both to answer for his freedom and make bold his acts. A tremor went through him. His soul plunged deep within itself to hear the voice of his mentor at its most profound depth. He opened his mouth to overwhelm the woman and to his horror what rushed from his lips, like the shriek of a bat, was an obscenity he had overheard once at a fair. (467–68)

At the same time, O'Connor ironically shows his vulnerability and the expectation that he account for disowning the call to be a prophet. The obscenity echoes as he retreats, but Tarwater's mind cannot "brook impurities of such a nature." His virginity foreshadows the rape scene at the conclusion of this chapter. But at deeper symbolic levels, O'Connor reveals a virginal human freedom that emerges in response to God's grace. The irony compounds because Tarwater now reveals his hunger "for companionship" equal to his craving food and water.

He accepts a cigarette and indulges in liquor offered by the devil under the guise of the man driving "the lavender and cream-colored car." O'Connor describes the effects: Tarwater felt himself pleasantly deprived of responsibility or the need to justify his actions. It is symbolic that he is stripped naked except for his untouched shoes, ironically recalling his "act of kindness" toward Bishop when he tied his shoes. Awakening with the symptoms of more than his hangover, Tarwater comprehends the rape as his face registers "some point beyond rage or pain." The "loud cry" that "tore out of him" identifies Mason's great-nephew as a victim and more. In this voice of lamentation we hear the collapse of Tarwater's claim to be self-made. It is not self-pity but the grief of the prophet uttered for the numbness and the despair of an entire people.

When he purifies the ground and the woods with fire, he unconsciously begins to reclaim a prophet's identity; the fiery coals that purified Isaiah's lips now purify Tarwater's eyes. Walter Brueggemann reminds that the tradition of biblical faith knows anguish as the door to historical existence, that embracing endings permits new beginnings.[26] So the sullen Rayber is the absolute antithesis of the lamenting Tarwater in O'Connor's novel of sin and grace. A yearning grows out of pain and grief as Francis Marion Tarwater crosses the bridge toward the shack. The "road home" now looks "like strange and alien country," but he cannot turn back before the "final revelation." In the shorthand words of biblical faith, "homecoming" is conversion.

In spite of Tarwater's facade of independence at the opening of chapter 12, the grieving notes of the woodthrush in the first paragraph are an ironic sign, much like the "grieving figures" (474) of the two chimneys at Powderhead. He returns to the scene where he had first silenced Buford's wife and her "nigger mourning" (357). Buford, astride the mule, raises his fist in a gesture interpreted as "half-greeting and half-threat" (476)—another instance of Tarwater's ambiguity. Once he realizes that the cross marks his great-uncle's grave and that Buford assumed his responsibility for the task, his "vision that seemed to pierce the very air" sees Mason amid a multitude feeding on the bread of life. He realizes that he hungers for this spiritual reality and that nothing on earth will satisfy him. His hunger becomes no longer a pain but "a tide" that prompts him to his prophetic mission to warn the children of God sleeping in the "dark city" of the terrible speed of God's mercy. Tarwater's compunction over his reluctance to accept his calling is symbolized by stooping at his uncle's grave and smearing a handful of dirt on his forehead. Reminiscent of Ash Wednesday, it is a prophetic recognition that from death and grief follows a new beginning, in the Christian pattern of the paschal mystery.

Brueggemann points to the prophet's alternative consciousness in the symbol of the cross. Jesus, in the tradition of Jeremiah, speaks of more than a criticism of what is deathly; his death is an act of solidarity and compassion that undermines the reigning consciousness. A people's numbness in the face of the entrenched power of the old consciousness gives way to new, transforming power. Rayber has exercised his own will to achieve such numbness—"and slammed [the door] on himself" (351); Tarwater submits to his vocation to be a prophet, embracing his uncle's grave under the sign of the cross and summoning others to Christ's grace. "There is no more radical criticism than...[to] announce that the power of God takes the form of death and that real well-being and victory only appear via death."[27] It is an ironic inversion of the stranger's earlier tempting Tarwater to deny the power of the cross: "...you can't be any poorer than dead" (352). And a compelling vindication of Mason, aptly described by Buford as "deep in Jesus' misery" (360).

Tarwater departs from Powderhead "off the way Buford had gone" (478). The humbling ritual act of smearing his head with dirt from his uncle's grave coincides with the self-humiliation of Jesus' incarnation. The fact that Buford rides a mule parallels Jesus' entry into Jerusalem for his passion and death, astride the poor man's donkey (John 12:14–15)—a symbolic farce from the prophet Zechariah, to shock hearers with an unmistakable sign of the Messiah's humility and self-emptying as the way to God's fullness.

In a 9 April 1960 letter to Dr. Spivey, O'Connor calls her novel "a very minor hymn to the Eucharist." The very term *Eucharist* in Greek means "thanksgiving" and she clarifies her meaning by admitting, "I believe that God's love for us is so great that He does not wait until we are purified to such a great extent that He allows us to receive Him" (*HB*, 387)—a source of immense, universal thanksgiving. Less than a year earlier she reveals to Spivey her ecumenical sensibility, speaking of the pain of the churches' division, admitting, "As far as I know, it hurts like nothing else."[28] In the same way, she insists on defending Christianity from distortions such as she finds in a Richard Chase novel. "This notion of grace as healing," she argues, "omits the fact that before it heals it cuts with the sword Christ said he came to bring" (*HB*, 411).

Karl Rahner provides perhaps a key to appreciate *The Violent Bear It Away* as a novel centered around a baptism and written as a minor hymn to the Eucharist. Tarwater uses the excuse that the formula for baptism, which he recites while drowning Bishop, is "words that just come out of themselves but don't mean nothing" (458). But since Augustine, the Catholic definition of *sacrament* states "that the word is an element of the sacramental symbolism." Rahner's analysis of the Eucharist insists upon the unity of Word and Sacrament: "It is only by their being constantly referred back to the words of consecration [from the synoptic gospels and St. Paul] that the species of bread and wine constitute the sign (*symbolism* in the Augustinian sense) that indicates and contains the presence of Christ."[29] What is true of bread and wine and the New Testament's institution narrative is also true of water and the gospel narrative's trinitarian formula for baptism. The post–Vatican Council II Catholic reform of the sacraments, simplifying, clarifying, and strengthening this unity of Word and Sacrament, opened new channels for ecumenical dialogue,[30] channels that O'Connor was already exploring in her fiction.

Over a ten-week interval in mid-1962, O'Connor writes a series of four letters to Emory University student Alfred D. Corn, offering an incomparable retrospect on her novel. Her empathy for this young man who fears that he is losing his faith is reminiscent of her concern for "A," the woman she served as confirmation sponsor, only later to see her leave the church. In the first letter, she cautions that he is too young to decide he does not have faith. The advice bears a striking resemblance to her portrayal of Tarwater's predicament. She reminds Corn that while college stimulates his intellect, it shrinks his imagination. Instead of absolute knowledge she prescribes that he cultivate Christian skepticism because "It will keep you free...to be formed by something larger than your own intellect or the intellects of those around you" (1163–65). The second letter echoes an insight on grace in her first letter, borrowed from Gerard Manley Hopkins: "Give alms." O'Connor appreciates how Hopkins was coaxing his agnostic friend, Robert Bridges, to look for God in Charity—"in the sense of love for the divine image in human beings." Romano Guardini's reflection on God's humility struck O'Connor with this very truth that "love does such things." O'Connor prompts Corn to pursue his demand for reason, "but remember that charity is beyond reason, and that God can be known through charity" (1166).

The last two letters addressed to Corn indicate that he has read *The Violent Bear It Away* and posed several questions to Flannery. She describes Rayber's struggling with his love for Bishop as "fighting his inherited tendency to mystical love." She writes to "A" on 5 March 1960 in similar language, describing Rayber's love for the idiot child as "the purest love I have ever dealt with." This very "terrifying purity" causes Rayber, who opts for selfish isolation, "to destroy it" (1124). If Bishop could not contain his love, she says, "he would then love everything and specifically Christ." But his choice at the moment where Tarwater drowns Bishop is "the Satanic choice" (1170) of preferring numbness and refusing to feel the pain of his loss. The final letter resurrects the question of her characters' free will. O'Connor's careful development of Rayber is corroborated by her insisting that his "psychological pulls" (1172) are strongest in the direction of loving Bishop, the direction he ultimately rejects. She argues against determinism forcing Tarwater to become a prophet by pointing to the presence of internal conflict in both characters as compelling evidence of their free will.

Flannery O'Connor's closing comment transparently reveals the power of her Christic imagination. She refuses to accept determinism as a philosophical worldview. In fact, she considers literature impossible in a determined world. "We might go through the motions but the heart would be out of it," a lesson she claims from writing two novels. The truth earned through the conflict experienced by characters in *The Violent Bear It Away* bears witness to her final sentence to the young Alfred D. Corn: "Mystery isn't something that is gradually evaporating. It grows along with knowledge" (1173–74).

Chapter Six

Mercy: *Everything That Rises Must Converge*

I keep seeing Elias in that cave, waiting to hear the voice of the Lord in thunder and lightning and wind, and only hearing it finally in the gentle breeze, and I feel I'll have to be able to do that sooner or later, or anyway keep trying.
        —Letter to Andrew Lytle, 4 February 1960

Nowhere does Flannery O'Connor crystalize her prophetic stance of hope better than in her final letter to the Emory University student, Alfred D. Corn, who had confided to her his struggles with faith in a deterministic, rationalistic world. "I don't believe Christ left us to chaos" (1173), she insists. In this August 1962 correspondence, only two years before her death, O'Connor—the orthodox Catholic—appeals to the work of the Holy Spirit in protecting the Church in truth. When morning dawns on the last day of Tarwater's saga of conversion and initiation in *The Violent Bear It Away*, the sun rose "majestically with a long red wingspread" (463). The imagery foreshadows the Pentecost Spirit who sends the young prophet into the world to announce the good news of God's unimaginable mercy. It sets a pattern for her mature fiction.

O'Connor's final legacy, the posthumously published collection of nine short stories entitled *Everything That Rises Must Converge,* marks her progress in finding a fictional voice that no longer relies exclusively on abrasive satire or the dark and disruptive grace of her early work, stories shouted for the deaf and drawn in large and startling figures for a nearly blind audience. She begins to mission her characters for life in the world with the ballast of Christian hope for the future. But more importantly, Flannery gives evidence that both she and some of her characters also hear the breeze whispering a gentler grace.

The effort to discern development in a fiction writer's creative imagination depends upon careful reconstruction of the author's canon. In O'Connor's case, the chronology of her stories is complex. For example, she excises one selection, "An Afternoon in the Woods," from *A Good Man Is Hard to Find* in early 1955 and revises it two years later for publication in *Partisan Review.* She includes the story in her second collection (published a decade after she originally completed the story), *Everything That Rises Must Converge.* Some commentators ignore the chronological sequence in which she wrote these stories and group them according to themes or internal connections.[1] The title O'Connor chooses for this final collection comes from the French Jesuit scientist and theologian Pierre Teilhard de Chardin and attests to her enthusiasm for his work that she begins to read in late 1959. His influence confirms her hope in the human community's progress toward fulfillment in the Christ event and in God's always-already-present reality of grace throughout creation. This chapter analyzes O'Connor's stories in chronological sequence in order to ascertain how her spiritual development, christological insights, and creative fiction gain new momentum. Midway in the chapter, a brief evaluation of Teilhard's influence upon Flannery will offer an orientation to assess his unique impact upon her imagination in the final stories.

"GREENLEAF"

Mrs. May, "a country woman only by persuasion" (508) after her husband's death, is another of O'Connor's rural widow characters. With an "iron hand" (511) she has turned the farm into a success. The prosperous farm reflects her own character as a self-made woman. Her hired man, Mr. Greenleaf, and his family offer the sharpest contrast at every point of comparison. The irascible Mrs. May judges everything as wrong in the Greenleaf family and indulges her own sons' ingratitude. She criticizes Mr. Greenleaf as "shiftless" (503) and begrudges his sons their education and the modernization of their thriving dairy farm financed by the G.I. bill's benefits. She resents that the Greenleafs "lived like the lilies of the field, off the fat that she struggled to put into the land" (509). Her contempt for Mrs. Greenleaf's emotional, pentecostal religious displays and "prayer healing" in the woods exposes her cold, methodic self-righteousness: "She thought the word, Jesus, should be kept inside the church building like other words inside the bedroom. She was a good Christian woman with a large respect for religion, though she did not, of course, believe any of it was true" (506).

Out of this conflict O'Connor introduces the story as mock-heroic comedy with the Greenleafs' escaped bull prowling in the night's moonlight through Mrs. May's hedges, "like some patient God come down to woo her" (501). This opening scene parodies the biblical text, frequently read in marriage liturgies, of the lover who gazes through the windows in search of the beloved (Song of Songs 2:8–16; 8:6–7). She resists the impulse to drive to Mr. Greenleaf's house and complain because she knows his rejoinder will be to compare his sons with hers, insisting that O. T. and E. T. would not make their mother come out in the middle of the night, but "do it theirself" (502). It touches a nerve. Scofield, who sells "nigger-insurance," and Wesley, who has a heart condition and teaches at the second-rate university, could not care less about what happened to their mother's farm. Neither of Mrs. May's sons is married, but the Greenleaf sons each have three children by French wives they married after the war. Wesley and Scofield taunt their mother about her self-sacrifice as she waits on their every need and makes excuses that they have "other talents" (507).

Mrs. May selfishly takes excessive credit for the way the Greenleaf boys "had risen in the world" (502) because she gave their father work fifteen years ago. When she finally searches for Mr. Greenleaf at their farm, her resentment over their government-subsidized milking parlor occasions a sharp exchange. He reminds her that all sons aren't alike. When she sarcastically thanks God for that fact, he turns her ridicule around to show that good country people like the Greenleafs are the biblical "salt of the earth." Mr. Greenleaf replies, "I thank Gawd for ever-thang" (514). (It proves ironic that Wesley May is on a salt-free diet, symbolizing the family's having lost its Christian identity and capacity for gratitude.) Mrs. May persists in seeing herself as the victim of other people's dependency. She registers surprise that O. T. and E. T. would let their bull run loose and jeopardize her dairy herd, after "all the nice little things I did for them" (518). But her condescending tone leads to a final irony: "Some people learn gratitude too late..." (519).

The final scene of the story takes place in the "green arena" encircled by woods. Mrs. May has forced Mr. Greenleaf to shoot the bull. She enjoys "the exhilaration of carrying her point"—a pride that betrays the controlling power she exercises over everyone. Standing in the center of the field, she is literally and figuratively in the "bull's eye." Just as she rests and closes her eyes, feeling tired, Mrs. May regains her mindset: before any judgment seat she would be able to say, "I've worked, I have not wallowed" (522). Her patronizing comment about Mrs. Greenleaf, an earth-mother figure whose prayer healings find her embracing the earth with her limbs, reminds the reader of the socially inferior woman's exclamation: "O Jesus, stab me in the heart!" (506). As the bull charges from the woods, Mrs. May stands in "freezing unbelief" until his horns pierce her heart. It is the prophet's symbolic metaphor of conversion, the new covenant of the heart. O'Connor describes her look as "a person whose sight has been restored but who finds the light unbearable." As Mr. Greenleaf shoots the bull, his weight pulls Mrs. May forward and she seems to whisper "some last discovery into the animal's ear" (524). In this revelatory moment, she encounters the dark and violent truth of her own lack of gratitude. Her heart is moved beyond the self-pity that accompanied her tears over a numb, loveless life with quarrelsome sons. Earlier in the story, the woods were imaged as "a black wall of trees with a sharp sawtooth edge" (511), fore-shadowing the ending of the miserly woman who even muses over "the perfect ending" of events with the bull goring Mr. Greenleaf. The real ending ironically demands Mrs. May's death in O'Connor's familiar portrayal of the humbling encounter with the transcendent.

"A VIEW OF THE WOODS"

O'Connor admits that the second story written for the collection is "a little grim" (*HB,* 175). A bitter multigenerational struggle within a family exposes layers of greed and conflicting claims of power. Mark Fortune, a wealthy landowner with a timely eye for "progress," attempts to ingratiate himself with his nine-year-old granddaughter and namesake, Mary Fortune Pitts. The real goal, however, is to control his "duty-proud" (527) daughter, who begrudgingly cares for him, and the son-in-law, Pitts, who profits from the use of the land but is frustrated from owning it. Not only does Mr. Fortune forbid them to drill a well and realize a degree of independence, but he also capriciously sells parcels of the property to outsiders because Pitts wants to buy it.

Fortune sees his granddaughter made in his own image and likeness—"a small replica of the old man's" face (525) and physical characteristics, complete with his intelligence, strong will, and driving temperament. He resists the family's attempt to win favor by naming their seventh child after him, but when she is born with his striking resemblance, he suggests that they name the baby after his mother. Fortune envisions the child's carrying on his habit of "making [the family] jump" in obeisance (527) after his death. He secretly arranges in his will for everything to be held in trust for Mary Fortune.

The opening scene finds both characters watching the construction at one of the lakeside lots Fortune has sold. No sooner are we into the story than we discover the dark evil that uncoils. Pitts's "ugly unreasonable resentments" (529) against Fortune turn directly in revenge against Mary Fortune. At regular intervals he summons her from the table for beatings. The description of the scene shows Fortune seated at the head of the table, displacing Pitts from the father's place of honor and authority. Every preference granted by the grandfather to the girl—only Mary Fortune was treated with respect, of all the family (526)—combines with every exclusion of Pitts by the old man, to erupt in the father's violence against the innocent child, but aimed at Fortune. The pattern is familiar to O'Connor from her southern culture. Masters had whipped slaves to discipline them, and so power manifests itself in both black and white men whipping wives and children into submission whenever they find themselves displaced or publicly shamed.

Fortune's response feeds the vicious circle. When he follows Mary Fortune and Pitts to confirm the beatings, he confronts the weeping, frightened child with taunts, encouraging her to reciprocate the blows. "Where's your spirit? Do you think I'd let him beat me?" But the combination of this psychological abuse and the father's physical abuse overwhelms her and she predictably denies the fact of the beatings.

The action of the story takes a new turn when Fortune retaliates by selling the lot in front of their house for a gas station. He does not anticipate Mary Fortune's disdain at the idea: "But that's where we play....We won't be able to see the view [of the woods]" (532). Their heated argument ends with mutual name calling. Mary Fortune accurately calls him "the Whore of Babylon" and names well the family's experience of captivity, like Israel under the Babylonian empire, under his oppression.

Fortune is oblivious to the cycle of abuse springing from the infighting of father-in-law versus son-in-law at the expense of the child. He considers Mary Fortune's refusal to stand up to Pitts as "her one flaw" (536). The grandfather is incorrigible about selling the prime lot and plans to buy her "a trifle" (538) to win back her allegiance. When the dark sky and humidity ominously suggest a tornado, it foreshadows a climactic scene of violence. Fortune decides that he "had been too generous" with his granddaughter. His misgivings are confirmed when the girl, "red-faced and wild-looking" (543), starts to hurl bottles when Fortune and Tilman sign the legal papers for the exchange of the lot. The old man suddenly recognizes that the girl's respect for Pitts is because he beats his daughter "for no just cause" (543). Jealous for the same respect, Fortune prepares to whip Mary Fortune.

The ensuing lethal violence shows Fortune striking her head three times against a rock. No sooner has he unwittingly killed the child than the "convulsive motion" of a stroke and heart attack takes his own life. Earlier, Fortune had stared twice at the dark woods revered by the family. Each time he failed to see any significance. His third look at the woods views red sunlight setting behind them in the early evening. He ponders "an uncomfortable mystery that he had not apprehended before,...as if someone were wounded behind the woods and the trees were bathed in blood" (538). It foreshadows the story's concluding scene of death, but symbolizes a greater spiritual reality.

As Fortune lies dying, he feels as if he were running through the woods toward the lake. In fact, he remains stationary. The trees "thickened into mysterious dark files that were marching across the water and away into the distance" (546). O'Connor herself explains that the woods symbolize Christ—walking on the water and on farther (1014). She writes to "A" that she has rewritten the story so that "the old man has more time to realize what he has done" (1013)—gone to hell (1011). Sally Fitzgerald points out that an earlier version of the story's ending avoided the "rather extreme verdict" (190) of Fortune's damnation and recognized the child's death as accidental. It suggests that "in the end both [Mary Fortune and her grandfather] had their eyes opened" (*HB*, 190) to a vision of God's loving presence. This alternative ending, even though discarded, suggests a subtle shift in O'Connor's imagination. For the moment, she decides upon the dark and disruptive grace imaged in the ending of violence. Love again miscarries through a legacy of stubborn selfishness and greed.

"THE ENDURING CHILL"

Five weeks before her death, O'Connor writes to her editor, Robert Giroux, "There is considerable rewriting I want to do on that one called 'The Enduring Chill'" (*HB*, 589), and suggests that he wait for a "new version" before putting the story into galleys. Her reservations about the story are repeated two weeks later in a letter to Catherine Carver: "I don't much like ["The Enduring Chill"] but I am afraid once I get to messing with it, I will make it worse" (*HB*, 593). This last of her short stories written in the late 1950s is a satiric comedy that pokes fun at Asbury Fox, an effete, young, would-be artist who scorned family and home for New York.

Asbury's "waiting mother" greets her returning, ill son. His irritability vacillates with the momentary "illusion" that Timberboro has been transformed into "some exotic temple for a god he didn't know." O'Connor's irony bristles further with Asbury's self-pity as he anticipates his own death. He judges that it will introduce her "to reality" and assist her in the process of "growing up" (547). As the story unfolds, Asbury's illusions compound. It is he who will be surprised by reality in this story of initiation.

When Dr. Block, the rural physician, is summoned, Asbury complains, "What's wrong with me is way beyond Block" (549). It is another form of his self-aggrandizement. The ailing twenty-five-year-old blames his mother for his failure. He writes a letter for her to read after his death, a letter in which "he forgave her for all she had done to him." He insists that "her way had simply been the air he breathed," and that she had domesticated his freedom. Asbury wallows in a torrent of self-pity: "I have no imagination. I have no talent. I can't create....Woman, why did you pinion me?" (554). This letter, the antithesis of forgiveness, again reveals Asbury's self-centeredness and the illusion that he is able to "face himself" or his mother. Asbury even mistakes the metaphor in the story's title; the "enduring chill" effect he intends the letter to have on his mother backfires. The chill that endures will come from the Holy Spirit who descends from the water stain on the ceiling above his bed, the figure of a "fierce bird with spread wings" and "an icicle crosswise in its beak" (555) that has both irritated and frightened him since childhood.

When Dr. Block finally returns with the diagnosis of undulant fever from the blood sample—"Blood don't lie" (557)—Asbury's vindictiveness and romanticizing of his death collapse as illusions. Even his attempt to aggravate his mother by calling the Jesuit priest to his bedside fails to meet his expectation that all Jesuits would be as "well educated" and "foolproof" (561) as the one he had met in New York, "a man of the world, someone who would have understood the unique tragedy of his death" (550). What Asbury failed to realize was the "icy clarity" of the earlier priest's comment: "'There is...a real possibility of the New Man, assisted, of course,' he added brittlely, 'by the Third Person of the Trinity'" (550). Such a conversion involves the deeper sense of community and life in Christ than Asbury, with his veneer of intellectualism and "artistic temperament" (551), realizes.

The brusque old priest chides Asbury for not praying and tells him to ask God to send the Holy Ghost—a direct link with the first Jesuit's advice. In an unwitting response that reveals Asbury's earlier failure to listen, he volunteers that the Holy Ghost is "the last thing I'm looking for!" The one-eyed priest, a victim of some unnamed violence or physical woundedness and therefore spiritually advantaged in O'Connor's universe, roars at the young man: "...the Holy Ghost will not come until you see yourself as you are—a lazy ignorant conceited youth!" He adds in an aside to the mother as he departs that Asbury is "a good lad at heart but very ignorant" (566–67).

O'Connor's craft as a fiction writer becomes evident in the structure of the story at this point. Asbury seeks to re-create "that experience of communion he had had" with the black farm workers the summer before when they smoked cigarettes together in the barn. He was working on a play about "the Negro" and sought their company to learn how they felt about "their condition." His illusions about that event—"one of those moments of communion when the difference between black and white is absorbed into nothing" (558)—coincide with his failure to comprehend that drinking unpasteurized milk (which the blacks refuse) is the source of his fever and illness. Asbury's drinking the milk is more a defiance of his mother's forbidding it—"That's *the* thing she don't 'low," the blacks tell him—than an offer of communion. The same "signifying" and "Tomming" that we saw in her earlier short story, "The Displaced Person," achieve comic effects here. Randall and Morgan mouth dishonest statements about Asbury's physical appearance and health: "I ain't ever seen you looking so well before" (569). It is a deft maneuver of self-ingratiation, and simultaneously a learned way of survival for the economically dependent workers.

The stirring in Asbury's "blurred eyes" at the end of the story yields to their appearing "shocked clean" after Dr. Block reveals that the unpasteurized milk is the source of his curable illness. The humbling experience completes his initiation. "The old life in him was exhausted. He awaited the coming of new life." And so it is that Asbury sees the Holy Spirit imaged in the water stain on the ceiling stir in motion. The "last film of illusion" is torn away as Asbury "would live in the face of purifying terror" (572). It is not difficult to hear the echo "in the back of Asbury's head as if his heart had got trapped in it and was fighting to get out" when Dr. Block first visits him. Here is an O'Connor character sent back into the world by the Holy Spirit, who gives life by liberating for community those captive to selfish, childish ways.

"THE COMFORTS OF HOME"

The opening words of "The Comforts of Home," another of O'Connor's short stories ending in brutal violence, succinctly characterize its protagonist: "Thomas withdrew...." The repressed rage of one of her quintessential intellectuals, a historian, ironically gathers momentum as the opening paragraph ends with a foreshadowing, "like a mob assembling." Here is a man who retreats from reality, much the same way that Rayber succumbs to numbness in *The Violent Bear It Away*. O'Connor portrays Thomas's ordeal: "Thomas loved his mother. He loved her because it was his nature to do so, but there were times when he could not endure her love for him. There were times when it became nothing but pure idiot mystery,...invisible currents out of his control" (575). Although he has inherited his deceased father's "reason without his ruthlessness," he also has the living legacy of "his mother's love of the good without her tendency to pursue it" (575).

When Thomas's mother graduates from taking boxes of candy to the families of newborns, scholarship recipients, or the sick, to having compassion for the jailed Star Drake (a.k.a. Sarah Ham), her contact with "real experiences" of human need threaten her

son's comfortable world. Thomas has only "contempt for a creature so pathetic" (575) as Star. He names her a "parasite" (580)
who will "ruin their peace" (591) as his mother progresses to
bring the nymphomaniac to dinner and eventually to invite her to
occupy the guest room. His fury turns against his mother because
she responds to the stepdaughter who was sexually abused by a
foster brother and fell victim to the "horror" of sadists and per-
verts. Thomas's mother redoubles her efforts to help Star, who
suffers from what she identifies as her "affliction" (578). Her
response to Thomas is to look compassionately at him because he
jealously challenges her inclusive love, claiming, "You can
choose—her or me" (573).

Thomas personifies a familiar character in Irish families,[2] a
type O'Connor knows from her heritage and Irish lore: the
unmarried son who faithfully remains with a widowed mother,
ostensibly caring for her needs but living as a parasite, indulged
by the mother who waits on his demands and whims. Flannery
shows a classic, comic moment from such an arrangement when
Thomas charges "like a bull" to discredit Star Drake as a "slut"
and calling her a parasite. Absent-mindedly, but totally in character, his mother disarms him, saying, "You'll have to use canned
cream this morning....I forgot the other." She nonetheless persists
in denying any faults in her son, appealing to him to think of "all
the comforts of home" and his morals: "No bad inclinations,
nothing bad you were born with" (582). O'Connor aptly writes
on the first page of the story Thomas's conviction, "She would
have to be shown"—and in the meantime, his mother counts on
his attachment to the electric blanket, symbol of his creature comforts, to pacify Thomas. It is another of her stories of domestic
life, replete with unhealthy family patterns and personalities
whose freedom to love is severely damaged.

Whatever the shortcomings of character development in this
story, the reader finds antecedents of the more human and convincing elements of Julian's torturous relationship with his
mother in the later story, "Everything That Rises Must

Converge." In the same way, Rayber's wrestling with the love of his "idiot child," Bishop, is more human and compelling, although it has familiar roots in Thomas's "idiot mystery" of love for his mother. The old lady's "general sorrow," the narrator tells us, "would have found another object" in the event that good fortune came the way of Thomas or Sarah. "The experience of Sarah Ham had plunged the old lady into mourning for the world" (587). Thomas may be an effective writer of history ("at his desk, pen in hand, none was more articulate"), but his encounter with the antics of Star Drake leaves him speechless, wooden, stunned, revolted, and outraged by her existence, "the very stuff of corruption" (580).

O'Connor describes Thomas as disturbed "in the depths of his being, somewhere out of reach of his power of analysis" (583). His logic-driven, intellectual passion for order makes Thomas a success in professional pursuits but a miserable failure in human relationships. The overemphasis upon the former and the absence of evidence for the latter cause this story to border on melodrama. Whether the threat he faces is an awakening of his repressed sexuality as some commentators emphasize, or the childlike jealousy that finds no satisfaction in responding to another's need for human dignity, a frightened Thomas becomes more dangerous as he is cornered without alternatives. He hears the voice of the devil's temptation as his father's shaming him into action. One even wonders about the relationship between Thomas's parents— who really is "the boss"? O'Connor hints at a complex father-son relationship without dramatizing it.

The narrator intimates that the father exploits others in the small town through the symbolism of his ability to "converse squatting" to their level. "By gesture he had lived his lie" (583), we are told. Never does the father outright tell a lie. It sets the stage for the son's placing of the gun that he thought was missing from his desk (only to rediscover it there after summoning the sheriff) in Sarah Ham's pocketbook—an act of deceit and betrayal. The irony is complete when she discovers his deception and he fires the gun at her, shooting his own mother, who throws herself forward to protect the girl. The greatest irony is that Thomas inadvertently acts with fatal results, when his habit is to whine and threaten but remain inert.

Sheriff Farebrother's arrival coincides with the climax of the story. He is described earlier as "another edition of Thomas's father" except for his Texas-style clothes. Moreover, he was "as easily dishonest" (585). He completely misreads "the facts" at the scene of the fatal shooting, interpreting it as Thomas's "nasty" plan to kill his own mother and live with the promiscuous Sarah Ham. O'Connor writes to John Hawkes in March 1961 to complain that readers expect her, as a Catholic writer, always to show someone being redeemed in her stories. She concedes a "symbolic redemption" through Thomas's mother, "who brings him face to face with his own evil" of preferring selfish comfort before charity. The sheriff, she points out, has the "devil's eye view," modeling the world's misinterpretation of the same events. She concludes by comparing Sarah Ham with Enoch and Bishop, unpredictable characters "who set the havoc in motion" (1146–47). The taciturn heart of Thomas resists the prophet's undertow in his mother's wider compassion and social concern. Once again, it takes violent grace to awaken such a character, or an audience equally complacent to the greater demands of social justice. In selfishly damning the whole universe (593), Thomas ironically condemns himself.

"THE LAME SHALL ENTER FIRST"

Near the beginning in O'Connor's seven-year process of writing *The Violent Bear It Away*, she writes to Sally and Robert Fitzgerald about her initial work on the novel and reveals an oblique connection with her short story "The Lame Shall Enter First." "I have a nice gangster of 14 in it," she reports, "named Rufus Florida Johnson. Much more in my line" (*HB*, 55). In retrospect, it becomes apparent that these early pages of her novel are excised and migrate into a short story in its own right. Her "gangster" reference connects the story to "A Good Man Is Hard to Find," also written in this early 1953 period. It becomes more and more apparent that five of the stories comprising her second collection are written during intervals while she is writing *The Violent Bear It Away*. This is the period when she struggles to make the characters in her second novel more human and credible than those in *Wise Blood*.

O'Connor's misgivings about "The Lame Shall Enter First" confirm the struggle to humanize her protagonists. About Sheppard she confesses in a 1962 letter, "I just don't know such a man, don't have any felt-knowledge of him" (1174–75). Despite a name that suggests one who cares for the vulnerability of his entire flock, Sheppard will come to confess—at first unwittingly—that he has denied and betrayed his own son, Norton, in order to fill "his own emptiness with good works like a glutton" (632). In the opening scene of the story Sheppard judges his ten-year-old son as selfish. Sheppard's prematurely white hair stands like "a brush halo," while the cross-eyed Norton's one eye "listed, almost imperceptibly, toward the outer rim" (595). The contrast between the righteous father and the damaged child ironically reverses by the story's end. Once again, O'Connor portrays an unbelieving protagonist who will come to a shocking revelation of spiritual reality, and a child with an innate capacity for spiritual vision hungering for initiation. She completes the cast of characters with fourteen-year-old Rufus Johnson, a personification of the devil, who plays the role of tempter.

Sheppard's job title is city recreational director, but his real satisfaction derives from Saturday volunteer work as a counselor at the reformatory. Under the guise of caring for neglected delinquents, he denies any grief for his wife, who died a year earlier— "I'm busy helping other people" (598), he tells Norton, trying to challenge the boy's selfishness. Sheppard's matter-of-fact, rationalistic way of dealing with her death also has the effect of causing him to overlook and dismiss Norton's deep feelings of abandonment and grief at the loss of his mother. He considers the child's emotional crying outbursts as more selfishness and abnormal grief. The dynamic between father and son exposes his psychological abuse of the boy by way of negligence; there is no evidence of affection between the two, only Sheppard's patronizing guilt imposed on Norton. The paroled Rufus Johnson, with an IQ of 140, captures Sheppard's imagination and emotions because he wants to make him into his own image and likeness; he has lost interest in Norton, who displays no intellectual curiosity; he judges his son to be dull and intellectually "average or below" (599). The resemblance between Sheppard and Rayber as well as Norton's likeness to Bishop in *The Violent Bear It Away* reveals the story's common root in an early draft of the novel.

Sheppard prides himself on his credentials and training for work with the juveniles at the reformatory. He self-righteously contrasts this with the dubious authority of the prison's priest-chaplain. Armed with social psychology, Sheppard accepts the challenge of developing Rufus's "potential" and invests himself totally in the teenager. He dismisses the criminal "mischief" as "compensation" for Rufus's clubfoot. His condescending approach comes forth when he tells the delinquent, "There are a lot of things about yourself that I think I can explain to you" (600)—but Sheppard ironically remains oblivious to the real truths about himself and how he compensates for the loss of his wife and the neglect of his son. Rufus confronts his counselor with a shocking response when he tells him that "Satan" makes him do what he does. His knowledge of the Bible momentarily elicits a "dull despair" from Sheppard. He indoctrinates Rufus with his secular atheism, telling him that this is the space age and "You're too smart to give me an answer like that" (600–601). As part 1 of the story ends, however, Rufus returns to biblical language and angrily tells Norton, "He thinks he's Jesus Christ!" (609). He acts perfectly in character because the demons in the New Testament are the first to recognize who Jesus really is

(Mark 5:1–10). The devil-Rufus cleverly exploits Sheppard's exaggerated sense of self.

When Sheppard hits upon the idea of a telescope to encourage Rufus's intellect, he does so under the guise of "the injustice" (603) the paroled boy suffers, living out of garbage cans and wearing rags. The excitement of "what he could do for such a boy" (602) by buying him a new orthopedic shoe and telescope ironically reminds the reader of his abandonment of Norton. When Rufus finally lets himself into the house with the key Sheppard gave him and decides to stay, the counselor marshals his reverse psychology to enlist the teenager's help to teach Norton what it means to share. He whips Norton one night when the child realizes that the intruder is sleeping in his dead mother's bed, to him a sacred place. Physical abuse, doled out in Sheppard's admitted anger, is added to the psychological abuse of neglect. O'Connor deftly images the absence of an emotional attachment: "[Norton] appeared so far away that Sheppard might have been looking at him through the wrong end of the telescope" (610).

A great irony in the story centers on the role Rufus plays in teaching Norton about spiritual reality from the scriptures. The juvenile offender knows that he is not going to the stars as an astronaut but to hell, unless he repents and believes in Jesus. The Bible's mythic language awakens Norton's imagination. He finds this alternative to his father's explanation of death as annihilation—"She doesn't exist"—to be more attractive and further quizzes him to discover that his mother is "saved" and "on high" (612). Meanwhile, Sheppard begins to behave like Mr. Fortune, distracted by the possibility that he may have failed by being too lenient with Johnson: "The boy would not respect him unless he showed firmness" (614). But the three episodes of the police accusing Rufus of breaking into and ransacking houses compound the plot with Sheppard's erratic misreadings of the youth's innocence and guilt.

The second visit to the brace shop for Rufus's shoe concludes with his rejecting it. Sheppard responds with a patronizing remark that labels his charge as immature, too childish for the new shoe. The night before this visit, Norton beckons to his father from his bed, only to have Sheppard stand unresponsive, "as if he saw nothing." Afraid of breaking Rufus Johnson's trust by having his son confirm or contest the delinquent's whereabouts at the time of the second accusation, Sheppard, like Rayber with Bishop, ignores Norton and denies him love. To heighten this action, the dawning consciousness of Rufus's ongoing crimes ironically affects Sheppard: "The failure of his compassion [for Rufus] numbed him" (625). Depressed and defeated, he now hopes Rufus will depart.

The final ironies of the story collide as Sheppard's self-deception and pride reach their apex: "He knew without conceit that he was a good man, that he had nothing to reproach himself with." But in the next moments he observes Rufus and Norton reading a stolen Bible. Norton's transformation is evident as his face shines and he looks alert: "[H]is eyes were a brighter blue than he had ever seen them before. There was a strange new life in him" (626). Johnson's symbolic act of eating the page of the Bible in imitation of the prophet Ezekiel's eating the scrolls when he is called by God proves ironic and, in part, blasphemous. But what is written on the scroll eaten by Ezekiel foreshadows the climax of the story: "Lamentation and wailing and woe!" (Ezekiel 2:9).

Norton sits at the telescope and his father communicates only to inquire about Rufus's whereabouts. Sheppard ignores the boy's excitement, "I've found her!" as he waves at his mother in the heavens. When the police return the third time with Rufus in tow, caught red-handed in crime, the shock of accusations of Sheppard's sexual advances ("Immor'l suggestions") staggers the counselor. But truth nonetheless comes from this devil-tempter, who admits that he wanted to get caught, "To show up that big tin Jesus!" (630). Sheppard denies the charges but persists in the illusion of Rufus's goodness, telling him in the religionless, sin-free language of social psychology, "You're not evil, you're morally confused" (631).

In the wake of Rufus's appeal to the biblical injunction, "The lame shall enter first," and an acknowledgement that Jesus—not "that lying stinking atheist"—can save him, Sheppard wallows in self-righteousness. His thrice-told denial, "I have nothing to reproach myself with," gives way to a recognition of his betrayal of his son, Norton. But too late come the compunction and remorse. "The image of himself shrivelled until everything was black before him" gives way to "a rush of agonizing love" and the revelation that he would be mother and father to his son. Running to kiss Norton and tell him he loved him, Sheppard discovers the "jungle of shadows," a modern crucifixion scene. The grieving boy's self-hanging was an effort to launch himself into space and be with his loving mother. Sheppard is left with the new consciousness of his own insecurities and the gluttony of good works that fed him, while failing to nurture Norton. Worse than a clubfoot is the unnamed spiritual deformity of a stony heart.

TEILHARD DE CHARDIN'S INFLUENCE

O'Connor's first mention of the French paleontologist, whose research in China included excavations at Chou Kou Tien near Peking, where the bones of Peking Man were found along with cinders that linked this civilization to the human discovery of fire, is a 25 May 1959 letter. There she recollects editor Robert Giroux's visit the week before, when he alerted her to a forthcoming book on Teilhard's thought and praised the "very impressive" Jesuit whom he had met shortly before the priest's death on Easter Sunday in 1955 (1097). Almost two years later she writes to "A" in defense of Teilhard, whose posthumously published writings were provoking condemnations and praise. In this February 1961 letter she confirms that she has now read "both books" and concludes: "...even if there were errors in his thought, there were none in his heart" (1144–45).

Her book review of Teilhard's *The Phenomenon of Man* is published in the local diocesan paper on February 20, 1960. The fiction writer describes how his vision of Christ and his love of science yield a memorable insight: "...his mind dealt in immensities." She appraises his study of evolution and the premise that all human life "is converging toward a point" which he calls Omega (the final letter of the Greek alphabet, symbolizing fulfillment); it is a definitive process that begins with Christ's resurrection and completed in Christ's Parousia, the Second Coming. Her accompanying review of Claude Tresmontant's book on Teilhard enthusiastically praises his contribution to spirituality. She focuses on Teilhard's work, liberating Christians from the caricature "which sees human perfection...in escape from the world and from nature." She appropriates from Tresmontant Teilhard's rediscovery of biblical thought: Nature is already fulfilled; "...creation is still in full gestation and...the duty of the Christian is to cooperate with it." She gravitates to Teilhard's emphasis upon "spiritualizing matter." The resonance between O'Connor and Teilhard, however, extends beyond her recognition that his work is "a scientific rediscovery" of St. Paul's thought. Spiritualizing matter, she insists, "is the path which the artist has always taken to his particular goals."[3]

Her second review of *The Phenomenon of Man* appears in a fall 1961 journal. She remarks that the poet, "whose sight is essentially prophetic," will recognize Teilhard as "a kindred intelligence." There are echoes of William Lynch's Christian theory of imaginative literature in her appreciation of the Jesuit scientist and theologian: "[Teilhard's] is a scientific appreciation of what the poet attempts to do: penetrate matter until spirit is revealed in it."[4] Meanwhile, she reviews Teilhard's *The Divine Milieu* and writes a review for the local diocesan paper. She lauds the book as a "religious" volume that gives perspective to the earlier *The Phenomenon of Man,* a scientific analysis of development through "the chemical, biological and reflective stages of life." The last line of this review is a most telling one, autobiographically revealing the effect of Teilhard's thought upon O'Connor's own imagination: "It is doubtful if any Christian of this century can be fully aware of his religion until he has reseen it in the cosmic light which Teilhard has cast upon it."[5]

Christopher F. Mooney's classic study, *Teilhard de Chardin and the Mystery of Christ,* includes three insights of special relevance to O'Connor's debt to Teilhard. The first concerns the christological problem with which Mooney's brother Jesuit struggled. In defining the universe not in terms of "cosmos" but of "cosmogenesis," Teilhard rethinks the total mystery of Christ as a genesis, or ongoing process of coming into being. "For the Person of Jesus the real Omega took flesh and became part of that evolutionary current for which he himself is responsible," says Mooney. The drama of sin and grace in O'Connor's fiction takes place through the freedom of her characters, participating in this evolutionary current. In Teilhard, "[Jesus'] work of salvation thus became rooted in space-time and destined to continue in the material world up to its fulfillment." The Christic genesis and the cosmic genesis become "one and the same."[6]

The second insight bears upon Teilhard's interdisciplinary method, what Mooney describes as an approach to the human mystery enabling us "to dispense with looking at the human person alternately from a scientific, philosophic and theological point of view." What Teilhard proposed was a single movement from one mode of knowledge to another—from the data of reason to the data of revelation. It is already a familiar path for O'Connor. Her anagogical way of seeing insists that as a literary artist she has an "enlarged view" that looks beyond the literal to the spiritual, the environs of palpable mystery, and returns her characters (and the reader) to reality.[7] Teilhard used the term *hominization* to name that critical point in nature when human persons move from instinct to thought. It evidences a critical complexity-consciousness, a higher degree of the mind's internal organization, and the human person as spirit. Teilhard described this capacity for what O'Connor calls her "enlarged view":

"More urgently than ever I feel that the great question in the depths of my being is one of a faith, a 'Christology,' that will give the fullest possible stimulation to the forces of hominization in us—or, which comes to the same thing, the forces of adoration."[8] Ruby Turpin's vision in "Revelation" becomes O'Connor's masterpiece, re-creating this urgent stimulation of hominization-as-adoration, as I will analyze momentarily.

The third and final insight concerns suffering as the deepest of mysteries. Mooney acknowledges Teilhard's firsthand experience of evil and suffering during service in World War I. He describes the French priest's use of biblical data concerning Christ's death and resurrection vis-à-vis the universe's genesis, or ongoing process of coming into being, "to show with certitude that in God's plan for mankind deficiency of matter is indeed meant to be the occasion for growth in spirit." In Teilhard's words:

> Suffering is still to be treated at first as an adversary and fought against right to the end; yet at the same time we must accept it in so far as it can uproot our egoism and centre us more completely on God. Yes, dark and repulsive though it is, suffering has been revealed to us as a supremely active principle for the humanization and divinization of the universe. Here is the ultimate meaning of that prodigious spiritual energy born of the Cross....A growth of spirit arising from a deficiency of matter. A possible Christification of suffering. This is indeed the miracle which has been constantly renewed for the last two thousand years.[9]

Growth in spirit is linked directly to the love of Christ fostering love among human persons. Christ conquers the world's inherent ambiguity and makes progress in the midst of suffering and death.

Mooney faults Teilhard's "strange tendency to depersonalize sin," but attributes this flaw to the then-contemporary theology of original sin. He asks if Teilhard "felt the terror of man's rejection of love too deeply to consider it objectively?" Could Teilhard's optimism, Mooney asks, have grown from a reaction to a personal temptation to pessimism? A passage from Teilhard's *The Future of Man* resonates well with O'Connor's images of a humble God and faith's vision as an alternative to the scandal of a God who would capriciously test human persons:

> No, God does not hide himself to make us search for him, of that I am sure,—much less to let us suffer in order to increase our merits. On the contrary, bent down over his creation which moves upwards to him, he works with all his power to give us happiness and light. Like a mother he watches over his newly born child. But our eyes are unable to see him yet. Is not precisely the whole course of centuries needed in order for our gaze to accustom itself to the light?
>
> Our doubts, just as our sufferings, are the price and condition for the perfection of the universe. Under these conditions I consent to walk right to the end along a road of which I am more and more certain, towards a horizon more and more shrouded in mist.[10]

More recently, Ursula King has interpreted Teilhard's contribution to spirituality. She identifies a passage from *The Future of Man* where Teilhard writes lucidly about love as liberation from enslavement, "the doom of ants and termites." "It is through love and within love," wrote Teilhard, "that we must look for the deepening of our deepest self, in the life-giving coming together of humankind. Love is the free and imaginative outpouring of the spirit over all unexplored paths."[11]

At precisely the moment when O'Connor admits that ours was not an age of great Catholic theology and "past time for a new synthesis" (1082), she discovers Teilhard. No wonder she writes in one letter during the last week of 1959 about the prophetic vision as "not a matter of seeing clearly, but of seeing what is distant, hidden. The Church's vision is prophetic vision; it is always widening the view" (1116). Flannery O'Connor's creativity, stirred by Teilhard, flowers in four short stories that lead from the environs of sin to renewed hope in the life-giving unity of humanity linked by bonds of unimagined love. But first she applies his Christology to a historical human drama.

Teilhard's Tenor: *Introduction to* A Memoir of Mary Ann

Teilhard's immediate influence on O'Connor's reflections is first manifest not in her fiction but her prose. In the spring of 1959, she receives a request from the superior of the Dominican Sisters from Our Lady of Perpetual Help Free Cancer Home in Atlanta. A girl named Mary Ann, who had lived under their care from the age of three until her death nine years later, suffered a grotesque tumor on the side of her face. "[O]ne eye had been removed, but the other eye twinkled, danced mischievously, and after one meeting one never was conscious of her physical defect but recognized only the beautiful brave spirit and felt the joy of such contact" (822). Now the nuns wanted Flannery to write Mary Ann's story. Most of all, they wanted her to communicate the "real impact" that Mary Ann had on the lives of each person she had touched.

In this poignant essay, O'Connor remembers how her first glance at the enclosed photograph of the child caused her quickly to put it aside. She describes the child's bandaged, "slightly out of place" features. "The child looked out at her observer with an obvious happiness and composure." Knowing that the sisters were the ones capable of writing Mary Ann's story, she declined but offered to help with editing. Nonetheless, O'Connor gazed at the photograph "long after I had thought to be finished with it" (823). She describes retrieving a volume of Nathaniel Hawthorne's stories and acknowledging that the great artist's daughter, Rose Hawthorne Lathrop, had founded the Dominican congregation who cared for Mary Ann. It is an uncanny connection for O'Connor. She is reminded of Hawthorne's story "The Birthmark," where a woman's slight facial defect shocks her husband as a mark of "earthly imperfection." The wife's question poses the mystery at the center of O'Connor's grotesques: "You cannot love what shocks you?" (824).

From another of Hawthorne's works, "Our Old Home," O'Connor describes an incident in a nineteenth-century Liverpool workhouse. A reserved English gentleman, "afflicted with a peculiar distaste for whatever was ugly," performs the heroic act of tenderly caressing a "loathesome child," with all the instinctive affection of its natural father. What is so compelling about this story is Rose Hawthorne's later discovery of this very incident of a six-year-old child, sick with scurvy and silently reaching out to be held, recounted in her father's own notebooks. O'Connor quotes Nathaniel Hawthorne's reflection on this vivid experience: "I should never have forgiven myself if I had repelled its advances."

As a result of O'Connor's effort on behalf of the Atlanta sisters, in December 1962 Robert Giroux published *A Memoir of Mary Ann*, written by the nuns with an introduction by herself.[12] Even though she describes it as "a story as unfinished as the child's face" (828), O'Connor acknowledges its impact in opening for her "a new perspective on the grotesque." She knew that she had always been able to write about evil—much like another story rendered with her father's literary gifts by Mother Alphonsa (Rose Hawthorne) and excerpted in O'Connor's introduction. This story from the foundress's account of "a flourishing slip with criminal roots" and a "gaze of satanic vigor" proves her point. While we might be dispassionate about evil, especially because it receives worthy literary expression and mirrors our own proclivity toward evil, the good proves to be another challenge.

> Few have stared at [the good] long enough to accept the fact that its face too is grotesque, that in us the good is something under construction....The modes of good have to be satisfied with cliche or a smoothing down that will soften their real look. When we look into the face of good, we are liable to see a face like Mary Ann's, full of promise. (830)

This unique essay in O'Connor's work is pure Christology. It resonates well with her appreciation of Romano Guardini's incarnate Christ as "the humble God" who bows, recognizing the dignity within our poor and paltry humanity. She reminds her readers that our age argues that the suffering of innocent children is reason to discredit God's goodness. She returns to the character Alymer in "The Birthmark," whom she sees multiplied: "Busy cutting down human imperfection, they are making headway also on the raw material of good." Dostoevsky's Ivan Karamazov, she points out, cannot believe if one child suffers torment; Camus' hero rejects Christ's divinity because of the slaughter of the innocents. O'Connor's lyric christological insight warrants a careful excerpt:

> In this popular pity, we mark our gain in sensibility and our loss in vision. If other ages felt less, they saw more, even though they saw with the blind, prophetical, unsentimental eye of acceptance, which is to say, of faith. In the absence of this faith now, we govern by tenderness. It is a tenderness which, long since cut off from the person of Christ, is wrapped in theory. When tenderness is detached from the source of tenderness, its logical outcome is terror. It ends in forced labor camps and in the fumes of the gas chamber. (830–31)

To sentimentalize human suffering with clichés or by smoothing down the rough edges of its shocking reality would lead, for O'Connor, to an illusory "tenderness" that erupts in dehumanizing violence. She elects to embrace Teilhard's theology of evil and suffering with what he names our "passive diminishments." In this light, Christian resignation to the will of God is not to be mistaken for passive submission; rather, Teilhard invites us to the positive function he assigns to Christian resignation: to climb in the light of the cross. Salvation is seen primarily not in terms of a reparation for sin, but in terms of "an elevating of created reality and a leading it to its fulfillment in union with God" through

Christ the Redeemer seen as Evolver. It becomes, in Teilhard's theology, a matter of radiating from Christ "the 'redemptive' qualities of the pain engendered by evolution."[13]

Both Teilhard and O'Connor see the Church's communion of saints as the key to the Christian understanding of "human imperfection and grotesqueries." She sees Hawthorne's "act of Christlikeness" springing into the tree of the Dominican Sisters founded by his daughter, and flowering in the life of Mary Ann. In O'Connor's words, "This action by which charity grows invisibly among us...is a communion created upon human imperfection, created from what we make of our grotesque state." The sisters had given Mary Ann "the wealth of Catholic wisdom" by teaching her "what to make of her death" (831). No wonder Flannery describes the Christian's creative action as preparing for one's death in Christ. In the case of Mary Ann, O'Connor celebrates her as "extraordinarily rich"—in grace. "Mary Ann's diminishment was extreme, but she was equipped by natural intelligence and by a suitable education, not simply to endure it, but to build upon it" (828). Such is the face of the good under construction in O'Connor's final short stories.

"EVERYTHING THAT RISES MUST CONVERGE"

Although O'Connor completed "The Lame Shall Enter First" after reading Teilhard, the dark and disruptive grace of that story ends in haunting violence and death. The story's origins date to 1952, when she began working on her second novel. But the short story fails to enjoy the "felt knowledge" of Sheppard that she achieved in Rayber; the absence of conflict paralleling Francis Marion Tarwater's choice between the contrary stances of Mason Tarwater and Rayber weakens the story's human drama. Mention of astronauts, space travel, looking through the universe with telescopes and microscopes testify to her development of the story through contemporary images and perhaps the hint of a wider vision. Before her 1961 title story for the second collection, there is faint evidence in her fiction of the deeper communion and harmony discovered in Teilhard's spirituality.

On her thirty-sixth birthday, 25 March 1961, O'Connor writes to her New York liberal friend, Maryat Lee, to tell her that she has just written a story that "touches on a certain topical issue in these parts and takes place on a bus" (1147). Given the context of their ongoing correspondence and debates about racial integration, O'Connor's provocative understatement about the subject matter of "Everything That Rises Must Converge" mirrors the story's parable quality.

As early as "A Good Man Is Hard to Find," the story of the escaped convict, O'Connor had tackled seemingly intractable social issues—in this case, the question of reformatories vis-à-vis her portrait of the human dignity and redemptive potential in the most perverse criminals. Allusions to institutional religion, the Holocaust, the welfare system, immigration, racial integration, class consciousness, and economics grow to become part of the matrix for her imagination.[14] Her final four short stories, written in the wake of her enthusiasm for Teilhard, usher readers into prophetic precincts. Each new protagonist rises to a new level of consciousness, a new vision of deeper communion and harmony, that mirrors the mystery of all creation converging and transfigured in Christ. Each of her sinful but redeemed characters progresses to a new way of living in the world.

The opening lines of "Everything That Rises Must Converge" herald the need for Julian's mother to "reduce." At the literal level, losing weight from her one-hundred-and-eighty-pound body is the concern addressed by her perfunctory Wednesday night "Y" class. But at the spiritual level, both Julian and his mother are swollen in a stubborn pride that only humbling can heal. St. Paul's antidote, especially for the survivor-Julian, is simply that he must decrease so that Christ (present in the dignity and collaborative effort of all peoples) might increase (John 3:30). It is frighteningly easy to read this short story and to miss the analogy between Christ's redemptive life, death, and resurrection and Julian's "entry into the world of guilt and sorrow" (500) as an affirmation of the way of discipleship.

Julian cultivates the familiar self-image of the victim in his relationship with his widow-mother. Like Saint Sebastian, he sees himself a martyr to his mother's racist attitudes, her nostalgia for the past, and her expectation that he will escort her to the Y. For all his claims that "He was not dominated by his mother" (492), he depends upon and exploits her indulgences, much like Thomas did his mother in "The Comforts of Home." Their tangled relationship exposes Julian's insecurity and poor self-image: "Everything that gave her pleasure was small and depressed him" (485).

Julian's determination to numb himself during his obligatory sacrifice for her pleasures only contradicts his claim that he is emotionally free from her. Like so many of O'Connor's protagonists, he habitually withdraws into his mind, "a kind of mental bubble" (491), from which he judges without being penetrated by the real world or by those inferiors he identifies as idiots. The irony of Julian's attitude is that it mirrors elements of his mother's attitude that he fiercely condemns. He can hardly see her or anything objectively. His perception that she lives in her own insular "fantasy world" (491), thinking that her sacrifices and the struggle have ended in victory, overlooks the fact that he has chosen to live in a version of the same unreality. When Julian acts upon his "evil urge to break her spirit" (489) and declares psychological war on her by treating her as a stranger, the young man unwittingly confirms his mother's assessment that he is ignorant of life and has not yet entered the real world, but has chosen to be "as disenchanted with it as a man of fifty" (492). The real alienation is Julian's estrangement from his true self.

The mother's wearing of the hat for the bus trip to the Y becomes O'Connor's telltale gesture that engages only later when Julian recognizes the mother of the black child, Carver, wearing the same hat. Julian interprets his mother's hat as "a banner of her imaginary dignity" (489). Her insistence that she knows "Who I am" harkens back to her great-grandfather, a former governor, and prosperous grandparents—including his grandmother, whose maiden name was "Godhigh"—a comic play on the claims of pedigree. O'Connor's mocking the nostalgia of Margaret Mitchell's novel (and the subsequent movie version), *Gone with the Wind,* echo here. The resistance of Julian's mother to the historical fact of slavery's demise ironically touches the metaphors of the story's title: "They should rise, yes, but on their own side of the fence" (488). In Teilhard's spirituality, rising to the consciousness of a new world (and not merely a privatized "new man") inevitably progresses to a point of convergence.

Julian's ambiguity about the family's decayed mansion symbolically compromises his politically liberal ideological stance on racial integration. While he now outwardly speaks of it with "contempt," he continues to think of it with "longing." It is a mansion that he had visited only twice before it was sold, but it recurs in his dreams. He insists that he, not his mother, could appreciate it, even in "its threadbare elegance" (488). The contempt erupts again on the bus when Julian imagines the myriad ways he could teach his mother a lesson. His indignation generates the perception of his mother wearing her hat like a banner of dignity, but "shrunken to the dwarf-like proportions of her moral nature" (495). Yet only moments before, when Julian moves to sit next to the well-dressed professional black man who boards the bus, his patronizing attempt at conversation ends in embarrassment when he has no cigarette for the match he has borrowed. In a poignant scene afterwards, his mother gazes at him, "but she did not take advantage of his momentary discomfort" (493). It is a signature of grace in O'Connor's fiction—and Julian cannot recognize or reciprocate her sublime humility or love. She has mercy on her son's inept and clumsy social skills.

When the black child Carver and his mother board the bus, Julian gloats at the lesson it will teach his mother, to see her prized hat worn also by the black woman: "Justice entitled him to laugh" (496). He fails to have mercy, and it demonstrates a truth advanced by his mother earlier in the story. When Julian replaces his tie to please his mother, he protests, "True culture is in the mind, the *mind*." She rebuts him by summoning Julian to the place of authentic conversion: "It's in the heart...and in how you do things and how you do things is because of who you are" (489). At a symbolic level, the pair of hats ironically symbolizes the convergence of the two women who seem to have diametrically opposed dispositions and histories. But they are, nonetheless, the primary teachers of the values and attitudes of children—the very ones from whom Julian and Carver learn love and hope.

Julian's mother employs her smile to attract Carver's attention. Despite her condescending offer of pennies (ironically bearing the face of the Emancipator, Abraham Lincoln), the narrator describes Carver escaping his mother's grasp and scrambling, "giggling wildly, onto the seat beside his love." It is spontaneous, a more natural and authentic action than Julian's sitting beside blacks on the bus as an act of reparation for the legacy of segregation. The child's mother slaps his hand and threatens to "knock the living Jesus out of you" (497)—the most explicit religious language in the entire story.

In the end, Julian and not his mother learns the lesson. He is forced to face "a new world and face a few realities for a change." As his mother suffers her fatal stroke, he voices his first words of affection, words he has denied her to this point: "Darling, sweetheart, wait!" Julian reverts to the child he really is, crying "Mamma, Mamma!" But now he is asked to become a man, entering the world of guilt and sorrow. His "Help, help!" whispers in a thin voice, "scarcely a thread of sound" (500). And in this humbled figure kneeling at his mother's side, one now hears a new dialogue about mercy that includes the voice Elias heard, the gentle breeze.

In a late 1961 letter to "A," O'Connor challenges her correspondent (who has recently left the Church) in the same way that

Julian is challenged at the end of this story: "You will have found Christ when you are concerned with other people's sufferings and not your own" (*HB*, 453). Julian's story progresses far beyond the discovery of Mr. Head and Nelson in "The Artificial Nigger" because it exacts from Julian the cost of discipleship in a complete communion that cannot hide behind ideology or in mental bubbles; it effects far more than the reconciliation between Mr. Head and his grandson. Julian's vocation is, after all, to be a *martyr,* one whose life and selfless redemptive suffering literally *witness* by reversing the sufferings of generations. The prophet's hope rebounds in the mission of such inclusive, suffering love.

"REVELATION"

The metaphor of "reducing" reappears in O'Connor's comic and poignant story of Ruby Turpin's transformation. From the moment she steps into the crowded, claustrophobic doctor's waiting room at the beginning of the story and sizes up the seating situation, it is apparent that this overweight farm wife has an enormous ego to match. Pushing her husband, Claud, into his chair and interfering with his efforts to rise tell us volumes about her controlling manner. The list of changes she would make in the running of the office, particularly the cleanliness of the waiting room—*if* she had anything to do with it—reinforces the reality of Ruby's bossy, judging personality. Her shallow self-deprecating remark, "I wish I could reduce," dissolves when the "stylish lady" tells her that your size makes no difference "as long as you have a good disposition" (634).

As Ruby scans the waiting room, she appraises the social standing of every person. Whether they fall into her category of well-dressed, "white-trashy," or "niggers," her elaborate scale of naming all the classes of people corresponds to her unfailing judgment of their shoes. Instead of counting sheep, Ruby falls asleep each evening by inventorying these clear-cut classes. The presence of Mary Grace, the daughter of the well-dressed and stylish woman, confounds Ruby because the college girl scowls and is visibly annoyed at the conversation as she tries to read her book entitled *Human Development*. Ruby's uncomfortable reaction to the girl combines with her pity that the girl not only is ugly, but acts ugly.

When the conversation turns to weather and the subject of picking cotton, Ruby takes the opportunity to criticize the way the "niggers" want to climb socially to the same social status as whites. Her explanation that her and Claud's diversified farming includes hogs elicits disgust and contempt from the "white-trashy" woman; Ruby counters with the thought that her hogs are cleaner than the woman's child. The conversation deteriorates as Ruby attempts to put the woman in her place, proclaiming, "There's a heap of things worse than a nigger....It's all kinds of them just like it's all kinds of us." Her patronizing sarcasm evokes from her peer, the well-dressed lady, the cliché "[I]t takes all kinds to make the world go round" (640)—deeply ironic in the wake of Ruby's bigotry.

Mary Grace's acne-marked face reddens as her internal rage mounts over the drift of the remarks. A Wellesley College student, she personifies the educated, politically liberal mindset that revolts at the South's racial attitudes and temperaments. Meanwhile, Ruby catches parts of the lyrics of a song on the radio ("But we'll all blank along/Together," and "We'll hep [sic] eachother [sic] out") in the waiting room and soberly agrees with its philosophy: "To help anybody out that needed it was her philosophy of life" (642)—it did not matter whether they were white or black, trash or decent. Ruby begins to congratulate herself that she has been blessed and is a "good woman" and "herself," for which she is thankful to Jesus—like the Pharisee in the gospel who believed in his own self-righteousness, thanked God, and held everyone else in contempt (Luke 18:9–14). She immediately turns and conspires with the mother of Mary Grace to voice condescending remarks (aimed at the daughter) about people with ungrateful, bad dispositions. It is the last straw that catapults Mary Grace into action, hurling her book at Ruby's left eye and wrestling her to the ground.

Ruby's intuitive powers prove to be her redeeming quality. Dazed by the violent eruption, she leans forward and looks into the girl's "brilliant eyes" (645), imploring, "What you got to say to me?" The narrator tells us that she waits, "as if for a revelation" (646). When the girl replies, "Go back to hell where you came from, you old wart hog," Ruby sinks into her chair. The doctor intervenes with an injection, hinting that perhaps the girl suffers from epilepsy or some infirmity contributing to her behavior. Ruby returns home, feeling as wounded and violated as if her house had burned down. Lying in bed, she is haunted by the image of a razor-backed hog bedecked with warts and horns. She weeps. Then, Job-like, she raises her fist in self-defense against her accuser.

Ruby and Claud arise to attend to the arrival of the Negro workers. As he takes the truck to meet them, Ruby ices their drinking water. Her action imitates the gospel's promise that if you give a drink of water to the least of your brothers or sisters, you do it for Christ. But Ruby's motives compromise her virtue. Earlier her bigotry paraded in a self-described manipulation: "I sure am tired of buttering up niggers, but you got to love em if you want em to work for you" (639). Ironically, she sees through the "signifying" and "Tomming" of the black workers who flatter her (much like in "The Displaced Person") and take sides against the girl, though Ruby confides in them the verbatim of the revelation. The dialogue ends with one worker saying, "Jesus satisfied with her!" But Ruby reacts by growling to herself, "Idiots!" (650)—aware of their ingratiating efforts and yet foreshadowing her realization that a deeper conversion to the Jesus ethic is asked of her.

Heading toward the pig parlor at sunset, Ruby glowers at the creatures. She recalls reading that they are the most intelligent animals, next to humans. Suddenly, her dialogue with God begins. When she questions, "How am I saved and from hell too?" Ruby touches the paradox at the heart of human existence.

Both sinning and graced, she shares with all people in the mystery of human freedom abused and properly used. But the grace cannot be earned or coerced; it is always already a present gift confirmed by Christ's life, death, and resurrection. Ruby's final question to God, "Who do you think you are?" echoes like a yodel in the hills and comes back, to interrogate her. O'Connor's imagery artfully describes the scene. An open-mouthed Ruby is speechless in her encounter with the ineffable. Her silence and vision, in the aftermath of Mary Grace's symbolic violence, suggests that she too encounters God in the voice in the gentle breeze that demands she account for her true identity. Her rigid muscles and fixed gaze suddenly, "like a monumental statue coming to life" (653), bend to absorb "some abysmal life-giving knowledge."

Perhaps of all O'Connor's fiction, no passage captures the Teilhardian image of the deepest communion and harmony as does Ruby's vision. With her hands raised in the priestly gesture of prayer, she envisions the "horde of souls...rumbling toward heaven." As in every good parable, the reversal of expectations surprises. And so, Ruby's classification of social order is reversed, with the "niggers," "lunatics," and "freaks" preceding the tribe of respectable people like Ruby and Claud who are at the end of the procession. The vision of their "shocked and altered faces" shows the truth O'Connor presents. It is because "even their virtues have been burned away" (654) that the mystery of mercy reveals how dependent they are on God's grace.

Now Ruby sees that she is called to a deeper discipleship, under the mercy of Christ. When her eyes fix unblinkingly on what lies ahead, she comes to accept with Julian (from the collection's title story) a true discipleship and hope. The story's early Holocaust reference, from her dream that all the classes are mingled and crammed into a boxcar for the gas ovens (hell), has worked through her unconscious mind. As Ruby rises to this higher consciousness of solidarity in suffering, hope abounds.

"PARKER'S BACK"[15]

In early 1961, O'Connor writes to a friend that she is working on a story originating in a newspaper clipping about a man who has Christ tattooed on his back. "This is obviously for artistic purposes as he also has tiger and panther heads and an eagle perched on a cannon" (1145). Already the metaphor of "icon" of Christ taps a rich religious tradition in the Eastern Orthodox Church.[16] Her appreciation of Teilhard's conviction that matter becomes spiritualized mirrors the sacramental action of painting icons. The use of natural pigments and the elements of the egg combine with the artist's prayer experience and an entire context of spirituality in the creation and ritual use of icons, particularly icons of Christ.

This story that O'Connor completes from her hospital bed just days before her death perhaps yields her most complete christological vision. The character of O. E. Parker and the action of the story move on three levels of consciousness: (1) shame, (2) conversion, and (3) transformation.

The striking resemblance between Parker and Hazel Motes is evident in their military service, their vehicles, their antiheroic sexual exploits, but most of all in the way their rationalist's mindset excludes any spiritual or invisible reality. In Parker's early conversation with Sarah Ruth, he deflects inquiry about his "saved" status: "...he didn't see it was anything in particular to save him from"(662–63). His dead-end secular quest is even manifest in his covering all his body except his back with tattoos because "He had no desire for one anywhere he would not readily see it himself" (659). In the first paragraph of the story, however, we discover Parker's deeper identity in a negative self-assessment: "He was puzzled and ashamed of himself" (655). This shame is deeper than any guilt imposed by external sources. It denotes an inner experience of alienation that results from the misuse of freedom— Parker's spiritual affliction.

Parker's experience as a fourteen-year-old, seeing the man at the fair who is covered head to foot with tattoos, awakens a sense of wonder in him. The muscle-rippling motion animating the "arabesque of men and beasts and flowers" touches a deeper ontological question in Parker. Never before had he thought about how extraordinary it was that he existed. O'Connor foreshadows the change of direction and ultimate destiny that will come with Parker's conversion: "It was as if a blind boy had been turned in a different direction" (658).

As Parker begins to place tattoos on his own body, his dissatisfaction grows with each additional tattoo. He begins with inanimate objects, an anchor and crossed rifles. They are ironic Christian symbols that he cannot yet interpret—the anchor, the symbol of hope; and the cross, a symbol of resurrection life. When he adds predatory wild creatures—the panther, lion, serpents, eagles, and hawks—they "literally penetrated his skin and lived inside him in a raging warfare" (659). These tattoos reveal his inner alienation and self-destructive behaviors.

After nine months of military service, Parker is dishonorably discharged for being AWOL. It is a symbolic rebirth after the customary term of gestation. He returns to the country, where there is "air fit to breathe" (659), but this is an ironic rebirth. Parker is Adam seeking Eve in the person of Sarah Ruth, to whom he offers the symbolic apple. O'Connor's craft in portraying this ironic Eden becomes a comic parody when Sarah Ruth fixes her "sharp eyes" on the "serpent" tattoo and her gaze unfolds in a "stupefied smile of shock, as if she had accidentally grasped a poisonous snake" (657). But we are warned that her perceptive powers are flawed when she mistakes the eagle tattoo for a chicken. Her naming Parker's chaos of tattoos "vanity" identifies the essence of original sin in pride. Even though unreliable in visual perception, Sarah Ruth ironically proves expert in "forever sniffing up sin" (655).

The story moves to its second level of consciousness, conversion, at the story's end when Parker returns home, bearing the tattoo of Christ on his back. Sarah Ruth's curt response, "It ain't nobody I know" (674), separates her from his conversion experience. But his progress to conversion comes only after he reexamines his life. The scene of Parker's violent expulsion from the pool hall shows the dawning of new consciousness:

> Parker sat for a long time on the ground in the alley behind the pool hall, examining his soul. He saw it as a spider web of facts and lies that was not at all important to him, but which appeared to be necessary in spite of his opinion. The eyes that were now on his back were eyes to be obeyed. He was as certain of this as he had ever been of anything. (672)

Remorse and compunction seize Parker as he recollects his negative stance toward God, others, and even himself and all reality. He awakens to realize how he abused his freedom in joining the Navy as an escape; in his lust and shallow commitment to Sarah Ruth. As he sobers up from the whiskey that he used to drown his emerging new consciousness, Parker realizes that "his dissatisfaction with himself was gone, but he felt not quite like himself. It was as if he were himself but a stranger to himself, driving into a new country, even though everything he saw was familiar to him" (672). O'Connor's presentation of the true country of grace is crafted through the creation of a character whose corruption and conversion are believable and compelling.

The movement to a third level of consciousness integrates the dominant eye imagery in the story. In O'Connor's fiction spiritual blindness is healed through the new vision that comes with religious conversion. Although Parker has adapted successfully to the mechanical world of the Navy ship, his eyes are described as "the same pale slate-color as the ocean, [reflecting] the immense spaces around him as if they were a microcosm of the mysterious sea" (658–59). It echoes a Teilhardian insight into the evolutionary process of life and the human connection to our origins in the sea. The "immense spaces" suggest the widening new context in which O'Connor places the Christ mystery and the rising human consciousness.

After the revelation when his tractor hits the tree, his eyes are described as "cavernous" (655) when, Moses-like, he sees the burning bush. At midnight on the second day at the tattoo artist's, Parker is forced to look at the image of Christ, using double mirrors: "but the face [of the Byzantine Christ] was empty; the eyes had not yet been put in....'It don't have eyes,' Parker cried out" (668). But the most deft contrast of eye imagery occurs while Parker spends the night at the Haven of Light Christian Mission. His nightmare is interrupted by longings for Sarah Ruth's "icepick eyes" when the eyes of the Byzantine Christ come to mind:

> Her eyes appeared soft and dilatory compared with the eyes in the book, for even though he could not summon up the exact look of those eyes, he could still feel their penetration. He felt as though, under their gaze, he was as transparent as the wing of a fly. (669)

Parker realizes that Sarah Ruth's eyes, by comparison, are no longer constricted, but dilated eyes, blurring her vision and distorting reality. When he is commanded to "look" at the finished tattoo, Parker's "vacant look" refocuses: "Parker looked, turned white and moved away. The eyes in the reflected face continued to look at him—still, straight, all-demanding, enclosed in silence" (670).

Although Sarah Ruth seemingly found the "word" she seeks when declaring Parker's tattoos "vanity of vanities," her naming of the tattoo of Christ an "Idolatry" denies the humanity of Christ and misinterprets the incarnation-redemption mystery. It also convinces the reader that her own biblical names are ironic. Her life is neither fruitful nor miraculously fulfilled in the new covenant in Christ, unlike God's work in Sarah, the wife of Abraham. Nor is she like Ruth, the Moabite woman, the foreigner who is included in the ironic mystery of salvation by marriage to one of Jesus' ancestors. Sarah Ruth's protest, "He don't *look*....He's a spirit," stuns Parker. O'Connor explains this crucial symbolic action in a letter to "A" just one week before her death: "Sarah Ruth was the heretic—the notion that you can worship in pure spirit" (1218). Ironically, Parker's wife has a "vanity of vanities" of her own. Her beating Parker with her broom, nearly knocking him senseless and raising "large welts...on the face of the tattooed Christ" presents the figure of the unresisting Lamb of God, the suffering servant, Christ's crucifixion and death. So that, when Parker cries "like a baby" at the conclusion of the story, O'Connor symbolically recognizes him as the "new man" in Christ. He leans against the pecan tree, literally and figuratively scourged, and yet embracing the symbol of resurrection faith.

Parker's reply to the artist's questions during the tattooing process—"Have you gone and got religion? Are you saved?"—epitomizes the stance of her unbelieving, secular characters: "A man can't save his self from whatever it is he don't deserve none of my sympathy" (669). By the end of the story the indelible tattoo symbolizes a transformation in Parker's very being. He is now the "Christ-bearer," literally "Christopher," bearing Christ's presence in the world. The mockery of the men in the pool hall, "O. E.'s got religion and is witnessing for Jesus" (671), now rings with irony. After the ensuing fight and Parker's expulsion from the pool hall, O'Connor describes the suddenly silent place, "as if the long barn-like room were the ship from which Jonah had been cast into the sea" (672).

Parker comes to share the prophet's vocation to tell the world of the speed of God's mercy. In the history of the Church, this image of Christ the Pantocrator emerged in the wake of the fourth-century controversies with the iconoclasts, heretics who broke and destroyed any likenesses of Jesus or Christ, the Risen One. The image of Christ the Pantocrator, traditionally seated above the rainbow (symbolic of God's love for the whole of creation), penetrates Parker's life with Teilhard's vision of all things converging in Christ.

"JUDGMENT DAY"

This final short story, "Judgment Day," written in longhand from O'Connor's hospital bed (1210), brings her work full circle. Her initial 1946 short story, "The Geranium," is transformed through various drafts into this sublime valedictory story about an old man's, Tanner's, homesickness. Exiled from Corinth, Georgia, to New York City, where he lives with a duty-bound daughter, Tanner's eyesight is failing and his body is crippled by a recent stroke. But his spirit gathers new momentum to animate his consciousness for death and the final things. His daughter impatiently scolds him for not watching more TV to distract him from thinking about "morbid stuff, death and hell and judgment" (686). Tanner shares with Mason Tarwater, the old prophet in *The Violent Bear It Away*, a preoccupation with the rite of burial—especially the return of his body to the holy ground of Corinth. He overhears his daughter's plans to bury him in New York City and considers it a broken promise, placing her in a precarious status somewhat like Francis Marion Tarwater. "Bury me here and burn in hell!" he confronts her (678).

Once again, O'Connor promotes a black man, Coleman—like Buford in *The Violent Bear It Away*—to carry out the spiritual desires of the old man. For thirty years Coleman has been paroled to Tanner. O'Connor deliberately presents them as ironic opposites. The black man and the white man, the law-abiding and the criminal. "When Coleman was young he looked like a bear; but now that he was old he looked like a monkey. With Tanner it was the opposite: when he was young he had looked like a monkey but when he got old, he looked like a bear" (679). Although Tanner calls Coleman a scoundrel and plies his artful "way with niggers" on him, he comes to discern in Coleman "a negative image of himself." Their "common lot" in "clownishness and captivity" (683) is a metaphor for Tanner's solidarity with his dearest friend, and the harmony and communion they live, even though he has yet to "decipher" this mystery of the human condition. Despite all his contempt for Doctor Foley (the landowner who is only part African American, with a mixture of white and Native American blood), who had wanted him to run a still—"the white folks IS going to be working for the colored and you might as well to git ahead of the crowd" (685)—Tanner's loyalty and concern for Coleman testifies to how they rise above both the violence and indifference he finds in New York. The note he writes for Coleman with his final, conserved energy fathoms the depth of his love: "STAY WHERE YOU ARE. DON'T LET THEM TALK YOU INTO COMING UP HERE. THIS IS NO KIND OF PLACE" (676).

Tanner's daughter scolds when he reports (with accumulated malice toward her "high and mighty" attitude) that "A nigger" has moved in the apartment next door. She commands him to observe the New York City protocols: "They ain't the same around here...just you mind your business and they'll mind theirs....Live and let live" (688). Tanner's efforts at greeting are met with the resistance his daughter predicts. At first he wonders if the neighbors are deaf and dumb. He mistakes the black man for a preacher and, assuming he is from South Alabama, asks about local fishing, only to evoke the chill response from the man that he is an actor. Tanner's third encounter meets more than a cold shoulder. The actor unleashes a vulgar retort and tells him that he is neither a preacher nor a Christian: "I don't believe in that crap. There ain't no Jesus and there ain't no God" (690). In a wave of rage he slams Tanner against the wall, causing a concussion and small stroke. The diminished Tanner is recovering from the effects of this violence when we meet him at the opening of the story.

In retrospect, Tanner regrets the decision to come to New York City. He sits lonely and homesick in the apartment, realizing he would prefer to be working the still for the wealthy black man in Corinth. The realization that "nothing was left in the chair but a shell" (685) unwittingly measures his Teilhardian progress, the spiritualization of matter. Tanner's virtual lameness as he struggles across the room and to the stairs reinforces this reality. He is another of the lame about to enter the reign of God. In a final moment before his daughter departs, he feels guilty. Despite his habitual denial of this gratitude as evidence that he is a "damned liar," it proves to be a moment of grace.

About to make his escape, Tanner stands and sways, waiting to get his balance. The posture is not without significance in O'Connor's fiction. At this moment of excitement, Tanner confesses his confidence by reciting Psalm 23, "The Lord is my shepherd...." Tanner falls halfway down a flight of stairs and lands "upsidedown." (The earlier suspicion that Doctor Foley secretly knew how long "it would take the world to turn upsidedown" [685] echoes with irony.) He has lost his balance, both literally and symbolically. The ultimate irony unfolds as the old man mistakes the black actor for his beloved Coleman. His final act is a plea, still identifying the man as "Preacher," to help him up because "I'm on my way home" (694). The indignity of the black man degrading Tanner by pushing head and limbs through the spokes of the banisters and pulling his hat over his face is a modern urban version of humiliation and crucifixion. O'Connor was familiar with the Bible through her own spiritual life and the ethos of the Bible Belt. She alertly knew that Psalm 23 is preceded by the classical example of a lament, Psalm 22: "My God, My God, why have you forsaken me?" This lamentation over being abused and scorned, laid low in the dust of death, appeals to God for deliverance. The psalm, however, ends in a hymn of praise. The fact that Jesus recites this very psalm from the cross connects Tanner's death to the remembrance of a merciful and faithful shepherd-God.

For all the racism in Tanner's background and culture, the irony lies in the New York City black actor inflicting racist violence upon the rural southern elderly man. Just as we saw in "The Artificial Nigger," O'Connor gives us a potent reminder of the complex, unresolved tensions of American racism. Explosive violence threatened when Tanner first met Coleman. Both characters resist the urge to use their knives. In the case of Tanner, it is some "intruding intelligence" that works in his hands. Tanner hid his vulnerability, his trembling hands, from the black workers by whittling crude figures. He disarms Coleman by crafting a pair of wooden spectacles for him. The much-abused and much-misunderstood black man finds that his urge to attack Tanner with the knife "was balanced against something else, he could not tell what" (683). Once again grace throws the balance against evil. He reaches for the eyeglasses and "with exaggerated solemnity" looks through them. When Tanner calls him "Preacher," he invests Coleman with new dignity. When he asks what Coleman sees, he replies simply, "A man." A follow-up question evokes the response, "A man that make theseyer [sic] glasses" (684). Only after framing the question in black or white categories does Coleman answer in the category of racial identity. From acts of grace rises a life's friendship. They both make alternative judgments, and mercy transforms them.

It may be more than coincidence that O'Connor entitles this final story "Judgment Day." She insists throughout her letters and essays that judgment begins in details seen by the eye. Whatever reality the artist consciously brings to the reader's consciousness ultimately contributes to the organic reality of the work of fiction. So Tanner transfigures Coleman with a gesture of grace. He urges the black man to wear the spectacles: "I hate to see anybody can't see good" (683). There is no better cue to the predicament of all her characters (and audience) or to O'Connor's gifted, anagogical imagination. Tanner's last words during his final encounter with the New York City actor accompany a gesture much like Ruby Turpin's in "Revelation." Raising his hand "light as a breath"—almost in a sign of prayer or blessing—he arrives at that Teilhardian Omega point where matter is spiritualized and consciousness rises to new heights. He implores "in his jauntiest voice" that the man help him stand because he is "on my way home" (694). The word "jaunty" denotes a *lively* awareness. In humiliation and finally in death, Tanner lives by grace with a new vision.

Conclusion

Flannery writes in a 1958 review of German theologian Karl Adam's *The Christ of Faith* that "The best way to understand the uniqueness of Christianity is by a proper Christology."[1] Her intuitive powers as an artist taught her, however, that the experience of knowing Christ comes out of the Church's "living self-awareness" constantly renewed through the centuries. O'Connor's fiction witnesses the way that the vitality of Christianity is poured out into a culture's literature, not constricted by "finished and inflexible" fossils of doctrine. She poignantly phrased this insight in an early letter to "A": "Conviction without experience makes for harshness" (949). The humanity of her characters proves to be a unique asset for avoiding harsh, doctrinaire, and abstract truths. Their lives become the raw existential material through which grace works. She follows the mystery of redemption in the sometimes densely tangled, but credible, lives of such characters.

And so, Flannery O'Connor celebrates the way she writes because of (not in spite of) her being Catholic. "[B]eing Catholic has saved me a couple of thousand years in learning to write" (966), she acknowledges. She brings her fictional grotesques and the audience of readers "home," to recognize the deepest longings for community and the hunger for shared meaning. Her modern imagination unfolds in irony after irony. Spiritual alienation yields spiritual presence. As early as 1955, O'Connor writes to "A," "I never have anything balanced in my mind when I set out" (970). She invariably follows her characters' freedom as they restlessly seek love.

In a rare personal comment about a mutual friend, O'Connor scolds "A" for her harsh comments about Caroline Gordon: "She may be basically irreligious but we are not judged by what we are basically. We are judged by how hard we use what we have been given" (1082). She insists that it is a willingness to struggle that is the true measure of the deepest spiritual reality. O'Connor understands fiction as stories that, unlike abstract teachings or formulas, "affect our image and our judgment of ourselves." She insists that such stories offer a means "to recognize the hand of God and imagine its descent" (858–59) in the reader's own life. Instead of advancing this imaginative engagement with fiction, she found that the larger culture persists in impoverishing the imagination and eclipsing the prophetic insights that a religious writer proposes. O'Connor challenges us to appreciate that the Catholic novelist in the South encounters the spirit in strange places and recognizes the spirit "in many forms not totally congenial." For that very reason such a writer "will see many distorted images of Christ" (859)—which ironically prove better than the total absence of images of Christ.

In language reminiscent of William F. Lynch, O'Connor invites her readers to "penetrate" beneath the extreme individualism of southern life and find "the human aspiration beneath it." She boldly asserts an inclusive vision of the "invisible Church," by professing that there is only one Holy Spirit, "and He is no respecter of persons":

> These people in the invisible Church make discoveries that have meaning for us who are better protected from the vicissitudes of our own natures and who are often too dead to the world to make any discoveries at all. These people in the invisible Church may be grotesque, but their grotesqueness has a significance and a value which the Catholic should be in a better position than others to assess. (860)

Flannery O'Connor makes no demand that her readers submit to a profession of Catholic faith. She does expect, however, that "you have a free mind and no vested interest in disbelief" (1038). In doing so, she stakes a larger claim for the Catholic imagination.

As she once rejected Evelyn Waugh's definition of a Catholic novel as one that "deals with the problem of faith," she enlarges it to include "a Catholic mind looking at anything" (1041). As one of America's most accomplished fiction writers, she knows that the writer must be "humble in the face of what-is." Therefore, only by staying within the limitations of the concrete, real world can fiction transcend those limitations (808). For O'Connor, the mystery of our existence is realized imaginatively only by freshly encountering it through the senses.

No wonder that "Revelation" ends with the imagery and drama of a procession entering heaven. It includes in the visible Church all those invisible members too easily overlooked and excluded. But more importantly, the procession witnesses to the process of convergence. All reality rises to a new consciousness in Teilhard's vision of fulfillment in Christ, the Omega point. It is for this very reason that O'Connor writes almost a year before her death: "If I set myself to write about a socially desirable Christianity, all the life would go out of what I do" (1183). The prophetic voice of the fiction writer, the artist as a realist of distances, rings true through her openness to the fact of the invisible Church.

Flannery O'Connor convinces readers that in the Christian vision we are asked to see Christ in others. But for some people, you have to squint hard. Three days after the date of her death, the Catholic Church celebrates the feast of the transfiguration on August 6. Just as Father Flynn watches Mrs. Shortley's peacock dance, raise its tail, "and spread it with a shimmering timbrous noise" as tiers "of small pregnant suns floated in a green-gold haze over his head" (317), he exclaims, "Christ will come like that!...The Transfiguration." The farm woman is lost in double entendres about Mr. Guizac, as yet unaware of the grace in her midst.

The incomparable art of Flannery O'Connor's imagination is the skill and tenacity with which she helps us to recognize that "eternity begins in time and we must stop thinking of it as something that follows time" (1001). Only a Catholic imagination invests history and the human with such compelling dignity.

Notes

INTRODUCTION

1. Joan Tucker Brittain and Leon Driskell, *The Eternal Crossroads: The Art of Flannery O'Connor* (Lexington: University of Kentucky Press, 1971).

2. Thomas Merton, "Flannery O'Connor: A Prose Elegy," *Raids on the Unspeakable* (New York: New Directions, 1968), 37–42.

3. *Ace of Freedoms: Thomas Merton's Christ* (Notre Dame: University of Notre Dame Press, 1993). See especially chapter 4, "Son of the Widowed God: Merton's Sapiential Reading of Fiction."

4. See my "O'Connor and Merton: Icons of the True Self in a 'Christ-Haunted' World," *The Flannery O'Connor Bulletin* 23 (1994–95): 119–36.

5. Among her letters to "A," O'Connor refers to Father John Mulroy in the context of mentioning several priests: "Fr. Mayhew turned up the next day, thank the Lord not the one before. He is about to be transferred to LaGrange and Fr. Mulroy to Athens. I guess you know Fr. Boyle died—33 years old" (24 February 1962). As quoted from Flannery O'Connor, *Collected Works* (New York: Library of America, 1988), 1159. References to this volume will be noted parenthetically in the text without any abbreviation and only the page number(s).

6. Flannery O'Connor, *The Habit of Being* (Letters Selected and Edited with an Introduction by Sally Fitzgerald; New York:

Farrar, Straus and Giroux, 1979). References to this volume will be noted parenthetically in the text as *HB* and page number(s).

7. Ibid., xv.

8. "Novelist and Believer," *Mystery and Manners* (New York: Farrar, Straus and Giroux, 1962), 165–66.

9. William F. Lynch, *Christ and Apollo: The Dimensions of the Literary Imagination* (New York: Sheed & Ward, 1960).

10. "The Nature and Aim of Fiction," *Mystery and Manners,* 79.

11. "Novelist and Believer," 158.

12. "On Her Own Work," *Mystery and Manners,* 118.

13. "The Catholic Novelist in the Protestant South," *Mystery and Manners,* 209.

14. See the excellent analysis by Ralph Wood, "Flannery O'Connor, H. L. Mencken, and the Southern Agrarians: A Dispute over Religion More Than Region," *The Flannery O'Connor Bulletin* 20 (1990): 1–21. I especially recommend his insight, "The brittle secularist and the crusty Catholic saw, as the [Vanderbilt University] Agrarians did not, that the real quandary of our time concerns not region so much as religion—and religion understood not so much as wistful theistic faith but as radical christological belief" (1).

15. "The Catholic Novelist in the Protestant South," *Collected Works,* 858–60. This later version of the essay was given as a lecture at Georgetown University on 18 October 1963.

16. "The Catholic Novelist in the Protestant South," *Mystery and Manners,* 191.

17. Walker Percy, *The Moviegoer* (New York: Random House, 1961).

18. "Novelist and Believer," 158.

19. Quoted in the brochure of the Flannery O'Connor Collection, Ina Dillard Russell Library, Georgia College, Milledgeville, Georgia.

20. "The Catholic Novelist in the Protestant South," 861.

21. This excerpt is from a letter to Eileen Hall, 10 March 1965.

CHAPTER ONE
DISCOVERING THE AUDIENCE

1. "On Her Own Work," *Mystery and Manners,* ed. Sally and Robert Fitzgerald (New York: Farrar, Straus and Giroux, 1969), 107. See also her additional comment, in the same essay: "Properly, you analyze to enjoy, but it's equally true that to analyze with any discrimination, you have to have enjoyed already, and I think that the best reason to hear a story read is that it should stimulate that primary enjoyment" (108).

2. "The Nature and Aim of Fiction," *Mystery and Manners,* 80.

3. This is from a letter to Carl Hartman, 2 March 1954. O'Connor here describes herself addressing the ladies' club, "I pretended I was Billy Ghrame [sic]." She quips in a letter to Sally and Robert Fitzgerald (8 May 1955) about her recent address to the Macon Writer's Club breakfast: "I have been wasting my time all these years writing—my talent lies in a kind of intellectual vaudeville. I leave them not knowing exactly what I have said but feeling that they have been inspired" (933).

4. This quotation comes from her essay entitled "The Grotesque in Southern Fiction."

5. "The Teaching of Literature," *Mystery and Manners,* 129.

6. "Writing Short Stories," *Mystery and Manners,* 96.

7. "The Nature and Aim of Fiction," *Mystery and Manners,* 84–85.

8. Ibid., 85.

9. Ibid., 65.

10. Ibid., 73.

11. Ibid., 79.

12. "Novelist and Believer," *Mystery and Manners,* 158.

13. "On Her Own Work," *Mystery and Manners,* 112.

14. Ibid., 208.

15. This quotation is from O'Connor's essay "The Church and the Fiction Writer."

16. "The Nature and Aim of Fiction," 83.

17. Ibid., 77–78.

18. Ibid., 79.

19. "Catholic Novelists and Their Readers," *Mystery and Manners,* 179.

20. "Writing Short Stories," 89.

21. Ibid., 90.

22. O'Connor states this in her essay "Writing Short Stories," *Mystery and Manners,* 105–6.

23. "The Nature and Aim of Fiction," 73–74.

24. "Writing Short Stories," 93.

25. "On Her Own Work," 111.

26. "The Nature and Aim of Fiction, 75. Emphasis mine.

27. "Writing Short Stories," 95–96, 102.

28. Ibid., 83.

29. "Catholic Novelists and Their Readers," 183–84.

30. "The Catholic Novelist in the Protestant South," *Mystery and Manners*, 191.

31. Ibid., 184.

32. Ibid., 208.

33. "The Fiction Writer and His Country," *Mystery and Manners*, 32.

34. "The King of the Birds," *Mystery and Manners*, 4.

35. "Writing Short Stories," *Mystery and Manners*, 91.

36. "Novelist and Believer," *Mystery and Manners*, 156.

37. Ibid., 155.

38. "The Church and the Fiction Writer," 146.

39. The tendency to exclude O'Connor's articulate expression of her Catholic Christian identity persists in O'Connor critical circles. An early instance is Stanley Edgar Hyman's critical judgment: "It is surely too early to evaluate Flannery O'Connor's work or place it in our literature, but some beginnings can be attempted. Two points must be made immediately. The first is that despite the prevailing opinion, she was primarily a novelist, not a short-story writer, and consequently her novels are better than even the best of her stories. The second is that any discussion of her theology can only be preliminary to, not a substitute for, aesthetic analysis and evaluation" ("Flannery O'Connor: 1925–64," *American Writers: A Collection of Literary Biographies*, vol. 8, Leonard Unger, editor-in-chief [New York: Charles Scribner's Sons, 1974], 357–58). In this book I follow William F. Lynch's critical theory (and O'Connor's explicit debt to his work) to demonstrate that the manner in which the imagination theologizes is more than preliminary; it is intrinsic to aesthetic analyses and critical interpretations of her fiction.

40. "On Her Own Work," 109. The context of this remark is her explanation of "the basis on which reason operates" in her short story "A Good Man Is Hard to Find."

41. For example, see Charles R. Meyer, *A Contemporary Theology of Grace* (Staten Island, New York: Alba House, 1971).

42. Karl Rahner, *Foundations of Christian Faith: An Introduction to the Idea of Christianity* (New York: Seabury, 1978), 131.

43. Ibid., 132–33.

44. Brian McDermott, "The Bonds of Freedom," *A World of Grace: An Introduction to the Themes and Foundations of Karl Rahner's Theology,* ed. Leo J. O'Donovan (New York: Seabury, 1980), 59–61.

45. "On Her Own Work," 118.

46. Ibid.

47. The letter is to Eileen Hall, 10 March 1956.

48. The essay in which O'Connor makes this observation is "The Grotesque in Southern Fiction."

49. Dietrich Bonhoeffer, *The Cost of Discipleship* (London: SCM Press, 1959), 35–41.

50. "Novelist and Believer," 165–66.

51. In the same vein, she speaks directly to the point in concluding her essay "The Catholic Novelist in the Protestant South." She argues, "I don't believe [the writer] can impose orthodoxy on fiction." Instead she insists that "our faith is deepened...by an encounter with mystery in what is human and often perverse" (863). She recommends that the writer who is "spurred by the religious view of the world" not overlook this integral reality. "He will forget that the devil is still at his task of winning

souls and that grace cuts with the sword Christ said he came to bring" (864).

52. "Writing Short Stories," 105–6.

53. "Novelist and Believer," 167.

54. O'Connor uses this description in a letter to Sally Fitzgerald, 26 December 1954.

55. "Novelist and Believer," 156.

56. "Writing Short Stories," 92.

57. "The Nature and Aim of Fiction," 68.

58. Thomas Merton, "Flannery O'Connor: A Prose Elegy," *Raids on the Unspeakable* (New York: New Directions, 1966), 37–42.

59. "Catholic Novelists and Their Readers," 181–82.

60. On fundamental option see Mark O'Keefe, *Becoming Good, Becoming Holy: On the Relationship of Christian Ethics and Spirituality* (New York: Paulist, 1995), chapter 3, "Dynamism and Integration: Fundamental Option and the Three Ways," 44–56; and James F. Bresnahan, "The Ethics of Faith," *A World of Grace,* chapter 12, 169–84.

61. "Catholic Novelists and Their Readers," 182–83.

62. "On Her Own Work," *Mystery and Manners,* 113.

63. This much-quoted remark by O'Connor comes from her essay "The Fiction Writer and His Country."

64. "Writing Short Stories," 97–98.

65. See George Kilcourse, "O'Connor and Merton: Icons of the True Self in a 'Christ-Haunted' World," *The Flannery O'Connor Bulletin* 23 (1994–95): 123–27. Cf. William F. Lynch, *Images of Faith: An Exploration of the Ironic Imagination* (Notre Dame: University of Notre Dame Press, 1973).

66. No doubt this metaphor harkens to the days of O'Connor's childhood when her mother, Regina, would borrow their cousin's electric car to drive her to school. The electric car's simple threefold operation—forward-neutral-reverse—would have been a familiar one.

67. The letter to Roslyn Barnes is dated 4 August 1962.

68. "On Her Own Work," 112.

69. "The Nature and Aim of Fiction," 82–83.

70. Ibid., 113.

71. See Edward Schillebeeckx, "The Role of History in What Is Called the New Paradigm," *Paradigm Change in Theology,* ed. Hans Kung and David Tracy (New York: Crossroad, 1989), 318–19: "If living human beings are the fundamental symbol of God *(imago Dei),* then the place where human beings are dishonored and oppressed, both in the depth of their own hearts and in an oppressive society, is at the same time the privileged place where religious experience becomes possible in a life style which seeks to give form to that symbol, to heal and restore it to itself: to express its deepest truth." Also relevant is Edward Schillebeeckx, *Christ: The Experience of Jesus as Lord* (New York: Seabury, 1980), 32: "[T]he constantly unforeseen content of new experiences keeps forcing us to think again. On the one hand, thought makes experience possible, while on the other, it is experience that makes new thinking necessary. Our thinking remains empty if it does not constantly refer back to living experience."

72. "On Her Own Work," 114.

73. O'Connor makes these remarks in a 9 December 1958 letter to Cecil Dawkins.

74. The letter to "A" is dated 8 December 1955.

75. The letter to "A" is dated 2 August 1955.

76. "The Nature and Aim of Fiction," 86.

77. "The Teaching of Literature," 132–33.

78. Ibid., 124–25.

79. See Brian A. Ragen, *A Wreck on the Road to Damascus: Innocence, Guilt & Conversion in Flannery O'Connor* (Chicago: Loyola University Press, 1989).

80. "The King of the Birds," *Mystery and Manners*, 5.

81. The letter to Alfred Corn is dated 30 May 1962.

82. Parker J. Palmer, "Contemplation Reconsidered: The Human Way In," *The Merton Annual* 8 (Collegeville: Liturgical Press, 1996), 22–37.

83. This letter to "A" is dated 2 August 1955.

CHAPTER TWO
MAKING GOD-IN-CHRIST BELIEVABLE:
WISE BLOOD

1. See Jon Lance Bacon, *Flannery O'Connor and Cold War Culture* (Cambridge: Cambridge University Press, 1993).

2. Norman Vincent Peale, *The Power of Positive Thinking* (New York: Prentice-Hall, 1952).

3. Fulton J. Sheen, *Peace of Soul* (Garden City, N.Y.: Garden City Books, 1949).

4. Joshua L. Liebman, *Peace of Mind* (New York: Simon and Schuster, 1946).

5. *The Correspondence of Flannery O'Connor and the Brainard Cheeneys,* ed. C. Ralph Stephens (Jackson: University Press of Mississippi, 1986), 210.

6. *HB,* 290. Letter to "A," 5 July 1958.

7. Thomas Merton, *The Seven Storey Mountain* (New York: Harcourt, Brace, 1948), 237–38.

8. Abraham Joshua Heschl, *I Asked For Wonder: A Spiritual Anthology*, ed. Samuel H. Dressner (New York: Crossroad, 1998), 39–40.

9. For a theological interpretation of the "God Is Dead Theology" see Langdon Gilkey, *Naming the Whirlwind: The Renewal of God Language* (Indianapolis: Bobbs-Merrill, 1969), especially chapters 1–4.

10. Quoted from R. J. Hollingdale, *Nietzsche* (London and Boston: Routledge & Kegan Paul, 1973), 64.

11. Ibid., 66–67.

12. *Mystery and Manners*, 91.

13. Mark Twain, *Adventures of Huckleberry Finn* (New York: Oxford University Press, 1996), 19. The exact line from Twain reads: "Well, I couldn't see no advantage in going where she was going, so I made up my mind I wouldn't try for it."

14. Walker Percy, *The Moviegoer* (New York: Random House, 1961), 7–8.

15. O'Connor's consciousness of this fact of exile and wandering colors her earliest short story, "The Geranium," with the character of Old Dudley.

16. Dietrich Bonhoeffer's expression, "cheap grace," suggests the same insight. See his *The Cost of Discipleship* (London: SCM Press, 1959), 35–41.

17. For a fuller appreciation of O'Connor's satiric presentation of Mary Brittle, see her letters about Dr. Frank Crane, an *Atlanta Constitution* columnist. In her first mention of Dr. Crane, she calls him "my favorite Protestant theologian (salvation by the compliment club)....He's a real combination minister and masseur, don't you think?" (935, from a letter to Robie Macauley, 18 May 1955). His columns are a probable source for her portrait

of Mary Brittle. See additional letters, *Collected Works* 958, 964, 966, 974, 1072, 1168–69.

18. "On Her Own Work," *Mystery and Manners,* 116.

19. Ibid., 117–18.

20. Dale Carnegie, *How to Win Friends and Influence People* (New York: Simon and Schuster, 1937).

21. For a complete analysis of the influence of Paul's conversion in *Wise Blood,* see Brian Abel Ragen, *A Wreck on the Road to Damascus: Innocence, Guilt, and Conversion in Flannery O'Connor* (Chicago: Loyola University Press, 1989). Richard Giannone, *Flannery O'Connor and the Mystery of Love* (Urbana and Chicago: University of Illinois Press, 1989), interprets *Wise Blood* according to a Pauline theology in terms of numerous excerpts from Paul's epistles in his first chapter, "The Price of Guilt."

22. Thomas Merton, *The Seven Storey Mountain,* 181.

23. "The Inner Experience," *Thomas Merton, Spiritual Master,* ed. Lawrence S. Cunningham (New York: Paulist, 1994) 295–96.

24. Merton, *The Seven Storey Mountain,* 165.

25. Thomas Merton, *The Wisdom of the Desert* (New York: New Directions, 1965), 11.

26. *HB,* 290.

27. Ibid.

28. Ibid.

29. New York: Holt, Rinehart & Winston, 1964.

30. Thomas Merton, "The Unbelief of Believers," *Faith and Violence* (Notre Dame: University of Notre Dame Press, 1968), 199, 201.

31. Thomas Merton, "Apologies to an Unbeliever," *Faith and Violence,* 205–6, 208.

32. Ibid., 210.

33. Ibid., 210–11.

34. Ibid., 213.

35. In Enoch's case, such knowledge is not always desirable. E.g., after stealing the mummy, he retreats to his room and sneezes: "His expression had showed that a deep unpleasant knowledge was breaking on him slowly" (98).

CHAPTER THREE
THE CHRISTIC IMAGINATION:
CREATIVE GESTURES OF A HUMBLE GOD

1. See Rose Bowen, "Christology in the Works of Flannery O'Connor," *Horizons* 14 (1987): 7–23, for an early attempt to gauge the christological "influences" of Karl Adam, Romano Guardini, Pierre Teilhard de Chardin, and Francis Durwell on O'Connor. Bowen's work, however, focuses upon these theologians' influence as traced in her nonfiction; Bowen claims an "impact on [O'Connor's] fiction" but does not offer any analyses or specific interpretations in the fiction.

2. Roberta Bondi, "Faith Matters: A Matter of Christology," *The Christian Century* 116:9 (March 17, 1999): 316.

3. William A. Sessions, "How to Read Flannery O'Connor: Passing by the Dragon," *Literature and Belief* 17 (1997): 198.

4. Paul Tillich, *Systematic Theology,* vol. 1 (Chicago: University of Chicago Press, 1951), 59–66.

5. From Guardini's *Berichte über mein Leben* (1984), as quoted in Robert A. Krieg, *Romano Guardini: A Precursor of Vatican II* (Notre Dame: University of Notre Dame Press, 1997), 27.

6. Ibid., 28.

7. *The Presence of Grace and Other Book Reviews,* comp.

Leo J. Zuber, ed. Carter W. Martin (Athens, Ga.: University of Georgia Press, 1983), 113–14.

8. Krieg's assessment of Guardini's 1937 book, *The Lord*, offers a striking description that makes O'Connor's attraction to Guardini even more plausible. One can see the parallel between Hazel Motes in *Wise Blood* and the audience for Guardini's kerygmatic theology: "*Der Herr [The Lord]* is directed to the 'heart,' to the whole person. It aims at a knowledge that is self-involving....In short, Der Herr is intended to facilitate encounters between Jesus Christ and all those who are searching for the truth" (152).

9. As quoted in Krieg, 32.

10. Ibid., 33.

11. Ibid., 13. Krieg captures Guardini's balance between the objective and subjective element in Catholic theology: "Once a person adopts the Christian *Weltanschauung* as known within Catholicism, the person stands not within a subjective and relative framework of other worldviews but within the horizon of meaning which is objective and absolute" (33). Krieg points to Guardini's 1984 autobiographical reflections that point to "this 'Copernican turn' of the believing mind" to capture the appropriate subjective dimension.

12. Ibid., 14. Krieg points to Guardini's early study of Max Scheler's phenomenology and his later contact with Martin Buber's phenomenology as distinct and enduring influences.

13. *Collected Works* 1015. In a 28 December 1956 letter to "A," O'Connor writes: "Apropos the Christ image business, the fall issue of Cross Currents has an essay on The Idiot as a Christ symbol by Msgr. Guardini....In my novel I have a child—the school teacher's boy—whom I aim to have a kind of Christ image, though a better way to think of it is probably just as a kind of

redemptive figure. None of this may work however; but I have made some progress these last three months or think I have."

14. Romano Guardini, *The Lord* (Chicago: Henry Regnery, 1954), 322.

15. Ibid., 323–24.

16. Jean-Marc Laporte, *Patience and Power: Grace for the First World* (New York: Paulist, 1988), 136.

17. "On My Own Work," *Mystery and Manners*, 111.

18. Ibid., 111–13.

19. "On Her Own Work," 112.

20. Ibid.

21. Guardini, 326.

22. See Karl Rahner, "On the Theology of the Incarnation," *Theological Investigations*, vol. 4 (Baltimore: Helicon, 1966), 105–20; also, his transcendental method is developed in *Foundations of Christian Faith* (New York: Crossroad, 1978), 285–305. In the latter work, Rahner assesses new approaches to orthodox Christology and recognizes the distinction between (1) the "act of faith" as subjective, involving the totality of the person; and (2) the "content of faith" as objective, i.e., expressed in the revered dogmas of the Catholic Church's tradition. His observation about Christology from "above" and "below" is especially helpful: "Only if this event of [God's] own in history [Christ in the incarnation], a history which, as lived out in divine and of course also in created freedom [humanity], determines [God] once and for all and hence becomes irrevocable, only then can we speak of an absolute and 'eschatological' event of salvation. The offer of himself [God's self] which becomes manifest in history as irrevocable must be his own reality in its createdness [Jesus], and not only in its divine origin. And this very own reality of his, which he can no longer undo as something which has been surpassed, must exist on

our side as our own real salvation, that is, on this side of the difference between God and creatures. This gives us an initial approach towards a Christology 'from below' which is objectively identical with the Church's classical Christology 'from above,' and which at the same time can also clarify the unity between incarnational, essential Christology and soteriological, functional Christology" (301). For a valuable historical and systematic overview, see also Elizabeth Johnson, *Consider Jesus: Waves of Renewal in Christology* (New York: Crossroad, 1990).

23. *The Presence of Grace, 55.*

24. Monika Hellwig, "Re-Emergence of the Human, Critical, Public Jesus," *Theological Studies* 50 (1989): 468. I am indebted to Krieg's work for reminding me of this reference to Hellwig's assessment of Guardini.

25. Krieg, 159–60.

26. *The Presence of Grace, 66.*

27. O'Connor's discriminating taste in literary criticism is evident in her remark to McKane in the same letter: "I never read all the articles in THOUGHT but there are always one or two I'm interested in. I am sending you a representative issue" (1088).

28. *The Presence of Grace, 75.*

29. See, for example, Jacques Maritain, *Creative Intuition in Art and Poetry* (Cleveland: World Publishing, 1953).

30. *HB, 58.*

31. To affix a precise date for O'Connor's first reading of Lynch's essay, "Theology and Imagination," is problematic. Her May 1953 letter to the Fitzgeralds (*HB*, 58) indicates that both they and O'Connor shared a certain familiarity with his work; she also is already familiar with the journal *Thought*. (It is interesting to note in this letter one of O'Connor's frequent malapropisms; she describes Lynch's article about the "anagogical" instead of the

"analogical.") However, in a 22 January 1956 letter to the Fitzgeralds (*HB*, 132) O'Connor writes: "The business of 'living in music' reminds me of a piece I am reading called 'Theology and the Imagination,' by yr friend, Fr. Wm. Lynch of *Thought*. It's about the manichean vs. the anagogical or Christian imagination. Have you seen it? I have at length subscribed to *Thought* and find it very valuable." Lynch's essay appeared in two parts, the first appearing in the spring of 1954 and the second appearing three issues later (winter 1954). Since O'Connor is not specific, it is plausible that she had read the initial essay earlier and is finally reading the second installment. Or she may actually have been rereading the initial essay. An annotated copy of the first essay is in the O'Connor Collection at Georgia College, Milledgeville, Georgia. In either case, whether she first read Lynch's initial essay, "Theology and Imagination," early in 1954 or early in 1956, his influence upon her writing in *The Violent Bear It Away* or in several of the short stories of *Everything That Rises Must Converge* coincides with the period of her writing which I analyze in chapters 5 and 6, below.

32. William F. Lynch, "Theology and Imagination," *Thought* 29 (spring 1954): 61. Lynch adds an alert remark in a footnote (81 n.7), "No one will understand that we are not pleading in these pages for a poetry that is formally Christic or religious. All we are saying is that something must reorientate our relation to the limited image, to the finite and the human, and that nothing short of a true Christology can give us the secure courage or theological energy necessary for this giant task." There are few more exact descriptions of O'Connor's fiction, for she does not plead for a "formally Christic or religious" literature—quite the contrary.

33. Ibid., 62.

34. Ibid., 67.

35. Ibid., 75.

36. Ibid., 66.

37. William F. Lynch, "Theology and Imagination II," *Thought* 29 (winter 1954): 542–43.

38. Ibid., 548–49.

39. "Theology and Imagination," 67.

40. Ibid., 68.

41. Ibid., 64.

42. Ibid., 68. In the second installment of his essay, Lynch contrasts the contemporary Manichaean theology with Greek tragedy and adds: "The dramatist, let us say in the *Oedipus,* has really faced into the finitude of man, to the finest point of helplessness, the collapse of human energy, death. It is by facing, without distraction, into the exceedingly concrete innards of what we may (for want of a better word!) call the finite structure of the fine and limited human situation that the extraordinary exaltations which belong to tragedy are evoked. Now exaltation can, indeed, only come from some form of the sublime but here the facts of the tragic text indicate that the sublimity is not in the greatness of man (his heroicity, his nobility in pain, etc.) but in the extraordinary depth of his finitude when it is, without distraction, really confronted" ("Theology and Imagination II," 536).

43. "Theology and Imagination," 68.

44. "Theology and Imagination II," 545.

45. Gerald J. Bednar, *Faith as Imagination: The Contribution of William F. Lynch, S.J.* (Kansas City: Sheed & Ward, 1996), 46. Chapters 2 and 3, "Lynch's Theology of Interpenetration: The Analogical Imagination" and "Faith as the Ironic Christic Imagination," are especially helpful discussions.

46. Ibid., 47–48. This distinction between "contraries" and "contradictions" lies at the heart of Lynch's theory of the Christic imagination. I find Frederick Asals's *Flannery O'Connor: The Imagination of Extremity* (Athens, Ga.: University of Georgia

Press, 1982) to be a useful and, at times, excellent interpretation of her fiction. He is especially adept in analyzing what he describes as her "posturing rebels" (233) and in drawing attention to her use of what Lynch calls the Manichaean rebellion in her characters: "Rebellion must therefore be the natural state of sinful man and not merely of the hypothetical modern man her essays and lectures seem so often concerned with" (229). However, Asals's recurring identification of the "dualities" and "dualistic imagination" (200) in her fiction and other writings gravitates toward the Manichaean disease against which Lynch cautions us. Since there is no reference to William F. Lynch's work or O'Connor's appropriation of his theory in Asals, the subtlety of the distinction between contraries and contradictories escapes his attention. The danger I find in Asals is that the "extremities" explored in O'Connor's images and the dualisms and the conflicts he repeatedly identifies can quickly collapse into "contradictories." This, I find, is to miss essential elements in her use of "contraries." Perhaps it is because of Asals's sharp segregation of the literary imagination from theology that he precludes the kind of interdisciplinary study undertaken by Lynch and, to a certain extent, by O'Connor. The most overt denial comes at the beginning of Asals's chapter entitled "The Prophetic Imagination": "The issues which [O'Connor's] work raises *are* more questions of imagination than of belief in the usual sense, and the exploration which follows will be more occupied with aesthetic than with theological discriminations, with such matters as temperament, tone, feeling, form, and patterns of action rather than with precise doctrinal points. For a writer of fiction, these are the primary issues, and while O'Connor's work certainly allows for the drawing of technical theological inferences, these need to be determined within the larger imaginative structures of her fiction, not outside of them. She did not, after all, pretend to be a systematic theologian. In fact, quoting Pascal, she insisted that her immediate concern as a writer was with the existential, not the theological, with the 'God of Abraham, Isaac, and Jacob and not of the philosophers and scholars'" (198). Following Lynch, I (like O'Connor) see that theology, in particular Christology, is not extrinsic to fiction but is the foundation for "the larger imaginative structures" of fiction. Chapters 5 and 6 of this book make that case in detailed analyses of the O'Connor texts.

47. Bednar, 50–51.

48. As quoted in Bednar, 52.

49. Ibid., 53.

50. Ibid., 55.

51. "Downward to the Infinite," *Time,* vol. 75, no. 21 (March 23, 1960): 82–83.

52. Lorine M. Goetz, *Flannery O'Connor: Her Life, Library, and Book Reviews* (New York: Edwin Mellen, 1980), 153.

53. William F. Lynch, *Christ and Apollo: The Dimensions of the Literary Imagination* (New York: Sheed & Ward, 1960), 126–33.

54. Ibid., 148.

55. Ibid.

CHAPTER FOUR
THE GOOD UNDER CONSTRUCTION:
A GOOD MAN IS HARD TO FIND

1. *Mystery and Manners,* 168.

2. Ibid., 30.

3. Ibid., 26.

4. "On Her Own Work," *Mystery and Manners,* 111.

5. *The Liturgy of the Hours* (New York: Catholic Book Publishing Co., 1976), vol. 2 (Lent, Easter), 405–6.

6. See Ralph C. Wood, "Where Is the Voice Coming From?: Flannery O'Connor on Race," *The Flannery O'Connor Bulletin* 22 (1993–94): 90–118.

7. Ibid., 113–14.

8. O'Connor's use of the term "depravity" to describe Mr. Head lacks the theological precision of Catholic theologians. In fact, the Catholic teaching insists that we are not totally "depraved" (a Calvinist doctrine), but rather "deprived" of grace. Because O'Connor was not a professional theologian, she occasionally misuses terms (much like her persistent misspelling of words). The context of her work itself affords the clarity of meaning that she intends—which is consistent with the Catholic emphasis.

9. "The Fiction Writer and His Country," *Mystery and Manners*, 26–27.

10. Thomas Merton, "Flannery O'Connor: A Prose Elegy," *Raids on the Unspeakable* (New York: New Directions, 1966), 42.

11. Ibid., 37–38.

12. Ibid., 41.

13. Thomas Merton, *The Hidden Ground of Love* (New York: Farrar Straus and Giroux, 1985), 564. This quotation comes from an 11 April 1959 letter to Daisetz T. Suzuki.

14. Thomas Merton, "The Inner Experience: Some Dangers in Contemplation (VI)," *Cistercian Studies* 19 (1984): 147–50.

15. The friction between O'Connor and Maryat Lee continued into late 1957. O'Connor refers to not receiving "your crusty note" to which Lee refers in her correspondence of 8 October 1957 (1045)—O'Connor suggests it was lost in the foreign postal delivery, Maryat Lee being in Japan at the time. In that same letter O'Connor reports that she had reread her last letter to Lee and admitted it to be "in part disagreeable, vain, and unclear" and says that while open to such interpretations, "None of these was

intended so put it down to my native idiocy." Undoubtedly, O'Connor's official biography by Sally Fitzgerald will shed light on this aggravated moment in the friendship.

16. "On Her Own Work," *Mystery and Manners,* 116.

17. Ibid., 115–18.

18. "Catholic Novelists and Their Readers," 184.

19. These definitions of the verb *cope* come from *The Oxford English Dictionary* (Oxford: Oxford University Press, 1971), 969–70.

20. In this 30 September 1955 letter to "A" O'Connor has also discussed Simone Weil's life as "both comic and terrible." She corrects "A" when it appears she has misunderstood Hulga as "a hypothetical Miss Weil." O'Connor also indicates that she had Hulga in mind as the character we find in "Good Country People" before she read Weil. She adds, "I couldn't write about Miss Weil because she is more intelligent and better than I am but I can project a Hulga" (958–59).

21. For an excellent discussion of the distinction between "guilt" and "shame" in Christian moral theology, see C. Ellis Nelson, *Don't Let Your Conscience Be Your Guide* (New York: Paulist, 1978).

22. This expression comes from a letter O'Connor sent to "A" in which she addresses her correspondent's decision to leave the Church. I find it an apt description of some of the same dynamics in her character Hulga.

23. It is striking to note that O'Connor faults herself on the smiling persona whose neurotic friendliness disguises an altogether different attitude. She writes in a 17 November 1956 letter to "A" about her participation in a Georgia literary awards event: "Each of us, of course, was preceded by a flowery introduction by Dying Voice....Finally it was over, but when these things are over, they are

just beginning as each and every one comes up and says a politeness to you and you shake more hands than Estes Kefauver. I must say I'm very good at it though—I expose every tooth in my head and insist that they all come to see me down on the farm."

24. Wood, "Where Is the Voice Coming From?" 105.

25. In O'Connor's "The King of the Birds" (832–42), she writes an important essay on raising peacocks and hens and interprets some of the symbolism that she associates with them. She includes telling observations such as: "Those [peacocks] that withstood illnesses and predators (the hawk, the fox, and the opossum) over the winter seem impossible to destroy, except by violence" (841); and, "Many people, I have found, are congenitally unable to appreciate the sight of a peacock" (836)—a remark that describes Mrs. Shortley and Mrs. McIntyre's obliviousness. It is in this essay that O'Connor parallels her metaphor of the peacock's tail as "a map of the universe" with the remark that when the cock raises his tail in a "shimmering arch around him....[m]eanwhile the hen goes about her business, diligently searching the ground as if any bug in the grass were of more importance than the unfurled map of the universe which floats nearby" (838).

CHAPTER FIVE
VIOLENT GRACE:
THE VIOLENT BEAR IT AWAY

1. Walter Brueggemann, *The Prophetic Imagination* (Philadelphia: Fortress, 1978), 13.

2. Ibid., 11

3. Ibid., 15

4. Ibid., 14–16.

5. Ibid., 18.

6. Ibid., 20–22.

7. Ibid., 39. Brueggemann develops these insights throughout chapter 2, "The Royal Consciousness: Countering the Counter-Culture," 28–43.

8. Ibid., 46, 49–50. Italics Brueggemann's.

9. Ibid., 50–51.

10. In a 23 April 1960 letter to Elizabeth Bishop, O'Connor writes: "[Catherine Carver] saw the book when the middle section was composed of three instead of six chapters. She told me it wasn't long enough and that it broke apart in the middle and that Rayber didn't come through—all of which was true. So I added all the business about the child evangelist and the chase through the city at night and that helped it no end" (1127). This structure, with three chapters focused upon Mason Tarwater at the novel's beginning, six chapters focused upon Rayber in the middle, and three chapters focused upon Francis Marion Tarwater at the end, is essential to any interpretation. Richard Giannone's helpful analysis of the novel in his chapter, "The Price of Love," in *Flannery O'Connor and the Mystery of Love* pays particular attention to her careful structure in this novel.

11. Brueggemann, 45.

12. "Among School Children," stanza 8, line 2, *Selected Poems and Two Plays of W. B. Yeats* (New York: Collier, 1966), 117.

13. Cf. "Renunciation, Freedom from Care, and the Recovery of Paradise," Douglas Burton-Christie, *The Word in the Desert: Scripture and the Quest for Holiness in Early Christian Monasticism* (New York: Oxford University Press, 1993), 213–35.

14. See above, pp. 101–07

15. Romano Guardini, "Dostoevsky's Idiot, a Symbol of Christ," *Cross Currents* 6 (1956): 359–82. Quotations are from pages 368–69, 371–72, and 382.

16. See George Kilcourse, "Ecumenism, Spiritual" *The New Catholic Dictionary of Spirituality* (Collegeville, Minn.: Liturgical Press, 1993) 334–37.

17. O'Connor's affirmation of the Protestantism of Mason and Francis Marion Tarwater could be judged as compromised by another statement in this 29 September 1960 letter to William Sessions: "One of the good things about Protestantism is that it always contains the seeds of its own reversal. It is open at both ends—at one end to Catholicism, at the other end to unbelief" (*HB*, 411). In light of the overarching appreciation of Protestant theology, I think it fair to interpret "reversal" in the sense of "reform." The Second Vatican Council (1962–65) was at this very time reversing some long-held Catholic beliefs and attitudes. Foremost among them was the recognition of the baptism of other Christians and their status as "churches and ecclesial communities" in the Decree on Ecumenism, nn. 13, 19–24. The council also described the Catholic Church itself as an *"ecclesia semper reformanda,"* a church always being reformed" (8). The same could be claimed for her neologism "crypto-Catholic" (1183) to identify Mason. One could interpret O'Connor on this issue much like Karl Rahner on the use of "anonymous Christian" to deal with the salvation of those who, without fault, never became Christians.

18. Roger Haight, "Sin and Grace," in *Systematic Theology: Roman Catholic Perspectives* (Philadelphia: Fortress, 1991), II, 107, n. 40.

19. At stake in this discussion is an understanding of *myth* that precludes a literal, historical Adam and Eve at some, as it were, time prior to actual history. Haight defines "symbol" as "any concept, word, event, thing, person, or literary expression that mediates an experience of transcendent reality" (89) that needs to be broken open as "an interpretation of ourselves" (90).

20. Ibid., 94–96, 98–101. Haight offers a succinct summary: "In sum, sin on the individual level may be described as a structure

and a process of human freedom that begins with a lack of an appropriation of God's grace but then qualifies every moment of a human being's existence in this world. This structure leads through concupiscence and temptation to the prior sin, that is, some measure of a lack of openness and surrender in self-actualization before God and according to God's will, and, more aggressively, a propensity against God and for the self. Sin emerges as a fallen condition only when it is actualized through human freedom. But at the same time it is not identical with any personal sin; it is a structured dynamic process of unfaith, a lack of trust and love that is prior to and underlies every personal sin" (100).

21. See Leo J. O'Donovan, ed., *A World of Grace* (New York: Seabury, 1980).

22. Ibid., 109–10.

23. *Mystery and Manners,* 175–76.

24. In a 30 November 1959 letter to Spivey, O'Connor is generous in distinguishing the Manichean from the Protestant vision; but she announces that in either case she is not ready in principle to accept his omission of Christian humanism and the place of literature and knowledge (*HB,* 360).

25. "Catholic Novelists and Their Readers," 182.

26. Brueggemann, 60–61.

27. Ibid., 91–95.

28. In the context of this letter, as elsewhere, O'Connor complains that Protestants do not recognize the Eucharist as "his actual body and blood," but prefer to think of it as "a symbol." For all her zeal, she fails to employ an adequate theology of symbol in making her assertion. For an appreciation of the contemporary Catholic theology of symbol, see the modern classic, Bernard Cooke, *Sacraments and Sacramentality* (Mystic, Conn.: Twenty-Third Publications, 1983).

29. Karl Rahner, "Christ in the Sacrament of the Lord's Supper," *Theological Investigations,* vol. 4 (Baltimore: Helicon, 1966), 292–93.

30. See Walter Kaspar, "The Joint Declaration on the Doctrine of Justification: Cause for Hope," *Centro pro Unione,* N. 57 (Spring 2000): 3–6.

CHAPTER SIX
MERCY:
EVERYTHING THAT RISES MUST CONVERGE

1. See Richard Giannone, *Flannery O'Connor and the Mystery of Love,* chapters 5–7, where he accepts the arrangement of the stories in the published volume, dividing the stories as: (1) a widow-widower group of three stories that center upon the anxiety of abundance; (2) a trilogy of stories that prepare her protagonists for "the new" by the Holy Spirit's conferring of a special understanding; and (3) three stories showing "the mysterious fulfillment of her comedies in the divine plan." I question Giannone's linking so directly all three of the second set of stories with Teilhard de Chardin's belief that the Holy Spirit confers "special understanding," "the source of Jesus' strength" that the Jesuit identifies with "the energy propelling creation toward unity." The first of this second set of three is written and published in *Harper's Bazaar* (July 1958) before O'Connor has read Teilhard de Chardin. The title story in the collection—bearing the most direct influence of Teilhard—the first story in the first set of three, was written in mid-1961, while the other two stories were published in 1956 and 1957. Cf. her 30 November 1959 letter to Dr. T. R. Spivey: "I haven't read Pere Teilhard yet so I don't know whether I agree with you or not on *The Phenomenon of Man*" (*HB,* 361). In a 2 January 1960 letter to "A" (*HB,* 368) she acknowledges that his work is "hard to read"—giving evidence that she has by that time read some of his work, without being specific.

As late as 7 May 1964, less than three months before her death, O'Connor writes to Elizabeth McKee (*HB*, 574–75) concerning the nine stories she wants in her final collection. The listed order of contents is not the order found in the published volume—and "The Partridge Festival" is replaced with the title story, "Everything That Rises Must Converge." She indicates, "This is not necessarily the order I want them in, but that can be worked out later with Giroux" (575). I find no evidence of her later suggesting a specific order to the stories, and I conjecture that Robert Giroux, her editor, consulted with Sally Fitzgerald to decide upon the order of the stories and the placement of the title story at the beginning.

2. In a similar vein, O'Connor remarks in a 14 November 1954 letter to Caroline Tate about the dissolving of Catholic identity in families, adding: "Part is from poor instruction and part from that awful jell the Irish manage to set their religion in. They pass it on from generation to generation. We all prefer comfort to joy" (926).

3. *The Presence of Grace,* 86–88.

4. Ibid., 130. This review originally appeared in *The American Scholar,* fall 1961.

5. *The Presence of Grace,* 107–8.

6. Christopher J. Mooney, *Teilhard de Chardin and the Mystery of Christ* (New York: Harper & Row, 1966), 61–63.

7. "The Nature and Aim of Fiction," *Mystery and Manners,* 71, 73. See also "On Her Own Work," ibid., 112–14.

8. From a 6 September 1953 letter in *Letters from a Traveler,* quoted in Mooney, 66. O'Connor read this volume and reviewed it in April 1963; cf. *The Presence of Grace,* 160–61.

9. From Teilhard's 1950 work, *L'Energie spirituelle de la souffrance,* quoted in Mooney, 114.

10. This excerpt is from Teilhard's *Comment je crois,* 1934, quoted in Mooney, 145.

11. Quoted in Ursula King, *Christ in All Things: Exploring Spirituality with Teilhard de Chardin* (Maryknoll, N.Y.: Orbis, 1997), 35.

12. Sally Fitzgerald's "Chronology" appended to *The Collected Works* details O'Connor's writing the introduction at the end of 1961 and sending the manuscript and introduction to editor Robert Giroux "for his opinion in early December [1961]" (1253).

13. Mooney, 120–22.

14. Cf. John Desmond, chapter 4, "Community in History: Imagining the Mystical Body," *Risen Sons: Flannery O'Connor's Vision of History,* 63–82. He develops an elaborate analysis of O'Connor's growing emphasis on "depicting the process of redemption in relation to the universal social order, the corporate body of the human community moving through history." Desmond describes the implications: "Individual refusals of this collective process are manifold, and the dire cost of return to this mystical community and collective process is repeatedly dramatized" (64).

15. For a fuller discussion of my interpretation of this story, see my essay, "'Parker's Back': Not Totally Congenial Icons of Christ," *Flannery O'Connor and the Christian Mystery,* ed. John J. Murphy, *Literature and Belief* 17 (1997): 35–46.

16. See L. Ouspensky and V. Lossky, *The Meaning of Icons* (Crestwood, N.Y.: St. Vladimir's Seminary Press, 1982) and A. Grabar, Christian Iconography: A Study of Its Origins (Princeton, N.J.: Princeton University Press, 1980).

Conclusion

1. *The Presence of Grace,* 55.